EXCAVATIONS AT TELL EL-BALAMUN

1995-1998

A.J. SPENCER

Published for The Trustees of

The British Museum by

BRITISH MUSEUM  PRESS

© 1999 The Trustees of the British Museum
Published by British Museum Press
A division of The British Museum Company Ltd
46 Bloomsbury Street, London, WC1B 3QQ

Set in Aldus PageMaker by A.J. Spencer
Printed in Great Britain by Henry Ling, Dorset

A catalogue record for this book is available
from the British Library

ISBN 0-7141-1933-4

EXCAVATIONS AT TELL EL-BALAMUN

1995-1998

Contents

Preface and Acknowledgements

This is the second volume devoted to the publication of the British Museum excavations at Tell el-Balamun and the information it contains adds directly to the account given in *Excavations at Tell el-Balamun 1991-1994*, which appeared in 1996. The majority of the results presented here concern the archaeology of the main temple of the site at various periods, together with descriptions of several associated structures. The latter include mud-brick buildings built for official purposes in and around the forecourt of the Thirtieth-Dynasty temple, as well as the foundations of two subsidiary monuments. Also described is the tomb of the official Iken, found a short distance to the north of the temple site above the remains of an enclosure wall of the New Kingdom. This tomb dates from the reign of King Osorkon I.

The successful conduct of the excavation has depended on the continued support of the Trustees of the British Museum and on assistance from various sources, particularly the Egyptian Antiquities Organization, now re-named the Supreme Council for Antiquities. We wish to thank Professor Gaballa Ali Gaballa, Secretary-General of the SCA, together with his predecessor Dr Abd el-Halim Nur ed-Din. We are also grateful to Dr Abdessalam Bakr, Director of Excavations and Inspectorates for the Delta, and Dr Mohamed Abd el-Halim Rizq, the former Director of the region. Thanks are also due to all the staff of the Antiquities Office at Mansura, particularly Mr Ahmed el-Sourougi and Mr Mohamed Abdel Fattah. During each season we have been fortunate to have the help of the Egyptian Antiquities Inspectors attached to the expedition: Mr Atef Abu el-Dahap in 1995-6 and Mr Yasser el-Sayed el-Gamal in 1997-8, with the assistance of Mr Ibrahim el-Saidi and Mr Ahmed Rabia Ahmed. To all we express our thanks.

We are also grateful to the following individuals for help with various matters, ranging from assistance with the acquisition or storage of equipment, to the preparation of drawings for publication and advice on the dating of material: Donald Bailey, Morris Bierbrier, Vivian Davies, Christian and Lisa Décobert, Günter Dreyer, Joyce Filer, Carla Gallorini, Rawya Ismail, David Jeffreys and Anthony Leahy. This publication has been seen through production by Teresa Francis and Nicola Denny of British Museum Press. Finally, it should be noted that the operation of the work at the site could not have been carried out so smoothly without the help of Gomaa Abbas Said Ali, guard of antiquites at Tell el-Balamun, and the members of his family.

Concerning the presentation of the material in this volume, the drawings of pottery are at 1:4 scale, unless otherwise specified. In the case of small objects of various materials the scales of the individual drawings are indicated on the plates. On the photographic plates showing excavated features each scale division of the ranging-pole measures 20cm.

Staff of the Expedition, 1995-98

A.J. Spencer	1995-8
Patricia A. Spencer	1995-8
M.A. Leahy	1995-6
Lisa M. Leahy	1995
Carla Gallorini	1995
Joanne Howdle	1995-6
Denise Ling	1996
Atef El-Dahap	1995-6
Yasser el-Sayed el-Gamal	1997-8
Ibrahim el-Saidi	1997
Ahmed Rabia Ahmed	1998

Introduction

The earlier seasons of excavation and survey by the British Museum at Tell el-Balamun included operations over a wide area necessary for the initial mapping of the ancient mound, the assessment of the surface pottery and the delineation of the enclosure walls and major buildings. This resulted in the identification of the two successive enclosures of the Late Period and their associated temples, together with the mud-brick casemate building at the south corner of the Inner Enclosure. The two small temples published in the previous volume were securely dated by foundation deposits to the reigns of Psamtik I and Nekhtnebef. The remains of these monuments and the surrounding enclosure walls lay close to the present ground surface, covered only by a thin layer of dust and mud, a fact which allowed rapid progress to be made in tracing the plans of the individual buildings or foundations. Conditions at the main temple of the site (Temple A, the temple of Amun) were very different, however, and the interpretation of its different building stages has required several seasons of large-scale excavation through deep layers of disturbed fill to supplement the preliminary investigations made in 1991 and 1994 (Spencer 1996, 36-42). This work, which forms the principal subject of this volume, has demonstrated that the northern sanctuary of Amun in Paiuenamon was equipped with a central temple of substantial size during the Third Intermediate Period, founded on the site of a temple of the New Kingdom.

As one of the largest of the Delta mounds, the site is likely to survive for a considerable time. It is, however, not entirely free from attrition caused by a variety of factors, the effects of which have been observed in the eight years since the commencement of the British Museum excavations. Surface erosion by wind in the dry summers and by rainwater in the winters has taken its toll, and the southeast wall of the Outer Enclosure, visible as an almost continuous surface trace in 1991, has now been reduced to a few patches of brickwork. The low-lying ground to the west of the main temple has been further eroded by rainwater and is regularly flooded in winter. In the most recent season this area was deliberately chosen for investigation as a priority whilst work there remained possible, resulting in the discovery of the north corner of the New-Kingdom enclosure wall, cut by two foundation-pits for subsidiary temple buildings, and the tomb of the official Iken. The results achieved in such difficult and unpromising areas demonstrate the potential for the recovery of significant information at Tell el-Balamun and at similar sites across the Delta. The scarcity of well-preserved standing monuments in Lower Egypt to match those further south is no sound basis for the determination of the relative importance of the two regions. Our assessment must depend on what archaeology can prove to have once existed, not on what happens to have survived above ground by chance.

1. The Main Temple of Amun (Temple A)

(a) Introduction

A basic plan of this temple has already been published (Spencer 1996, pl.9), using information gained from the excavations of 1991 and 1994. Three major elements were recorded in the building: an extensive front courtyard, a wide pylon or pronaos and the rectangular rear portion of the building around the shrine. These features all belonged to the latest reconstruction of the temple in the Thirtieth Dynasty, built over the remains of an earlier temple of the Third Intermediate Period with a different layout. The older level was mentioned only briefly in the previous volume because good evidence for its existence was not detected until the 1995 season, when the monograph was already at an advanced stage of production. Several important foundation deposits, discovered in 1995, were likewise mentioned in the earlier publication with the minimum of detail. These discoveries, which are fully published in the present report, add significantly to the available information on the development of the main temple, with implications for the general history of the city at Tell el-Balamun.

Intensive study of the Amun-Temple was carried out in the seasons from 1995 to 1997, with the objective of recovering as much as possible of the original ground-plans of both the Twenty-second Dynasty and the Thirtieth-Dynasty monuments. Although virtually all the stone masonry of the temple of Amun was removed in antiquity, much of the plan can be reconstructed from the remains of its extensive sand-filled foundations, which have remained sufficiently well preserved to define the limits of the monument. These foundations include elements from both building phases, which it has proved possible to distinguish through a study of the stratigraphy of the site. The more complicated arrangement of the temple substructure for the earlier building stage is shown in plates 5, 7 and 8, and reconstructed plans, showing the relative positions of features from each phase, are given on plates 2, 4 and 6. It should be noted that the number of columns in the colonnade on plans 2 and 6 is estimated.

(b) Overview of the temple layout

The rear part of the building is marked by a low, rectangular area of around 80 x 40 metres, in which all the inner rooms were located: the halls and chambers around the sanctuary, which, in the latest phase, probably consisted of the granite naos which lies in pieces not far from its original position (Spencer 1996, 37, pl.8b). The interior of this rectangular space consists of a huge foundation-pit, the whole of which originally had been filled with sand to form the basis of the stone temple-platform. Much of this sand remains in place, although its level has been reduced by the intensive and repeated pitting of the site. This kind of destruction, motivated by the quarrying of stone, extraction of sand and general treasure-hunting, has been particularly severe in the rear part of the building and has eliminated any possibility of recovering the arrangement of the internal walls. Not only has the stone platform of the temple been removed, but also a good deal of the foundation sand has been quarried out and replaced by pits full of broken stone chippings and mud. The date of the final reconstruction of the temple has been established, however, thanks to the discovery in 1995 of an intact foundation deposit of Nekhtnebef in the rear south corner of the sand-bed (below, pp.26-7). Since the inner chambers of the Thirtieth-Dynasty temple stood on the same spot as those of its earlier counterpart, the refurbishment of the foundation-pit by Nekhtnebef has removed any traces of the older building in this area. However, in front of the rectangular area of the 'inner temple' it was possible to detect elements of both building phases from the surviving foundations.

The entrance to the site of the 'inner temple' originally consisted of a large pylon, dated by foundation deposits to the Third Intermediate Period, almost certainly to the reign of Sheshonq III. The width of the foundation for the pylon was approximately 52 metres, which presumably indicates an intended size of 100 cubits. This was actually the second pylon of the building which, in common with other elements of the Third Intermediate Period temple, was completely demolished sometime during the fifth century BC. In the Thirtieth-Dynasty reconstruction this pylon was either rebuilt as an entrance to the new temple or perhaps replaced by a pronaos-type hall, occupying a slightly smaller area.

In front of the Second Pylon are two parallel sand-filled foundation-trenches extending for about 40 metres, to join the rear of another, larger pylon (the First Pylon). The most likely purpose for the parallel trenches would have been to support a colonnade, rather similar to those of the Twenty-fifth Dynasty at Karnak. The First Pylon, at the front end of this colonnade, was a massive structure about 74 metres wide and 12 metres deep. All four corners of its foundation were found to have been disturbed in antiquity and no foundation-deposits were recovered, despite deep excavations at each corner. Consequently, good evidence is lacking to confirm whether this pylon and the colonnade were also constructed by Sheshonq III or whether they were added in the Twenty-sixth Dynasty, although there are indications from stratigraphic observations that the latter view might be correct. The area in front of this great pylon contains additional sand-filled foundations for some kind of entrance gate or portico.

This plan was not followed in the Thirtieth-Dynasty building. Instead of a narrow colonnade along the axis of the temple and a massive front pylon, a wide forecourt was created with walls extending from the ends of the new pylon or pronaos on the former site of the Sheshonq III pylon. The lateral walls of this forecourt passed over the destroyed remains of the earlier First Pylon, which, by the time of the Thirtieth-Dynasty reconstruction, had been hidden by accumulated fill into which the later wall foundations were cut. Details of the remains of both levels of the temple are given below, beginning with the older phase. The following description begins with the rear part of the monument, which might be considered an odd place to begin, but this allows the less complex remains situated between the back of the temple and the Second Pylon to be dealt with first, before discussing the more complex foundations of the First Pylon and later forecourt.

The temple from the Twenty-second to Twenty-sixth Dynasties

(a) Introduction

As mentioned in the foregoing section, it was not possible to identify any elements of the Twenty-second Dynasty building phase in the rear part of the temple, to the south-west of the Second Pylon, owing to the foundations of the Thirtieth Dynasty having been recut in the same area. Certainly, some part of the 80 x 40 metre area behind the pylon of Sheshonq was occupied by the inner chambers of the Twenty-second Dynasty temple, but whether these extended for 80 metres like those of the later building is unclear. The Nekhtnebef temple might have been of greater length than the one it replaced, which would perhaps explain the fact that the rear wall of the Outer Enclosure of the temple complex is located some 20 metres further to the south-west than the corresponding wall of the Saite Inner Enclosure. In fact, Nekhtnebef seems to have utilised the cut-down remains of the Inner Wall to form a convenient limit to the foundation-pit, so it is possible that his architects decided to extend the length of the temple in order to take advantage of this older brickwork. A similar situation seems to have occurred at Tanis, where the Thirtieth-Dynasty temple foundation was set against the wall of Psusennes (Montet 1935, 58-63; Brissaud 1992, 118).

The sand-filled foundation-pit of the Second Pylon provided the most accurate evidence for the date of the older temple so far recovered, in the form of several foundation deposits. In 1995 excavation of all four corners of the pylon foundation was carried out deep into the foundation sand and, where necessary, below the subsoil water-level, in an exhaustive search for accurate dating evidence. Intact foundation deposits survived at two of the corners: the front left (north) and rear right (south); part of a disturbed deposit was also recovered at the rear left (west) corner. The front right (east) corner had been completely destroyed by later pitting.

(b) The Second Pylon and its foundation deposits

Rear corner of the north-west wing of the pylon
The first corner to be investigated was the rear left (west) angle, where work began by removing the mud-brick packing of the Thirtieth Dynasty, noted in 1994, to reveal the sand-bed below extending right into the true corner of the foundation-pit. The rubble and mud was gradually cleared from the interior of the foundation, which had been cut by numerous deep pits of late-Roman date. A limestone model mortar was found in the redeposited fill, 230cm from the left side of the foundation and 175cm from the rear wall. Slightly deeper, a fragment of an uninscribed malachite plaque was found, 175cm from the left side of the substructure and 30cm from the rear, at a relative level of about 35. This plaque lay in disturbed fill, but had probably been dug up from the deposit below. A second fragment of it was found a little deeper in the same spot. More sand appeared as the excavation went deeper and the bases of most of the later pits were passed, but a few of the pits were very deep and continued into the subsoil water. The area below the location of the plaque fragments was excavated into the water-table, draining the water by baling into a sump. Part of a foundation deposit was found (Cat.**103**), including some sherds from red siltware cups, a calcite hemi-disk inscribed for a priest of Amun named Hor and a fragmentary silver plaque. A late-Roman pit through the area had destroyed the rest, although the fragmentary malachite plaque found in the higher rubble almost certainly belonged to this deposit, since the parallel deposits from the other corners included a plaque of this material. The same is unlikely to be true of the model limestone mortar, however, because this type of object was not represented in any of the other deposits of the Third Intermediate Period phase. It is more characteristic of Late-Period deposits, and may have belonged to the Thirtieth-Dynasty refoundation (a similar model mortar was present in the foundation deposit of Nekhtnebef at the rear of the temple). The total material recovered in this corner was as follows:

Limestone model mortar from the rubble fill (probably later)
Fragmentary plaque of green malachite (found in rubble)
Calcite hemi-disk inscribed for the priest Hor
Corroded silver plaque, incomplete, text lost
A few red siltware pottery fragments: when sorted by shape and fabric there were pieces from four conical cups and one small dish, of the same types as those from the front corner deposit, described below. The original total may have matched that at the front: four cups and three dishes.

Front corner of the north-west wing of the pylon
A trench measuring 4 x 3 metres was dug in this front corner of the north-west wing of the pylon and excavated progressively down to clean sand. The surface dust contained a mixture of Ptolemaic and Roman sherds, including a small piece of Memphis Black Ware, part of a spouted flask, fragments of an African Red Slip Ware bowl and ribbed body-sherds from amphorae. More compact earth fill was encountered a little deeper above the north-west end of the foundation, with pottery fragments dating from the first Persian Period, deposited after the destruction of the pylon. Within this area was a pit containing a large red siltware pottery jar, which had been broken in antiquity and repaired with binding (colourplate 1a and pl.9a). The rim of this vessel lay at relative level 123. The style of the vessel places it in the fifth or fourth century BC. The pit in which it lay was located just within the north-west edge of the foundation and it descended into the top of the sand-bed, but further towards the interior of the pylon foundation there was no pottery, only masses of limestone rubble. The fact that the pottery vessel and associated fifth-century BC fill remained undisturbed by the Thirtieth-Dynasty rebuilding of the temple shows that whatever feature replaced the pylon in the later design - whether a new pylon or a pronaos with engaged columns - was not as wide as the older monument. Additional evidence for this view is provided by the fact that the sand-trench for the foundation of the Thirtieth-Dynasty forecourt wall ran on for about 2 metres into the area of the earlier pylon foundation (see below, p.26 and Spencer 1996, 39-40 with colourplates 2c, 3a).

The top of the foundation-pit was preserved to relative level 84 at the front of the north-west wing of the pylon, cut into the ground with hardly any brick revetting of the sides, unlike the rear edge, which was extensively reinforced with mud-brick. In the upper-level fill outside the front edge were examples of Persian-Period pottery, including specimens of types A.2.10, A.5.10, A.5.28 and A.5.39 of the corpus published in 1996, but at greater depth were the vessels drawn in plate 9b. These comprised a shallow bowl, part of a much larger bowl with an internal rim, and a rounded jar with an external pink wash. All these items were made of red siltware and they resemble the forms of certain vessels from the area of the grain-silos beside the New-Kingdom enclosure wall, dating from the Twentieth to Twenty-first Dynasties (see Chapter 4 and pls.71a, 72-75). Their presence in front of the Second Pylon shows that the occupation area of this period extended well into the later temple site. Excavation was continued through the broken stone rubble to reveal clean yellow sand. Embedded in this, 160cm from the north-west side of the foundation and 100cm from the front edge, was a curious lump of mud of circular shape, but conical in section, with bits of limestone within it and below it. The origin of this feature is unclear; it may have been simply a chunk of muddy earth which fell accidentally into the foundation during the filling of the sand-bed. It is visible in colourplate 1a.

At slightly greater depth a complete foundation deposit was revealed in the sand, just above the subsoil water at a relative level of 9. The cluster of objects lay 71cm from the front of the foundation-pit and 228cm from the north-west edge, and covered an area of 55 x 72cm. The objects were distributed as shown in the photographs on colourplate 1b, plate 10a-b and the drawing on plate 11a. They comprised the following (see Cat.**104**):

1   A thin brick of dense, black mud
2   Gilded wooden plaque with an inscription of the priest Hor
3   Silver plaque, corroded, with the same text as last
4   Calcite hemi-disk with an inscription of the priest Hor
5   Bronze plaque inscribed for the priest Hor
6a-b   Fragments of a green malachite plaque, uninscribed
7   Group of faience beads, including rings, spheroids and cylinders
8   Piece of rough hard limestone
9   Two rough pieces of black granodiorite
10-13 Four fragmentary conical cups of red pottery
14-16 Three low dishes of red pottery
17   Green faience plaque with no surviving inscription
18   Green faience plaque with remains of an illegible text in black paint

The numbers of the above list refer to those on the plan in plate 11a. Illustrations of the individual pieces are given on colourplate 1c and plates 11b and 100.

Front corner of the south-east wing of the pylon
A 4 x 3 metre trench dug on this corner of the pylon went down through a mass of deeply pitted limestone rubble and mud fill to water, with no intact foundation sand preserved. All of this rubble was contained in deep pits, which had been refilled with dumped material after ancient quarrying. Fragments of Roman glass and pottery were noted in the fill, as was a fragment of worked basalt. The brick-lined face of the foundation-pit was eventually revealed on the south-east side, and later at the north-east, or front. All the higher parts of the brickwork had been damaged by the pitting of the area. Dumped in the bottom of one of the pits in the east corner of the foundation was a large circular limestone block, which had been either a column base or an unfinished drum from a column, possibly re-used in the pylon. The block was 1.88 metres in diameter and 35-40cm thick, and there was a shallow groove across the top where an attempt had been made to cut it (pl.13a). The upper surface of the stone lay at relative level 37. The area around this block was tested deep into the water, but no sand was encountered, only masses of broken stone in the bases of the pits, so it was not surprising that the foundation deposit was lacking.

14

Rear corner of the south-east wing of the pylon

Excavation of this corner was situated next to the old trench ES3 of the 1991 season, into which it was eventually extended. Mud-brick had been used to reinforce the sides of the foundation-pit, and three courses were preserved at the top of the south-east side, although this revetting may well belong to the Thirtieth-Dynasty phase. A trace of the Thirtieth-Dynasty forecourt wall foundation-trench, largely cleared of its sand and refilled by mud flow, was detected coming into the main foundation from the south-east.

Inside the main foundation was a great deal of rubble in old stone-quarrying pits, which went down to considerable depth before foundation sand was reached. From the rubble came a rough piece of quartzite sandstone, possibly a material sample disturbed from the foundation deposit below. The surviving sand of the foundation was not revealed until the subsoil water-table had been reached, at a relative level of -10. The water was drained by baling and the excavation continued to greater depth to reveal a complete foundation deposit similar to the one at the north corner (Cat.**105**). The objects were recovered from wet sand between relative levels -35 to -40, in a cluster centred 100cm from the side wall of the foundation and 70cm from the rear (pl.12a). This deposit had a similar configuration to that from the front of the left side of the pylon, and some of the objects bore identical inscriptions of the priest of Amun named Hor. Fortunately for the problem of dating, there was also one plaque with a royal cartouche of a king Sheshonq, who is most probably to be identified as Sheshonq III (see Chapter 6). The objects are shown in plates 12b and 101, in addition to colourplate 2a-b. The deposit contained the following objects:

1   Large brick of black mud
2   Calcite hemi-disk inscribed for the priest of Amun, Hor
3   Gilded wooden plaque, originally inscribed with the same text as last
4   Two pieces of a corroded silver plaque, no text remaining
5   Malachite plaque without inscription
6   Bronze plaque with an inscription of the priest Hor
7   Faience plaque in two pieces with traces of black paint
8   Green faience plaque with a cartouche, most probably of Sheshonq III
9   Green faience plaque without inscription
10   Two rough pieces of granodiorite
11   Broken model of a limestone mortar
12   Fragment of corroded iron
13   Group of faience beads, including rings and cylinders
14   Eight red-brown siltware pottery cups in fragmentary condition, now restored

(c) The parallel sand-trenches of the colonnade foundation

Further work was carried out in 1996-7 at the centre of the pylon of Sheshonq III, close to the axis of the temple. Trenches in this area revealed more of the foundation sand, but no more deposits. The disturbance of the area by late-Roman pitting had been very severe and some of the pits continued well into the subsoil water. Part of the front of the foundation-pit was cleared, its edge surviving to relative level 121, at the junction of the pylon foundation and the end of the north-west sand-trench of the colonnade. Unfortunately, a huge later pit had destroyed the stratigraphic link between the colonnade foundation and that of the pylon, so it was not possible to establish whether the pylon and colonnade had been built as one project, or whether the colonnade had been a later addition to the face of the pylon. The colonnade trench had been cut into the same ground as the pylon foundation but did not go as deep, descending to an irregular base at relative levels ranging from 16 above datum down to zero. From the sand in the bottom of the trench came a rim from a siltware jar of Type D.1.51. The base of the trench consisted of hard mud with bands of broken limestone fragments - all material which had been part of the older ground into which the temple foundations were cut.

The north-west side of the colonnade foundation was first detected in the 1991 season, below an area of limestone pavement of Roman date (see Spencer 1996, 41-2). Following the discovery of the Sheshonq III pylon, the idea of two parallel sand-filled trenches for the foundations of a colonnade extending along the temple axis from the face of the pylon seemed plausible, and excavations were made to check this hypothesis. The second sand-trench for the south-eastern side of the colonnade was soon revealed and the link between these two trenches and the foundation of the much larger First Pylon was then explored. The colonnade trenches are each approximately 4 metres wide, with an intervening space of 10.2 metres. They run for a distance of 39 metres from the face of the pylon of Sheshonq III to the rear of the First Pylon (pl.5). The connection between the foundation of the latter pylon and the two trenches shows that the entire system of foundations for the colonnade and the First Pylon was cut as a single project. Although it is not possible bc absolutely sure whether these elements were built by Sheshonq III or belonged to a Saite addition to the building - owing to the problem of the discontinuity in the stratigraphy at the face of the Second Pylon, mentioned above - there is some other evidence to suggest a Saite date. Immediately to the north-west of the First Pylon lay a small temple, situated in the classic location of a barque-station dependent on the main temple (see Chapter 4). The processional axis from this building was blocked by the construction of the First Pylon, so the chapel would seem to have been built at a time when the Second Pylon formed the front of the Amun-Temple, implying that the colonnade and First Pylon were indeed added later. These monuments cannot be later than Saite because of the clear stratigraphic evidence for their complete destruction during the first Persian Period.

(d) Connection of the colonnade foundation with the face of the Second Pylon

The excavation immediately in front of the Second Pylon on the axis of the temple revealed an interesting feature concerning the arrangement of the parallel trenches for the colonnade. The usual width of about 4 metres for each of the trenches is reduced to 2.5 metres from a point about 9 metres in front of the pylon. This reduction was accomplished by a divergence in the alignment of the outer edges of each trench, bringing them closer to the axis of the temple. In the narrowed sections, however, the original width was regained for a short interval by creating a curved scoop into the inner side of each foundation trench, as shown in plates 13b and 14. The lengths of these curves were in the range of 3.5 to 4 metres and their widths between 1.8 and 2.1 metres, but the sides of the cutting were quite irregular and sloped inwards at greater depth. A discolouration in the sand at the point marked 'X' on the plan was followed down for 1.2 metres to the irregular surface of the mud side of the foundation, where a patch of reddish-brown material, probably a decayed wooden object, was all that remained of the source. Between the curved portions and the face of the pylon the trench resumed its 2.5 metre width. The purpose of this arrangement can only have been to provide a foundation for some feature immediately in front of the Second Pylon, probably an attached gate of the Egyptian *sbḫt* type (pl.6). The excavation of these details also revealed the full 6 metre width of the original pre-temple ground between the curved portions of the two parallel sand-filled trenches, at a relative level between 120 and 125. Embedded in this ground was the jar rim drawn on plate 71b, no. 7.

The pre-temple ground was buried under a deep deposit of quarrying rubble in which some large blocks of limestone had been buried (pl.17a), derived originally from the temple buildings but in some cases re-used in the Roman Period. Three large blocks were scattered across the axis, their sizes being 117 x 119 x 45cm, 100 x 79 x 73cm and 100 x 70 x 65cm. The largest example bore a few traces of register lines, showing that it had once been part of a temple building. Just to the west, on the inner edge of the north-western sand-filled trench, was a fourth large block measuring 117 x 72 x 63cm, which had to be moved since it began to fall onto the sand. This block, visible in plate 13b, was covered with oblique chisel marks from working. Under the large stone were some smaller slabs of more regular shape which had quite clearly been recut for use in Roman masonry. In the rubble beside these a limestone fragment from the inscribed back-pillar of a statue was recovered (Cat.2). From the overlying fill came a small, illegible coin, a complete fired brick measuring 23 x 11 x 6.5cm and fragments of others embedded in pink plaster. Ptolemaic to Roman pottery fragments were also recovered in this area and the shapes which could be identified are drawn on plate 16, nos. 1-7.

Some *in-situ* masonry was found on the edge of the opposite foundation-trench, south-east of the axis, consisting of a few courses of small blocks of limestone (pls.17b, 18a). The lower two courses were founded on the pre-temple ground at relative level 121 and might have belonged to part of the original temple pavement in front of the Second Pylon. Two further courses had been added above these in the Roman Period, since there was a layer of typically Roman plaster between the different levels. All the masonry had been quarried out until very little remained. From the fill above this masonry came evidence of Roman activity in the form of fired bricks, fragments of pink plaster and marble wall-facing. A model of a column-drum in glassy faience was also found here (Cat.**47**) as well as a number of fragmentary glass inlays (Cat.**49**). A few pieces of Ptolemaic to Roman pottery and glass from here are shown on plate 16, nos. 8-12.

The nature of the original pre-temple ground was tested in the axis between the two sand-trenches, and also at the north-west side of the excavation, in an area untouched by the temple foundation. In both locations it was found to have the same composition of compact black mud interspersed by layers of broken limestone, presumably from the demolition of some older building in the vicinity, but not actually on the same spot, since the quantity of broken stone was not sufficient. A section showing part of the pre-temple ground was cleaned and recorded over the outer edge of the north-western sand-trench (between points A and B on the plan in plate 14). It shows how the level of this ground has been reduced since the destruction of the temple by the repeated pitting of the area, clear profiles of the pits being visible.

Notes on the profile over the outer edge of the north-western sand-trench (pl.15)
This profile shows a section over the north-western edge of the colonnade foundation in front of the Second Pylon, with part of the sand-filled foundation-trench on the left and the pre-temple ground on the right, both buried under disturbed deposits from the repeated destruction and quarrying of buildings in the area. The chronological sequence of the section begins with the pre-temple ground [k], which, as elsewhere in the temple site, consists of alternate bands of compacted earth and limestone debris. This ground rises to a maximum relative level of 125, but was probably higher originally. The edge of the sand-filled foundation-trench was cut vertically through the layers of the original ground, but some of the height of both the sand and the pre-temple ground has been cut away by the pit [j], which was sealed by stratum [f]. This layer of earth and sand, together with the higher levels of destruction rubble [e,d,c] probably extended to the south-east across the temple sand-trench [m] before being truncated by the foundation-trench of a Roman wall [g] and later by the huge robbers' pit [b]. The block [h] belongs to the footing of the wall; the top of the block was covered with pink cement characteristic of Roman constructions. The great quantity of broken limestone in all the contexts [b] to [d] came from the destruction of the Pharaonic temples and of the Roman buildings in the area.

On the right-hand side of the profile, the various layers were cut by the large late pit [a], which descended as far as the first layer of broken stone within the pre-temple ground. This pit was subsequently left to fill up gradually: the first accumulation at its base consists of wind-blown dust. Above this is a stratum of dumped builders' waste: earth, stone fragments, sand and sherds. More dust blew in to cover this debris, a little sand was dumped (probably extracted from the temple foundation in other pit-digging), then additional dust gathered above the sand. A stratum of broken mud-bricks was thrown in, followed by a litttle more sand, before a final deposit of wind-blown dust sealed the pit at surface level.

This extremely 'busy' section illustrates the extensive activity which took place in the area after the demolition of the temple, with the erection of Roman buildings and their subsequent destruction, followed by intensive and repeated pitting.

The length of the section described above was only 2.8 metres, but the same kind of stratification was also noted in a separate excavation trench of 3 x 4 metres, situated 2 metres further to the north-west. Deep in this ground a small area of settlement debris was recovered containing a few sherds, which appeared to date from the end of the New Kingdom.

(e) Connection of the colonnade foundation with the rear of the First Pylon in Area RP1-2

The angles made by the two sand-trenches with the rear of the foundation of the First Pylon were slightly offset, the internal corners turning some 4 metres short of the location of the external angles (pls.3 and 5). The interior angles turned towards the temple axis for 3 metres to meet a central strip of the original ground, left in place between the two great sand-pits on which the towers of the pylon once stood. Against both sides of the central strip and just one metre distant from the rear corners, some mud bricks were revealed on the top of the foundation sand at a relative level of 80, arranged as shown in plates 20a-b. The dimensions of the bricks were 38 x 20 x 9cm. Their position suggested that they might have been intended to cover the locations of foundation deposits, but an investigation below the bricks revealed no traces. Both clusters of bricks lay at the base of pits and appeared to have been rather disturbed (see the profile, pl.19). It is possible that the pits were cut during the robbing of foundation deposits covered by the bricks, or even that the bricks themselves had been dumped in the pits as rubbish. The latter possibility is supported by the presence of some additional mud-bricks, which clearly had been discarded in the base of another rubbish-pit, situated just 50cm distant from the north-western brick cluster. The sand under the bricks in the two corners was not clean like the surrounding sand of the foundation, but was contaminated with bits of stone and mud. At a relative level of -35, well under the subsoil water, a layer of black mud was encountered as the bottom of the sand was reached. Since these corners are essentially still within the ends of the colonnade foundation-trenches, this depth for the sand cannot be taken as being the same as that within the foundation of the First Pylon itself, where the base of the sand was not revealed. The bottom of the north-western colonnade-trench had also been exposed at its junction with the Second Pylon, but at a higher relative level of 16 (see above, p.16).

The connection of the foundation of the south-eastern wing of the pylon with the south-eastern trench of the colonnade exhibited an interesting ancient baulk which had separated the two areas until, presumably, the final stages of preparation. This was probably necessary for easy access across the site and might also have been related to the different depths of the two parts of the foundation. The baulk crossed the widened part of the colonnade foundation-trench at the rear of the pylon, a distance of 6.9 metres, but its removal prior to the filling of the foundation system with sand was not completely carried out. Its remains extend 2.6 metres from the original strip of ground down the axis of the temple, beginning at the same level as this pre-temple ground for the first 80cm (relative level 105), but then cut down in a series of curved steps to progressively greater depths, whilst at the same time narrowing from 120cm to 100cm (pl.21a). The descent of this part was traced to a relative level of 1cm above datum before it dropped into wet sand in the middle of the foundation trench. On the opposite side of the trench a similar but rather smaller excrescence appeared, the remains of the other end of the baulk, here cut into a curved ridge, projecting slightly into the pit and tapering away to a point. This effect will be familiar to those with experience of supervising the moving of large masses of earth, such as excavation dumps or surface mud, in Egyptian excavations. Each worker cuts the earth before him, but frequently a piece of ground between two workers will be regarded as the responsibility of neither, and it is left as a projecting mass, exactly the same as the feature observed in the temple foundation. The ancient foundation system for the temple was obviously excavated with tools unsuited to precise work - the ancient equivalents of the modern Egyptian hoe, the *turiya* or *fas*, so it is not surprising that the hard earth sides of the pit show exactly the same kind of curvature which occurs in all modern digging with these tools, brought about by the characteristic angle of the blade. This minor piece of ancient evidence gives an interesting sidelight on ancient constructional methods.

In the clearance of the junction of the colonnade foundation and that of the First Pylon a considerable quantity of broken stone was found in the overlying fill, together with pottery fragments of the late-Roman Period. The stone was the product of the quarrying of the temple and consisted chiefly of roughly broken fragments of limestone. One piece of interest was recovered from the fill above the north-west side of the colonnade: part of a limestone doorsill with a cut-away section at one end for a pivot-block. The remaining part of this slab was 74cm in length by 56cm wide, with a thickness which varied between 12 and 16cm (see pl.24b).

(f) The axis of the temple

The strip of earth which separates the two halves of the first pylon foundation is a preserved part of the Twenty-second Dynasty ground-level, left as an ancient baulk along the temple axis. It is not a built feature, but simply a piece of earth left undisturbed by the cutting of the foundation-pits around it, just the same earth as exists between the two sand-trenches of the colonnade or against their exterior edges. These areas of the the original ground into which the foundation was dug are of interest because they represent the stratified deposits which had accumulated on the site of the temple prior to its construction in the Twenty-second Dynasty. Close to the temple axis they consist of hard brown or black mud with embedded layers of limestone chips, but very few sherds or other settlement debris. The small amount of pottery recovered from the mud seems to date from the end of the New Kingdom. Some parts of the outlying limits of the temple foundation, however, such as the end of the north-west wing of the First Pylon, were cut into fill more characteristic of domestic settlement with remains of brick features, carbon deposits and sherds, dating from the Twentieth to Twenty-first Dynasties (see Chapter 4).

In most areas the pre-temple ground-level now lies between 80 and 120cm under the present-day surface. For a distance of 19 metres from the corners which it makes with the colonnade foundation-trenches, the central strip extends towards the front of the temple with a width of about 4 metres, although the cutting of its edges is rather irregular. It then narrows gradually to a width of 2 metres in the region of the front gate, perhaps to allow for the positioning of deep masonry foundations on either side (colourplate 2c). Despite the irregularity of the axial piece of original ground, there is no doubt that it was left deliberately by the builders in order to facilitate the laying out of the temple. Leaving a strip of ground along the axis would have allowed for easier measurement of distances, not only along the axis, but also as offsets to the edges of the sand foundations on either side. That this procedure occurred is confirmed by the discovery in Trench A1 of a limestone slab marked with the axis line of the temple, set into the surface of the central strip near the front of the building (pl.21b). This axis-marker was for use only during the setting-out of the temple, because it would have been covered by the pavement as construction proceeded. There must have been at least one other marker at some point along the axis, in order to be able to sight a line between two points, but its location has not yet been discovered.

The excavated axis-marker consists of a roughly square slab of limestone, 15cm in thickness, measuring 72.5 x 66.5cm. It had been set into the ground with its upper face flush with the surrounding surface at a relative level of 84. The actual axis line was positioned 46.5cm from the south-eastern edge of the slab, but only 26cm from the opposite edge. The fact that the line was not in the middle of the slab suggests that it was cut after the stone had been set into the ground. This view is supported by the fact that, although the slab itself was not accurately centred within the strip of earth, being 152.5cm from the south-east side and 172cm from the north-west, the marked line falls exactly in the middle of the strip, which has a width of 3.97 metres at this point. The axis-slab was lifted (and replaced in precisely the same position) to check for a possible foundation deposit below but there was only the usual black earth of the pre-temple ground, from which part of a pottery jar-rim was retrieved, probably dating from the eleventh century BC (pl.71b, no. 10).

The original strip of ground on which the axis-marker rests was found to have been covered by a stratum of clean sand, cut in places by two large pits from the surface. These pits, filled entirely with sterile rain-washed mud, increased in depth towards the south-west and descended into parts of the pre-temple ground. In those areas not destroyed by the pits, the stratigraphy revealed a stratum of broken limestone over the clean sand layer, including some large slabs which had once formed part of the temple pavement. This was laid on the sand, but as the original top of the sand is not preserved it is difficult to establish the exact relative level at which the pavement of the Twenty-second Dynasty temple was located, but it was probably no lower than 225. From the relative levels shown on the plan in plate 7 it will be noticed that the height of the original ground along the axis rises slightly from the front of the temple towards the rear, which may be related to the rising floor-level in Egyptian temples as the sanctuary is approached. Some pieces of broken limestone were found in the fill above the axis-stone, including one with remains of an inscription in hieroglyphs. The piece was smoothed on two faces and the inscription ran vertically (Cat.**4**). This and the other limestone fragments had been discarded in redeposited fill containing a little late-Roman pottery, probably evidence of quarrying.

(g) Position and size of the First Pylon

The two sand-filled foundation-pits for the towers of the First Pylon are separated by the axial strip of ground discussed in the foregoing section (pl.5). The full extent of the pylon was traced during the 1995 and 1996 seasons by the cutting of numerous excavation trenches. These produced ample evidence for the destruction of the pylon during the first Persian Period, and the consequent accumulation of structures and deposits from this age above the remains of its sand-bed. Details of these post-destruction levels are given in Chapter 2. The pylon foundation itself consists of two roughly rectangular sand-filled pits, each measuring about 36 x 14 metres, the limits of which extend to a maximum distance of 39 metres to either side of the temple axis. This excavation, like the sand-filled trenches of the colonnade foundation, was cut into the existing ground-level of the Twenty-second Dynasty. The cutting of the pit was not very regular, as is evident from the divergence of the rear edge of the pylon foundation from a straight line at right-angles to the temple axis (pl.5). On both sides the rear edge was found to have been cut too far back as the distance from the axis increased. Evidence to show that the builders were not too concerned about minor deviations from the exact alignment was clear from the presence of undulations and irregularities in the cutting of the sides of the foundation, as also observed in the sand-filled trenches for the colonnade.

(h) Tracing the foundation of the south-east wing of the First Pylon

From the central connection with the colonnade foundation, the rear of the pylon was first traced towards the south-east, in a series of small excavations (reference numbers E6 to E11, pl.3). The first of these tests to be dug, E11, missed the edge of the pylon foundation owing to the unexpected irregularity of the ancient alignment, but succeeded in revealing some of the interior sand at relative level 54. During the removal of some of this sand some of the remainder fell away from the south-west profile to expose the face of the foundation-pit just behind. The position of the succeeding trenches was then adjusted to take the divergence of the foundation into account. These trenches revealed the edge of the pit and part of the sand-bed which it contained, overlaid by a layer of broken stone rubble from the destruction of the temple. Later features and deposits above the sand and rubble are considered in the description of the post-destruction phase (Chapter 2). The depth to which the foundation had been cut down by the later activity on the site increased as excavation proceeded further from the temple axis, as can be seen from the relative levels for the original pre-temple ground at the edge of the pit, and for the sand itself (pl.7). Beginning near the axis with readings of over 100, the levels on the foundation edge drop to 66 in Trench E10 and 55 in Trench E9. The descent continues through Trenches E7-8, with a relative level of 45 observed in the link cut between these two excavations. Part of the rear of the pylon in this area had been overbuilt by several pottery kilns, and it is possible that the destruction of the foundation was connected with the removal of sand for use in the mixing of pottery clay. At a distance of just over 28 metres from the axis, the higher foundation-trench of the Thirtieth-Dynasty forecourt wall was encountered, cut through the level containing the pottery kilns and into the older pylon foundation. Excavation outside the line of the Thirtieth-Dynasty forecourt showed that the pylon foundation continued to the south-east, although the preserved level was falling even deeper than before, down to a relative level of only 14. The rear edge of the foundation could still just be observed, however, at a point 33.5 metres from the axis, but beyond this point detection became impossible. Trench E6, situated on the rear corner of this wing of the pylon, failed to reach any remaining sand, revealing instead only redeposited fill from two phases of destruction, the first in the fifth century BC and second in the late Ptolemaic Period. The front angle of the pylon had also suffered total removal through the Ptolemaic pitting observed in Trench E5 (see Chapter 2). No front edge to the sand-bed was found in Trenches E2 or E3, because E2 was sufficiently close to the temple axis as to lie above the extended sand-bed of the monumental approach to the pylon, and therefore contained a continuous stratum of sand, and E3 had been too greatly disturbed in the Persian Period. The difficulty of tracing the south-eastern limit of the foundation as the level of the sand fell below the water-table led us to transfer our attention to the opposite wing of the pylon in the hope of finding better-preserved remains.

(i) Tracing the foundation of the north-west wing of the First Pylon

The excavations at the south-east side of the pylon had already shown that the foundation extended a considerable distance from the axis, and exceeded the width of the forecourt of the Thirtieth-Dynasty temple. Exploration of the opposite wing of the pylon was not intended to repeat this information but to extend it by the identification of the limits of the foundation. Accordingly, trenches were dug along the rear edge of the pylon, from the region where it was crossed by the later forecourt wall towards the north-west. The first trench of this series (W5) was situated just within the Thirtieth-Dynasty forecourt, and was designed to intercept the interior edge of the foundation-trench of the forecourt wall as a control on the precise location. This excavation of 4 x 3 metres revealed foundation sand of the pylon at relative level 31 on the south-east side, sloping down towards the north-east. Eventually clean sand of the foundation was exposed over the full area of the trench, but the back of the foundation-pit was not found. A small extension to the south-west showed that the trench had missed the edge by approximately 50cm, owing to the deviation of the side of the foundation from a right-angle with respect to the temple axis. This was the same problem as occurred in Trench E11 on the opposite wing of the pylon. Above the sand in Trench W5 was fill from the first Persian Period and also some late-Roman features, the most striking of which was a brick-built lime-kiln in the south corner. Details of this and other remains from the upper levels are given in Chapter 2.

Having confirmed the position of the rear of the pylon foundation on this side of the temple, additional excavations were made to trace it around its north-western limits, as had been attempted previously for the south-east wing. Trench W6 was dug some 2.5 metres further from the temple axis, to reveal a bed of well-preserved sand from the foundation of the pylon. This sand had survived to a maximum relative level of 44, the highest portions being at the south-west side. It was noticeable that the best-preserved sand filling always occurred at the edges of the foundation, presumably because it was easier to extract sand from the middle. The back of the foundation-pit passed across the south-west profile of this trench and continued to the north-west. A third excavation (W7) placed initially some 37 metres from the axis, and later extended for another metre, finally located the rear corner of the pylon foundation. This angle at the back of the north-west wing of the pylon was not at all regular, but consisted of a rather wide and meandering curve, cut into the pre-temple ground surface. The identification of the corner was hindered by the presence of several pits, some cut through the upper post-temple destruction fill into the older levels, but others actually being pre-temple pits contained within the ground into which the pylon foundation had been cut. The original ground in this area was very clearly the product of the stratified accumulation of settlement fill, with clearly visible pits and mud-brick features. These belong to the continuation of the occupation-area of the Twentieth to Twenty-first Dynasties which forms the subject of Chapter 4. One of the chief activities in the excavation was to distinguish this pre-temple domestic fill from the post-temple Persian-Period fill, which was not simply overlaid on the former, but also sunk into it in deep pits.

This rear corner of the foundation was subsequently found to be the only one of the four outer corners under the First Pylon to contain a substantial quantity of the original sand above the ground-water. Trench W7 was extended to the north-east in order to be sure it included a sufficiently wide area below the original location of the actual masonry of the pylon and the whole corner was excavated deep into the sand and below the water by using a motor pump, allowing the sand to be searched for any foundation deposit down to a relative level of -89. Unfortunately the region which would have lain beneath the angle of the pylon was found to have been dug out in the Persian Period and refilled with broken pottery jars in a great dump, which expanded in area as it descended into the sand. Even at the lowest limit reached, the sand-bed was still found to be discoloured by mud introduced through this disturbance, together with further examples of the intrusive pottery (see Chapter 2).

The edge of the foundation-pit at the back of the north-west wing of the pylon was preserved to relative level 57 at the rear of the corner, but dropped into the water-table (about relative level 10) as it went around the end of the pylon. Further excavation was undertaken to trace the edge across the end of the pylon and to try to find the front corner of the foundation-pit. The small trench W8 about 5 metres north-east of the rear corner revealed traces of the edge of the pylon foundation at a low level, buried below muddy fill of the first Persian Period, deeply cut by Roman pits. A larger excavation further to the north-east (W9) exposed settlement refuse of the fifth century BC right down into the water-table, where it had replaced the sand filling of the foundation. Along the north-west edge of this trench, however, a trace of the original sand appeared at water-level, confirming that the foundation had extended over the area. The excavation was extended to the north-west and north-east to reveal more sand, rising in level as it approached the edge of the foundation-pit. Eventually, the front corner of the pylon foundation was found with some of the sand filling preserved within it (colourplate 4b). Part of the pre-temple ground at this corner of the foundation rose to relative level 77, consisting of fill of the Twentieth to Twenty-first Dynasty around the mud-brick wall of a grain-silo, which had been truncated by the foundation-pit of the pylon. The remaining sand, however, lay at a relative level of only 1cm over datum. Attempts to trace the front of the pylon foundation were complicated by the fact that the sand was present only right within the corner and vanished to inaccessible depths as soon as work proceeded further along the front edge. Eventually the approximate position of the front of the foundation-pit was revealed only by a discontinuity in the stratigraphy between pre-temple settlement deposits and post-temple destruction fill. Study of the south-west section of the excavation revealed a similar interface between the pre-temple ground and the mud which had filled the foundation after the sand had been removed. The nominal distance across the end of the pylon foundation between the front and rear angles of this wing was 14 metres, although the size of the pylon itself would have been smaller, since foundations were always rather wider than the masonry they supported. The position of the end of the foundation lay 39 metres distant from the axis of the temple. For discussion of the dimensions of the pylon which stood on these foundations, see Chapter 6.

(j) The interior of the First Pylon foundation

Several excavations were made between 1994 and 1996 inside the area of the First Pylon foundation, although those cut in the earlier year were dug before the true nature of the foundation had been identified. The trenches produced one of two results: either they revealed the sand-bed, covered by varying amounts of later fill, or they simply went down through redeposited debris all the way into the subsoil water. The date of the overlying deposits was usually the fifth century BC, with sometimes a little Ptolemaic or Roman material above, and the absence of sand in certain areas was simply the result of it having been quarried out to great depth before being covered by these later deposits. Had it been possible to go sufficiently deep below the water-table, it is almost certain that all the trenches in the area would eventually have reached undisturbed foundation sand: the presence or absence of sand in any particular trench depended only on the depth to which it had been removed by post-destruction activity, and its place taken by later fill. The sand-bed was originally prepared to a standard level corresponding approximately to relative level 125 throughout the foundation, but only small areas close to the axis have survived to the full height. Excavations in Trenches W3 and W4, near the inner end of the north-west side of the pylon, revealed foundation sand at relative levels ranging from 54 to 91, but in Trench W2 all the original sand above water had been replaced by later fill, with the usual stratigraphy of mixed Roman and Ptolemaic traces near the surface and fifth-century BC below. Near the middle of the front of the opposite wing of the pylon sand was present in Trench E2 at the low relative level of 34 under a deep mass of compacted later deposits, but the sand level dropped below the water-table only about 6 metres further to the south-east, at the end of Trench E3. Excavations in Trenches E5 and E6 at the far south-eastern end of the foundation failed to reach any sand, but here it had been replaced by Ptolemaic fill rather than with material from the first Persian Period. (Or, more probably, the Persian stratum had itself been removed completely by the later Ptolemaic activity).

Although the excavations inside the foundation produced little information on the structure of the pylon, they were most valuable for the study of the destruction of the monument in the fifth century BC, and the subsequent overbuilding of its foundation. Details of these overlying levels are given in Chapter 2.

(k) The approach to the First Pylon and the temple entrance

Excavation at the front of the temple revealed the location of an entrance to the earlier phase of the monument (Twenty-second Dynasty to Saite), the site of which had been overbuilt by a gate of the Thirtieth-Dynasty temple. The first task in the excavation of the gate area was the removal of a large dump, created during ancient quarrying of the temple and lying directly above the axis. The south-western half of this mound was removed in the 1995 season down to the base of the dump at relative level 195. Evidence from elsewhere in the courtyard suggests that this was the ground-level in the first century BC, before the late-Roman quarrying of the temple, which took place some 500 years later. The direction of the tip-lines in the dump showed that it had been thrown from the direction of the interior of the court.

Many loose bands of sand, interspersed with layers of broken limestone rubble, make up this dump, but there was little pottery or other man-made material. A few fragments of fired bricks, the base of a clear glass bottle and small fragments of bronze were the only items noted. At the south-east end of the dump were a few mixed sherds, mostly of coarse siltware, but including a finer red sherd from a Ptolemaic cooking-pot and the neck from a Cypriote flask of the seventh century BC. Some lumps of pink plaster below the middle of the dump were similar to the bedding of a pavement found in 1991, located some 30 metres south-west of the gate. Probably parts of the pavement, which may once have approached closer to the gate, were destroyed by the quarrying and thrown into the dump. All the material in the mound was completely mixed, of course, being anything which happened to be lying around during the quarrying operations.

Excavation below the base of the mound began as an initial trench of 7 x 3 metres, but was subsequently extended as necessary to follow various features, as indicated on plate 22 (Area TG1). The fill above the temple level in this region lacked any later built structures and consisted only of various layers of redeposited material: sand, limestone rubble and rain-washed mud. This was removed to reveal a bed of clean yellow sand over the whole area, clearly intended to serve as a foundation layer. Later work has shown that this sand belongs to the front part of the vast foundation of the Third Intermediate Period to Saite temple, the majority of which still remained to be discovered in 1995.

The sand rose highest (relative level 97) in the middle of the excavation, along the temple axis, and bedded into it were two courses of mud-bricks which had formed the foundation for the threshold of a gate (colourplate 2c, pl.23a-b and the plan on plate 22). The bricks were laid in a row 5.3 metres long, terminating to the south-east at a block of limestone, which must have belonged to the base of the stone jamb. At the opposite end the equivalent stone had been robbed out, but its original position could still be detected. The size of the mud-bricks was in the range 40-41 x 20-21 x 8-9cm and the joins had been filled with sand only. The relative level on top of these bricks was 102, much too low for them to have belonged to the Thirtieth-Dynasty temple, and they were probably part of the sub-structure of a gate belonging to the earlier phase of building. The excavation was extended to the south-east to reveal many fragments of limestone and some larger blocks scattered over the sand. The fact that both phases of temple building included a gate in this area makes it difficult to ascribe these stone fragments to one or the other stage of construction, particularly as the stratigraphy has been disturbed by late-Roman pits. That this stone debris derives from the south-eastern masonry jamb of the gate is certain, but it probably includes fragments from both the Twenty-second Dynasty and Thirtieth-Dynasty monuments.

The upper surface of the sand lay at relative levels which varied between 56 and 23, depending on the extent to which it had been cut by pits from above, but it was found to be present over the whole area of the extended trench. The sand was everywhere covered by a layer of limestone fragments from the destruction of the temple masonry, buried in turn by a stratum of mud, which in some places contained broken mud-bricks. Earth fill containing pottery of the fifth century BC had accumulated immediately above this layer, as in so many other areas of the temple foundation. Details of the pottery from the overlying strata around the gate are given in Chapter 2. An examination of the foundation-trench of the Thirtieth-Dynasty forecourt wall, where it entered the excavation to the south-east of the temple gate, showed that it had been cut through the layer containing the pottery and also through the mud and broken stone layers, until the base of the trench descended into the extensive yellow sand bed. This stratigraphic detail is good evidence for the conclusion, also drawn from the results of other excavation trenches, that the Thirtieth-Dynasty rebuilding of the temple took place over the layers of mud and mixed debris which had accumulated on the site since the destruction of the earlier temple sometime after 525 BC.

The sand along the axis of the gate and below the mud-bricks of the threshold did not go very deep, but descended only for about 30cm below the level of the top of the mud-bricks before reaching the surface of the axial strip of pre-temple ground, mentioned above in section (f). This is the same layer of sand as was found to cover the area of the axis-stone, some 6 metres to the south-west. In this area of the gate the central strip was only 2 metres wide (colourplate 2c). Embedded in it were a few sherds from ceramics of the twelfth to eleventh centuries BC, suggesting a continuation into this area of the settlement deposits of this age in the angle of the New-Kingdom enclosure wall, some 40 metres to the north-west. How far the central baulk continued to the north-east beyond the brick threshold is un-clear: a test-trench sunk some 7 metres in that direction, on the north-east side of the ancient dump which covered the temple gate, failed to identify it with any certainty.

Among the stone fragments near the gate was a particularly large block of quartzite, which on close examination proved to be the lower half of a sculptured triad depicting Ramesses II with two divinities, almost certainly Amun and Mut (Cat.1). This sculpture lay inverted in the mud fill above the sand-bed; the presence of mud between the stone and the sand suggested that the block had been dumped not long after the destruction of the Twenty-second Dynasty temple (pl.24a). It had then gradually become buried in fill, which was cut by later pits: these were filled up with rain-washed mud. That it remained exposed for a considerable period after being discarded is shown by the weath-ering of the stone, and by the presence of grooves worn into it by persons removing powdered stone for magico-medicinal purposes. Not being of limestone, it is the sort of piece which was commonly rejected during the quarrying of temples, the main objective of which was lime production. A descrip-tion of the sculpture and its inscriptions is given in Chapter 5.

The sand-bed in the gate area was found to extend for a distance of at least 17 metres to each side of the temple axis; it also continued in a south-westerly direction, to merge with the great foundation-pit of the the First Pylon. The extent of this sand was established through the excavation of Trenches E1, E2 and W1, all of which reached clean sand above the level of the water-table. At the front of the temple the limit of the sand was also traced in the eastern part of Trench TG1 and in Trenches TG2-5 (pls.25a-b). This part of the foundation system probably belonged to some kind of monumental ap-proach to the pylon, occupying an area about 34 metres wide by 10 metres deep. At the front of this area, immediately outside the position of the front wall of the Thirtieth-Dynasty forecourt, the width of the foundation-pit of the temple narrows to just under 22 metres, as shown on the plan in plates 5 and 7. The front of this narrowed portion of the temple foundation contained a great mass of broken limestone in a pit which sloped to the north-east into the subsoil water. The foundation sand under this rubble also plunged below the water-level, making it impossible to be sure about the position of the end of the foundation system, although it is unlikely to be far away. The broken stone almost certainly came from the destruction of some kind of monumental portico in front of the First Pylon. The photo-graph in colourplate 4a shows the sand against the edge of the foundation in Trench TG3 together with the pit in the profile of the overlying layers of fill and mud.

The Thirtieth-Dynasty reconstruction of the temple

(a) Introduction

A complete rebuilding programme of the Amun-temple was initiated by Nekhtnebef, together with the construction of the new subsidiary Temple B and the Outer Enclosure Wall. The new Amun-Temple was constructed on the site of the destroyed Twenty-second Dynasty monument, the ruins of which had become covered by fill and rubbish of the fifth century BC, as indicated above. The site seems to have been levelled prior to the digging of the necessary foundations for the new building. At this stage the upper parts of features which had been built over the older temple ruins, such as the pottery kilns of the Persian Period above the First Pylon, were cut down to a uniform level. The foundations were then cut into the levelled surface of fifth-century BC deposits according to the new plan of the building, in which the front area would be made into a large open courtyard, at the back of which was a new pylon or a pronaos on the site of the pylon of Sheshonq III. To the south-west of this feature lay the inner part of the temple, occupying the same position as in the earlier design, but possibly of increased length. Where parts of the new foundations overlapped those of earlier date, the sand filling of each phase could often be distinguished by differences in colour. A description of the archaeology of the Thirtieth-Dynasty temple has been published in an earlier volume (Spencer 1996, 36-42), and the details given here are intended to supplement that account with more recent discoveries.

(b) Additional information on the forecourt and pronaos

Through certain detailed investigations carried out since the publication of the previous report, a few additional comments can be added to the description given in that volume. The alignment of the south-east side of the Thirtieth-Dynasty forecourt, assumed to mirror the north-west side, has now been confirmed to do so by excavation. The foundation-trench of this wall was discovered in the 1994 season when considerable parts of the north-west perimeter of the forecourt were traced. In 1995 a cross-section of the sand-filled foundation-trench was cut on the south-east side, and the results of this work are described below, p.35. The wall foundation was also cut in the 1996 season by our excavations along the rear of the foundation of the earlier First Pylon, between Trenches E7 and E8, as shown on the profile drawing on plate 38. In 1997 a portion of the foundation-trench was cleared at the south-east of the courtyard in association with the excavation of the mud-brick structure N1. This long building was positioned along the interior face of the south-east side of the court and appears to have been constructed under Nekhtnebef or soon afterwards. It is described in Chapter 3.

During the work on the forecourt in 1994, a drain made from cylindrical sections of pottery was discovered, extending in front of the forecourt wall to the north-west side of the temple axis (Spencer 1996, 40-41). The presence of a ceramic pipe-section on the inner side of the forecourt wall had been noted, and the suggestion made that the drain had passed under the wall to carry off rainwater from the courtyard. The remainder of the drain inside the forecourt was excavated in the 1996 season, when a further seven wheelmade ceramic sections were found, extending the drain for a distance of 4 metres into the forecourt. Each section had a diameter of 28cm at one end and 32cm at the other, to fit together, and the lengths were between 55 and 58cm. The separate elements had been arranged with the wider diameters towards the south, showing that the intended direction of flow was from the interior of the court to the outside. This supports the suggestion that the drain was contemporary with the temple and was designed to drain the courtyard, a very necessary provision in view of the substantial winter rainfall in this part of Lower Egypt. Ancient disturbance of the area had resulted in all the sections being broken and the top half of their circumferences sheared off. The level of the pipe rose towards the southern end; there might originally have been more sections, but the rising level had ensured their destruction so near to the pitted surface.

The site of the Second Pylon of the Twenty-second Dynasty temple was reworked by Nekhtnebef for the creation of a new feature, which could have been a new pylon or a pronaos with engaged columns at the front, as seems to have been preferred in temples from the fourth century BC. The proportions of the foundation-pit would seem to indicate that a pylon would have been more likely; if a pronaos was chosen, it must have been of limited depth, perhaps with only a single row of internal columns in addition to the engaged columns of the facade, like the pronaos of the temple of Khnum at Elephantine (Ricke 1960, plan 4). The walls of the Thirtieth-Dynasty forecourt met the sides of this pylon or pronaos as described in the previous volume (Spencer 1996, 39-40). Further consideration of this link led to the conclusion that the facade of the new temple occupied a slightly smaller area than the older pylon of Sheshonq III, because the foundation-trench of the forecourt wall did not end flush with the edge of the earlier pylon foundation but extended into it by about 2 metres. This overlap was betrayed by the different colours of the sand filling of the older and later foundations at the north-west side of the temple (Spencer 1996, colourplates 2c, 3a and plate 10). The counterpart to this situation on the opposite side of the temple was far less clear owing to the poor state of preservation of the remains. Although traces of the foundation-trench of the forecourt wall were detected as it entered the main foundation of the pylon/pronaos, all the original sand filling of the trench had been removed and replaced by water-laid mud.

(c) A foundation deposit of Nekhtnebef at the rear southern corner of the temple

The corners at the back of the temple had been partly investigated in 1991, but were re-cleared to greater depth and over a wider area in 1995 to take advantage of a lower water-table. The western corner was found to have been completely destroyed by pitting in Roman times, but intact clean foundation sand was found in the southern corner at a relative level of 40-50, under a mixture of surface mud, our own 1991 backfill and ancient pit-fill. The sides of the foundation of the temple had been reinforced extensively with mud-brick, almost certainly during the Thirtieth-Dynasty building operations. An intact foundation deposit was found near the corner, only slightly above the water-table at about relative level 10. The compact cluster of objects was situated 40cm from the south-east side of the pit and 60cm from the south-west, or rear wall (colourplate 3a). A line of discolouration around the deposit, enclosing the corner of the foundation, might indicate that the objects had been placed in a pit dug into an older sand-bed during the rebuilding of the temple. The sand inside this pit contained fewer inclusions of stone chips and mud than that further away from the edges of the foundation.

The deposit consisted of a quartzite model grinder on top of a quartzite model saddle-quern, at the north-east side of the group, with a blue faience cup to the south-east of these. To the south-west of the querns stood a model limestone mortar-vessel, to the east of which was a large faience plaque. Next to this, again on the east, was a second faience cup, lying on its side. These objects were lifted to reveal a mass of sand cemented together with an exudation of gypsum, going down into the water. The whole block was undercut and taken complete to the house, where the remaining items were extracted: seven more intact plaques, plus one of corroded bronze, a decayed piece of lead, three fragments of iron corrosion, a lump of bitumen, four pieces from two model bricks and a mass of white oxidised material. A list of all the items is given below. For additional information, including details of the exact content and distribution of the texts, see Catalogue entry **106**, colourplate 3b-c and plates 101-102.

Model limestone mortar
Model quartzite grindstone of curved shape
Model quartzite quern
Two blue faience cups, both fragmentary
Large green-glazed faience plaque inscribed for Nekhtnebef on each side
Hollow gold plaque, inscribed on both sides with the names and titles of Nekhtnebef
Silver plaque, inscribed similarly to last
Chalcedony plaque, inscribed with royal titles on one side and the prenomen of the king on the other
Green felspar plaque, inscribed on one side only with the names and titles of Nekhtnebef
Red jasper plaque, inscribed on both sides with the names and titles of Nekhtnebef
Green malachite plaque without inscriptions

Blue glass plaque, imitative of lapis-lazuli, inscribed on one face only with a text giving the names and titles of Nekhtnebef, followed by the epithet: '(may he) live forever.'

Remains of a decayed metal plaque, perhaps of lead

Corroded bronze plaque, inscribed with traces of a text which contained the names and titles of Nekhtnebef

Three fragments of iron from between one and three plaques

Piece of black bitumen

Four fragments from two model mud-bricks

Corroded white material, probably from a decayed plaque of metal

The whole area of this corner of the foundation was searched below the subsoil water to check whether there might have been another foundation deposit from the earlier building phase of the Twenty-second Dynasty, but none was found. Had the older temple been of shorter length, then the deposits would in any case have been sited further to the north-east. Dumped in the mud over the sand were two large broken blocks of basalt with remains of inscriptions (one seen in 1991 bore only part of the hieroglyph *iri*. The more extensive text of another block read: *...wrt mry di ʿnḫ*). It is unclear as yet whether these blocks belonged to the reconstructed temple of Nekhtnebef, or are actually Ramesside material, re-used by Nekhtnebef in the foundation-platform (pl.29a-b). A fragmentary basalt statue of Ramesses II was found in 1992 in fields north of the *tell*.

2. Destruction and overbuilding of the Amun-Temple

(a) Introduction

The arrangement of the surviving elements of the temple of Amun has been described in the previous chapter, with an account of the excavation of the temple level. Much additional information on the history of the site and the sequence of temple building was gained from an examination of the overlying strata, composed of a mixture of debris from the destroyed temple and fill derived from domestic or industrial activities of later periods. These levels and the antiquities contained within them are described below with reference to the individual excavation trenches opened over several seasons, so that the exact provenance of particular objects or pottery can be established in relation to the various parts of the temple. Owing to the great extent of the temple foundation, particularly the vast First Pylon, excavation to recover the plan had to be carried out through the use of numerous small excavations at selected points, since excavation of the whole area down to the level of the sand-bed would have been a colossal undertaking, and one unlikely to provide much more information that that achieved by more modest techniques.

The stratigraphy of the site shows clearly that the temple of the Twenty-second Dynasty to Saite Period was destroyed sometime in the fifth century BC and its masonry almost entirely removed, after which dust, mud, and various kinds of occupation debris accumulated over the sand-bed of the foundations to a depth of between one and one and a half metres. It is interesting to record that the demolition of the temple seems to have been achieved without much smashing of the stone, as the thick deposits of stone chips which are the usual sign of this activity are lacking. In the previous British Museum excavation of the temples at El-Ashmunein, the late-Roman quarrying of the monuments had left compacted layers of limestone chips up to half a metre in thickness as evidence for the breaking-up of the masonry, especially on the site of the pylons. By contrast, the modest scatter of fragments over the foundation sand of the pylons at Tell el-Balamun shows that these structures were dismantled systematically, block by block.

The stratum of fifth-century BC fill which covered the site of the destroyed temple was later cut by the foundations for the new temple of the Thirtieth Dynasty, founded sometime in the reign of Nekhtnebef (370-343 BC). The renewed temple of Amun does not seem to have remained in use beyond the last half of the first century BC, however, when late-Ptolemaic secular buildings and rubbish-pits encroached upon its front courtyard. Excavation of the temple revealed this same stratigraphic sequence in many areas, but most clearly in the south-eastern side of the forecourt. In the central part of the earlier temple, above most of the length of the colonnade foundation between the two pylons, the stratigraphy had been so greatly disturbed by Roman building activity, and later by stone-robbing, that nearly all the fill above the foundation sand was found to have been redeposited during this time. The same was true for the area immediately in front of the Second Pylon, described in the previous chapter. Small areas of localised late-Roman pitting were also encountered at various other points, such as close to the front of the temple in Trench TG1, but the older stratigraphy could still be identified around the areas cut by the pits. That the fifth-century BC and Ptolemaic strata once existed right across the temple site is suggested by the fact that the former level is present above the north-west edge of the First Pylon, although the erosion of the ground has removed any overlying Ptolemaic material.

The general pattern of the stratigraphy described above was recognised during the excavation of the numerous trenches required to explore the plan of the temple. Although the sequence of the different fills, pits and foundation-trenches has been established through study of the relationships of these features in the ground, the dating of the different strata above the temple sand-bed depends on the pottery and objects recovered from each layer. This material is presented in the plates with indications of the areas in which different groups were found. To complement these illustrations, the description below gives an account of the features encountered in the levels above the destroyed temple, including references to certain pottery types already drawn in the previous report (Spencer, 1996). For the positions of the different trenches mentioned in this account, see the key-plan on plate 3.

(b) The front of the temple

Trench TG1

First indications of the presence of a fifth-century BC destruction-level over the ruins of the Twenty-second Dynasty temple were noted in the area of the temple gate (TG1), where the rubble and mud immediately over the foundation sand was overlaid by fill containing fifth-century BC pottery. Above this was disturbed fill left from the activities of the stone-robbers, the only item of interest from which was part of a pottery dish (or lid) of Ptolemaic date (shape as the example in Spencer 1996, pl.54, 8). Across the axis of the temple much yellow sand was encountered at a fairly high level under the surface mud, but it proved to be redeposited sand brought from elsewhere. Somewhat deeper, most of this sand disappeared to reveal the fifth-century BC fill, followed by hard dark mud and stone chips. Finally, the concentration of broken stone increased immediately above the temple foundation sand. From the fill above this deposit of mud and broken stone came fragments of pottery vessels of the first Persian Period, listed below.

Material from the fifth-century BC stratum above the temple level in TG1:

Parts of two large bowls of coarse red siltware (pl.26, no.1).
Rim from a deep siltware bowl with an external rim (pl.26, no.2)
Part of a small vessel of fine beige marlware with black paint on the rim (pl.26, no.3)
Four small dishes of coarse red siltware (pl.26, no. 4)
Small pink marlware bowl (pl.26, no. 5)
Thick-walled bowl of coarse red siltware ware (pl.26, no. 6)
Two examples of a siltware shouldered jar (pl.26, no. 7)
Two examples of a siltware shouldered jar, wider neck than last (pl.26, no. 8)
Upper part of a shouldered jar of red siltware (pl.26, no. 9)
Rim of a small red siltware jar (pl.26, no. 10)
Coarse red siltware jar with an external rim (pl.26, no. 11)
Very coarse red siltware rim from a jar (pl.26, no. 12)
Sherd from an imported Cypriote vessel, decorated with black paint (pl.26, no 13)
Rim and neck from a fine small imported vessel, probably Cypriote. Fine pink/orange fabric with red paint on the exterior and around the interior of the rim. (pl.26, no.14)
In addition to the above, there were also examples of the following vessel types from the corpus of forms published in Spencer 1996: A.3.96; A.4.36; A.5.10; A.5.39; D.1.29; D.1.63 and D.2.66.

Trench TG2

This test-trench was cut to investigate the edge of the foundation-pit for the Twenty-second to Twenty-sixth Dynasty temple at the south-east side of the temple gate, the opposite side being located in Trenches TG3-5. Immediately below the surface mud was a layer of broken limestone from the destruction of the forecourt wall of the Thirtieth-Dynasty temple, the foundation-trench for which had been cut into fifth-century BC fill. A few Ptolemaic and Roman sherds were present in the top of the rubble layer, including the neck of a local amphora (shape as in Spencer 1996, pl. 46, no. 13). From just below the broken stone layer came several examples of small pottery dishes (pl.27a, nos. 1-4) and the top of a Phoenician amphora (pl.27a, no. 6). From lower down in the fill came some more siltware dishes of the same type as certain examples from Trenches TG1 and E1-2, shown on plate 26, no. 4 and plate 32b, nos. 2-3, and some small fragments of Cypriote vessels with black-painted decoration (pl.27a, nos. 7-9. The rim from a siltware shouldered jar was found just above the sand-bed of the temple foundation (pl.27a, no. 5). A faience spacer-bead was also recovered here (Cat.**55**).

Trenches TG3 and TG4
Like trench TG2, these excavations were dug to investigate the configuration of the edge of the pre-temple ground at the front of the temple, where the sand-bed narrows for the entrance. Trench TG3 was dug originally in 1995 during investigation around the Thirtieth-Dynasty forecourt wall. After cutting through about 40cm of compacted surface mud, mixed fill of earth with pockets of stone chips and sand was reached. Below this level the excavation descended over most of the area of the trench through a compact mass of broken limestone fragments into the clean sand of the temple foundation system, with part of the original pre-temple ground along the north-west edge of the trench. Trench TG4 exposed the continuation of this edge to the corner where the sand-bed widens in front of the First Pylon. Sherds from the mixed fill above the temple sand were mostly of the fifth century BC, with a few intrusive Ptolemaic fragments.

Pottery from TG3:

Very coarse siltware wide-mouthed jar (pl.27b, no.10)
Shouldered jar of red siltware (pl.27b, no.2)
Necks from red siltware jars (pl.27b, no.3-7)
Coarse red siltware vessel (pl.27b, no.11)
Upper part of a jar of Ptolemaic date, with traces of handles at the sides (pl.27b, no.8)
Part of the neck from a Ptolemaic jar with two handles, with a white wash on the exterior and inside the rim (pl.27b, no.9)

All the above pieces came from the fill between the surface mud and the top of the deeper stone rubble. This context also contained examples of the following pottery types from the corpus published in the previous volume (Spencer 1996). The number of examples follows the type designation in parentheses: A.4.10 (3); A.5.10 (3); A.5.48 (3); A.5.58 (1) and D.1.24 (1). In the deeper layer of stone rubble the following ceramics were noted: Types A.5.10; A.5.15; C.6.112; D.1.49; and D.2.53. There is little significance in the position of this pottery except that it overlies the temple level, because the contexts are not sealed except by the surface mud, which is probably quite recent.

Trench TG5
This trench was cut to follow the edge of the sand-bed extending to the north-west side of the temple entrance (see Chapter 1). The area was covered by very compact surface mud, compressed by the vehicle tracks which had formerly run across it. Below this mud was a large dump of broken pottery jars of the usual fifth-century BC destruction phase, this material having been thrown down into the edge of the foundation of the temple after removal of most of the sand filling. The forms of the pottery are shown on plate 28. The smaller pieces (nos. 1-3 of the plate) came from the top of the dump and the jars from lower down, but this might be only the effect of the heavier items falling to the base of the slope. The bowl fragment (no. 3) is from an imported Cypriote vessel of a fine orange fabric with a trace of a black-painted circle on the side. Many duplicates of the jars were present, and one example bore a rough potmark, made before firing (no. 7).

Trenches A1 and A2 on the temple axis
The excavation of these trenches produced no remains of note above the temple level, as the upper fill consisted almost entirely of compact rain-washed mud in old pits. Some limestone fragments found in a late-Roman pit under the mud have been noted in Chapter 1.

(c) The rear central part of the First Pylon foundation

Areas RP1 and RP2

Excavations were made in 1996 within an area of some 95 square metres at the rear of the pylon, to investigate the link between its foundation and the two parallel sand-trenches of the colonnade. The sand of the temple foundation in this area was found to be well preserved, rising to around relative level 100, and the excavations revealed the edges of the original ground into which the foundations had been cut. Details of the temple level have been given in Chapter 1. The overlying strata consisted of a mixture of layers of sterile rain-washed mud, and earth fill containing sherds and fragments of stone. In this region the material in the upper level was Ptolemaic to Roman, rather than fifth century BC as found further from the temple axis. This is the result of Graeco-Roman activity in the central part of the temple site, probably associated with the late pavement in the vicinity. Persian-Period fill may well have been present at one time, but it was later replaced by this more recent disturbance.

The fill above the junction of the south-eastern trench of the colonnade foundation and the rear of the pylon contained a preserved patch of pink plaster bedding from a Roman pavement, probably part of the one found in 1991. The new area of plaster covered an area of approximately 3.5 x 1.5 metres. It had been partly cut by a later pit, found full of rain-washed mud, and overlay a prepared foundation of hard mud, levelled stone fragments and fired bricks (see plates 18b-19 and the description below). This had been built up over the temple sand, in the angle between the edge of the south-eastern colonnade trench and the central strip of pre-temple ground. Among the stone fragments below the plaster layer was one with remains of an inscription, showing a Sed-festival hieroglyph (Cat.**5**).

Notes on the profile at the rear of Area RP1 (pl.19)

This section was situated at the north-west side of the excavation in RP1, above the edge of the temple sand-bed (see the plan on pl.3). It presented a typical example of the disturbed stratigraphy above the temple level in this area. The profile extends from the rear edge of the temple foundation - some of the pre-temple ground is included in the lower levels on the south west - over the sand in the interior. Below a fairly recent deposit of rain-washed mud in the surface pit [a] were remains of some pink plaster and fired bricks from the bedding-layer of a pavement [b], actually the continuation of the limestone pavement found in 1991 some 10 metres to the south-west. Associated with this plaster was a block of limestone and some compacted crushed shell, a material not uncommon in foundations of Roman buildings [k]. Below the plaster stratum was an older pit containing limestone rubble and plaster fragments [m] and under this was a continuous layer of very hard, black mud with a few embedded blocks of limestone [c]. This was followed by another stratum which continued right across the full length of the section, consisting of a mixture of earth, stone fragments and pockets of sand [d]. Below this, apart from the pit [f], all the deeper layers predated the destruction of the Third Intermediate Period temple. The successive fills on the south-west [g,h,j] were all part of the pre-temple ground, cut vertically at the edge of the foundation-pit for the introduction of the sand filling, much of which remained in place [e]. In this area the original ground consisted of a succession of soil fill [g], bricky fill [h] and mud with stone rubble [j]. The clean sand of the interior of the temple foundation had been cut by the pit [f], which had become refilled with discoloured sand containing chips of stone and pieces of mud-bricks. This pit was situated exactly above the cluster of mud-bricks which might once have formed the cover of a foundation deposit, as described in Chapter 1. The base of the pit had broken through the mud-bricks and the deposit, if there was one, was probably removed during this operation.

Excavation extended across the full width of the south-east side of the colonnade foundation at the point where it widened to join the sand-bed of the First Pylon. A small quantity of Ptolemaic and Roman pottery was noted, including some painted sherds, lying in the redeposited fill above the sand (see list below and pl.33). A fragment of marble wall-facing with traces of an inscription in Latin was also found (Cat.**6**).

On the western side, in Area RP2, the upper fill consisted of redeposited mud and stone fragments, with some areas of more recent disturbance refilled by wind-borne dust. Remains of vegetation buried under the sterile mud deposits indicated that the area had been dug out previously in modern times. A few late-Roman items were noted, particularly characteristic pieces being two sherds of African Red Slip Ware and a glass fragment, but there was much less pottery here than in RP1. Above the junction of the north-west colonnade foundation-trench and the back of the First Pylon there was a concentration of limestone fragments, including the fragment of a doorsill mentioned in the account of the temple plan (above, p.18).

Material from the fill above the temple sand-bed in area RP1. All items except the first are of Ptolemaic to Roman date:

Relief fragment with Sed-festival hieroglyph (Cat.**5**).
Fragment of marble wall-facing with part of an inscription (Cat. **6**)
Sherd from a red siltware cooking-pot (form as one from Trench W3 on pl.33, no.2)
Small red siltware plate (pl.33, no. 3)
Siltware dish (pl.33, no. 4)
Small siltware lid (pl.33, no. 5)
Flared red siltware jar-rim (pl.33, no. 6)
Jar of hard red siltware with a flared rim (pl.33, no. 7)
Part of the rim from a very large coarse siltware vessel (pl.33, no. 8)
Rim from a large siltware jar (pl.33, no. 9)
Two siltware jar-rims (pl.33, nos. 10-11)
Siltware vase with ribbing on the shoulder (pl.33, no. 12)
Two painted sherds from a Ptolemaic vessel, decorated in purple-red on an orange ground (pl.33, nos. 13-14)
A similar decorated sherd from a separate vessel (pl.33, no. 15)
Small dish with an external rim (for shape, see Spencer 1996, pl. 56, no. 2)
Body sherd of African Red Slip Ware
Two spikes from local amphorae
Fragment from the glass base of a vessel
Bronze nail (Cat.**33**)

Material from the other side of the temple axis in area RP2:

Part of a limestone doorsill (pl.24b)
Two small body-sherds of African Red Slip Ware
Glass fragment
Large pieces of broken limestone
Fragment of red granite

Trench E12
Additional excavation adjacent to the north-east end of area RP1 was carried out in 1997 by the cutting of Trench E12, covering 3 x 4 metres, directly over the rear inner corner of the pylon to check the well-preserved sand-bed for any foundation deposit, although these are not normally associated with the interior angles of pylons and no traces of any deposit were found. Below approximately 90cm of overlying fill, the sand was exposed over the majority of the area at a relative level of 80, but its upper surface had been contaminated by mud and stone fragments. A mud-filled pit was detected on the south-east side containing some body-sherds from late-Roman amphorae; in the base of this pit lay a large, plain block of limestone from the temple masonry, resting on the sand. This block measured 116 x 88cm, with a thickness of 38cm and its upper surface lay horizontally at relative level 118. Despite its horizontal position, the block had obviously been dumped back into the pit. Two other pits containing mud and limestone fragments were also noted in the north and east corners of the excavation. These pits contained some sherds of Ptolemaic to Roman date: part of the rim from a cooking-pot and

a fragment of a shallow dish. The pit in the east corner also contained several pieces of fired bricks. The sand became cleaner at a depth of 50cm below the top of the original pre-temple ground along the axis, except in the pits at the north and east, which continued to greater depths. At the south-west side of this excavation the remains of the ancient baulk, described in Chapter 1, began to appear. Excavation was continued into the ground-water to a relative level of -80 without revealing any evidence for a foundation deposit, nor reaching the bottom of the sand.

Material from Trench E12

From the upper fill:
A few Roman sherds
Fragment of glass
Half of a very corroded coin
Limestone fragments

From the mud-filled pit on the south-east side:
Several body-sherds from late-Roman amphorae

From pits in the sand on the north and east:
Dish fragment (pl.33, no. 16)
Siltware jar neck (pl.33, no. 17)
Part of a cooking-pot rim (pl.33, no. 18)
Pieces of fired brick, especially from the pit in the east corner

(d) Trenches to the south-east of the temple axis

The exploratory trenches E1, E2 and E3 were dug in 1995 to investigate the extent of the sand-bed of the temple and the stratigraphy of the overlying levels. The results in trenches E1 and E2 were similar to each other, revealing the temple sand to be overlaid by a thick layer of fifth-century BC fill, which had been cut by Ptolemaic pits.

Trench E1

Just below the present ground surface were some large and fragmentary vessels of coarse red siltware pottery, including the side of a shallow bin, 92cm long and 32cm high. This rested in the centre of the trench; around it were the lower parts of three large siltware jars embedded in the ground (pl.30a). Of the largest there remained only fragments of the rounded base, but in the west corner of the trench was the lower part of an ovoid jar with a narrow, rounded base and a maximum diameter of 18cm (pl.31a, no. 1). Another vessel, to the north of the fragments of the bin, had been of more rounded shape, with a diameter of 21cm. This jar had once possessed two loop-handles at the sides, although these had been broken away (pl.31a, no. 2). The pottery was associated with scanty remains of mud-brick walls at each end of the trench, eroded to only a single course of bricks. This high level dated from the Ptolemaic Period: a characteristic spindle-bottle (pl.32a, no.1) and a basalt weight were also found (Cat.**18**). At a lower level sherds of fifth-century BC jars and dishes were recovered, similar to examples from Trench E2, described below. The forms of these ceramics are shown on plate 32b, numbers 1-8. Parts of only two examples of the large platter were found (number 1 on the plate), but the other shapes were more numerous. There were eight examples of small dishes (as numbers 2-3 of the plate), fifteen silt jar-rims as numbers 4-6, six of number 7 and six of number 8. The clean yellow sand of the Twenty-second Dynasty temple foundation was reached over the whole area of the trench at relative level 8. The north-east end of this trench was arranged to cut the edge of the Thirtieth-Dynasty forecourt wall foundation, so that it was possible to confirm that the latter had been dug through the fill containing the Persian-Period pottery.

Trench E2

This trench of 3 x 4 metres was situated to the south-west of Trench E1, above the position of the front edge of the First Pylon. As in Trench E1, there was much Ptolemaic pottery in the upper level, consisting of heavy domestic coarse wares. Part of a red siltware jar, with a low ring-base 15cm in diameter, lay near the south corner (pl.31a, no. 3) and some body-sherds from a separate jar were embedded in the fill in the same area. In the west corner a broken red siltware jar was found in a pit on the edge of the trench; this vessel was 60cm high and 48cm in diameter (pl.30b). To the east of this jar were a crushed amphora of Nile siltware and part of the body of another large storage jar.

The trench cut through several large rubbish-pits, the outlines of which were clearly visible in the sections. The most impressive example, in the south-east profile, descended from the present-day surface to relative level 36, cut into the hard Persian-Period fill which overlay the sand bed of the pylon. This fill consisted of successive layers of muddy earth, as indicated on plate 31b, much of it the product of mud-brick decay. The remains of three pottery ovens had been dumped in another pit near the eastern corner of the trench. In the pits was some discarded Ptolemaic pottery, including a fine jug with remains of a red slip on the upper part of the exterior (pl.32a, no.3). This vessel was found inside a fragmentary red siltware storage-jar.

Earlier pottery, of the fifth century and perhaps early fourth century BC, was recovered from intact horizontal strata of fill below the pits, especially in the north-west part of the trench. The variety of forms was very limited, but those which did occur were present in large quantities. There were twenty coarse plates (form as pl.32b, no.1), over forty silt jar-rims (pl.32b, nos.4-7), a further twelve rims from jars with thicker rims (pl.32b, no. 8) and twenty-three dishes (pl.32b, nos.2-3). It is worth noting that a similarly restricted assemblage occurred in Trench W5, above the north-west wing of the First Pylon (below, p.42). Among the sherds from Trench E2 was one fragment from a Phoenician amphora. Eventually the temple sand-bed was reached over the full area of the trench, sloping from relative level 34 on the north-west to 25 on the south-east. The sand was covered by a stratum of limestone chips and mud, as around the temple gate, the remnants of the demolition of the earlier temple.

Trench E3

This narrow probe-trench of 5 x 1.5 metres was extended to the south-east from the side of Trench E2, in an attempt to check the extent of the sand layer in that direction. Once again, the surface dust contained Ptolemaic settlement pottery, comprising several fragmentary siltware jars (pl.32a, nos.4-9), the lower part of one bearing remains of red-painted decoration. A few very small fragments from Memphis Black Ware bowls were noted. At the south-west side of the trench was a small area of mud-brick a couple of courses thick, which might have belonged to the corner of Building N1, discovered subsequently in the 1997 season (see below, Chapter 3).

The layer containing the pottery did not descend more than 30cm below the surface. At this depth a few rough blocks of limestone were encountered at the north-east side, under which there was empty mud fill to the north-west, but some settlement fill on the south-east. This became more dense, with the frequent appearance of layers of carbon and burned soil, as the subsoil water-level was reached. Pottery fragments from this deep level were once again of the fifth century BC, although less abundant than in Trenches E1 and E2. The narrow baulk between Trenches E2 and E3 was later cut down to the level of the sand, which was seen to drop as it went towards the south-east, going into the water. A deep probe-pit was dug in the south-eastern end of Trench E3, but no sand could be dredged up from below the water; it had evidently been cut down by the settlement deposits to an inaccessible level.

Trench E4: Cross-Section of the Thirtieth-Dynasty forecourt wall foundation

A trench some 1.6 metres wide was cut across the foundation of the forecourt wall of the later temple, at a point 14.4 metres along the right (south-east) side from the front right corner. This section revealed the greenish sand filling of the trench and the different layers of fill into which it had been cut, and those which accumulated above it after the destruction of the wall (pl.53). All the layers directly above the foundation of the temple wall had been dug through in late-Roman times to remove the last blocks of stone, and the space was then refilled with redeposited material and surface mud. This upper level was subsequently pitted in places: it contained stone fragments and bits of pottery of mixed periods, chiefly Ptolemaic to late Roman. Among these pieces was the enigmatic object shown as no.5 on plate 54a. Some brick features built over the wall line following the earlier demolition of the visible masonry were cut by this second stage of quarrying for the foundation blocks. Part of the section was cut back to link the observed stratigraphy beside the temple wall with the fill below the brickwork of Building N2 (see Chapter 3), to reveal that the latter structure had been built while the temple wall still stood. The foundation of this building rested on fill which accumulated against the outer face of the stone wall. By the time of the secondary occupation of the building by squatters the temple wall had been demolished, so that some of their added brick structures could run unimpeded across its original position.

At a deeper level the sand-foundation in the wall-trench became more clearly defined as the surface pits did not descend very far. The width of the sand-bed was about 1.9 metres, although it appeared to have been cut too wide at the bottom, then adjusted by the addition of mud-brick to retain the edge of the trench. On the north-west side of the trench were mud-bricks embedded in hard mud, from which came a pottery mould for an eye-amulet (Cat.**60**). Siltware pottery fragments from deep in the fill into which the foundation-trench had been cut were of the fifth century BC and comprised the following examples:

Two saucers of type A.2.10
Jar-rim between types C.5.8 and 10
Jar-rim with high neck (pl.54a, no.2)
Jar-rim between types C.5.41 and C.5.44
Jar-rims of types D.1.26; D.1.49 and D.1.52
Jar with external rim (pl.54a, no.1)
Body-sherd with part of a handle
Part of a pottery counter (not catalogued)

Further examples from the north-west end:
Three bowls, of types A.4.36; A.4.38 and A.4.44
Two very rough saucers like type A.2.10, but more irregular
Two jar-rims like type C.4.16
Five rims of small jars: four as plate 54a, no.3; one as plate 54a, no.4
Cooking-pot with a debased handle on rim: like the form in Spencer 1996, pl.54,2
Small base cut into a rough vessel (pl.54a, no.6)

The presence of this pottery in the deeper fill matches the stratigraphy inside the temple forecourt, particularly in Trenches E1 and E2 and around the temple gate, where sherds of the first Persian Period were found above the destroyed remains of the Twenty-second to Twenty-sixth Dynasty phase of temple building. No remains of the sand-bed for the First Pylon of the temple were found in the trench, because it had all been replaced by later deposits - the sand of the Thirtieth-Dynasty forecourt wall-trench and the surrounding fifth century BC fill - to levels below the water-table. Similar stratigraphy was noted in another cross-section of this same side of the forecourt wall some 8 metres further to the south-west, cut in 1996 during investigation of the rear of the First Pylon of the earlier temple phase (below, Trenches E8-E7).

Trench E5
An area of 4 x 3 metres was dug inside the front outer angle of the south-east wing of the First Pylon. This trench lay immediately to the north-east of Building N2, described in Chapter 3, a fact which might account for differences in the stratigraphy from that observed in the trenches within the area of the Thirtieth-Dynasty temple forecourt. Trench E5 contained Ptolemaic fill without any traces of structures. Ptolemaic pottery fragments and part of a terracotta figure (Cat.**69**) were recovered from the surface dust. The pottery fragments from this high level are shown on plate 40a, nos. 7-8. Also found

were fragments of two jars of the same types as examples from Building N2, illustrated on plates 61, no.4 and 62, no.13. At a depth of 50cm there were many fallen bricks in the fill, perhaps from the adjacent large building. On the south-east side was a layer of settlement fill above a stratum containing many fragments of broken limestone. Only the north-east half of the trench was taken down below this level. Below the stone rubble was fairly empty soil, except at the east corner, where a patch of small stone fragments was observed, probably in a pit. From this deposit came two fine red ware Ptolemaic bowls, one with a red slip on the interior and upper part of the exterior (pl.40a, nos. 4-5). Slightly deeper, broken limestone again appeared, particularly towards the north-west side. A pottery lid was found here (pl.40a, no. 1), together with several bowl-rims of the kind published in Spencer 1996, pl.45, nos 4, 6; and a red ware cooking-pot like the one shown in ibid, pl.54, no.1. Three small fragments of green-glazed faience were noted in the fill. At greater depth in the south-east part of the trench was a patch of burned earth containing the following Ptolemaic pottery:

Part of a jar of a fine hard red fabric, with an external dull red slip (pl.40a, no. 6)
Two fine red ware pottery dishes or covers (pl.40a, nos. 2-3)
Part of a small vase in a hard, pink fabric with remains of an external pink slip, running over into the inside of the rim (pl.40a, no. 10)
Red siltware jar (pl.40a, no. 9)
Two bowl-rims, as Spencer 1996, pl.51, nos. 27-29
Another bowl, as Spencer 1996, pl.51, no.28
Red siltware flask-neck, burned black, shape as Spencer 1996, pl.54, no.7

The presence of these ceramics at a level just above the subsoil water-level is evidence for deep pitting of this area during the Ptolemaic Period, which may have removed a stratum of fifth-century BC remains similar to that observed elsewhere above the destroyed pylon. It would seem very probable that the disturbance to the ground took place during the preparation of the area for the construction of the mud-brick building beside the temple forecourt. With this extent of later activity, it is not surprising that no trace of any foundation deposit had survived in this angle of the pylon.

Trench E6
As part of the programme of searching for good dating evidence for the First Pylon, a trench of 3 x 4 metres was excavated over its rear south-east corner, placed above the position of the original masonry rather than the edge of the foundation-pit. The west corner of this trench was situated immediately adjacent to the east corner of Trench E7. At the surface the excavation cut through part of an overlying mud-brick wall of Building N2, embedded in muddy fill with few sherds. Some Ptolemaic sherds were found in a shallow pit in the east corner, including parts of a bowl and a situla with partial exterior red slips (pl.40b, nos. 1-4). Another Ptolemaic pit went down to water at the south, and was found to contain a local amphora-neck copy of the Dressel 1B form, small rim fragments from two red-slipped bowls (pl.40b, no. 5), part of a ring-based bowl, also with an external red slip (pl.40b, no. 6), and a neck from a shouldered jar (same form as on plate 61, no.2). Deeper in the trench a little earlier material was encountered, but only at the west side. The sherds comprised a few bread-platter pieces, a base from a Rhodian amphora of the fourth to third century BC, and a Phoenician amphora sherd, probably dating from the fifth century BC.

(e) Excavations along the rear of the south-east wing of the First Pylon

The deep trenches cut to trace the rear of the First Pylon foundation produced some of the most interesting evidence for the use of the area after the destruction of the Twenty-second to Twenty-sixth Dynasty temple. The stratification was similar to that observed elsewhere within the south-east side of the Thirtieth-Dynasty forecourt, but the fifth-century BC level was found to contain not only rubbish-fill, but also built structures in the form of several pottery kilns. These had been founded directly above the layer of broken limestone which occurred on the top of the foundation sand, a situation which suggests that they were established soon after the destruction of the temple. Details of ceramics and other material from this area are given in the notes on the individual trenches, below. These trenches are described in an order which follows the sequence of their excavation, which began close to the axis of the temple and was extended towards the end of the pylon. The locations are shown on plate 3.

Trench E11

The surface dust contained a few fragments of Roman pottery, including a piece of Egyptian Red Slip Ware, but immediately below this level was a large pit containing broken stone fragments and Ptolemaic sherds. This pit had been cut right down to the level of the destroyed temple foundation, and had removed practically all traces of the older fifth-century BC deposits. The stratification showed that the fill had been dumped from east to west. In addition to sherds from pottery vessels, two terracotta fragments (Cat.**70, 71**) and a stamped amphora handle (Cat.**99**) were found. Two new forms of Ptolemaic pottery are shown on plate 39, nos. 1-2, but several examples of shapes published previously were also noted, as follows:

Parts of three small red siltware dishes of the form shown in Spencer 1996, pl.56, no.2
Base of a plate of Memphis Black Ware, as Spencer 1996, pl.51, no.21
Base of the same shape as last, but in fine red ware
Several fine red ware bowl-rims like that shown in Spencer 1996, pl.53, no.9

Trench E10

In this excavation the Ptolemaic level was restricted to the highest stratum and it included the bottom two courses of a mud-brick wall on the south-west side. This brickwork probably belongs to the lowest courses of the wall of Building N1. A fragment of a blue glass rod was found in the Ptolemaic level. Under the Ptolemaic remains were deposits of the fifth century BC, lying directly over the broken temple stonework and sand-bed. In the Persian-Period fill were several pieces of very coarse red siltware pottery covers, with large projecting handles at the centre. These handles took the form of a cone of clay, with finger-imprints near the base to allow a good grip. An example with part of the centre of the original lid attached at the base is shown on plate 104a, no. 1. Perhaps these covers were used to close off the tops of the kilns in the vicinity (see below). Parts of two small, perforated covers were also found (pl.39, no. 3) together with a spoiled pottery jar. A bowl fragment like one published in Spencer 1996, pl.63, no.19 was found in the north corner. A few large bricks, 37 x 20 x 12cm in size and burnt red, were found in the lower part of the post-temple fill. These, it later became clear, had come from the back of the pottery kiln in the adjacent trench E9.

Trench E9

A thin layer of Ptolemaic fill, with fragments of mud-brick, was found to lie above the remains of an earlier pottery kiln, situated on the north-west side of the trench in the fifth-century BC stratum. The top of the kiln had been cut by a large pit, situated in the baulk between Trenches E10 and E9. Along the other three sides of the trench, however, the surface level was composed of between two and three courses of solid mud-brick, probably the foundation courses of the main north-west wall of Building N1. This wall, the full extent of which was not discovered until 1997, passed right over the position of Trenches E10 and E9 (see Chapter 3). Around the kiln under this Ptolemaic level the ground contained much red and black burned earth, together with more examples of red bricks from the destroyed walls of the kiln, like the ones found in Trench E10. These bricks had not been intentionally fired but had been burned during the operation of the kiln. More pieces from coarse siltware lids or covers of large diameter were found, and it is possible that these may have served as covers for the kilns. Other items from the fill around the kiln comprised the following:

Rim of a stone bowl (Cat.**23**)
Red siltware lid (pl.39, no. 4)
Siltware jar-rim (pl.39, no. 5)
Rim and shoulder from a red siltware jar (pl.39, no. 6)

The kiln in the north-west profile had an internal diameter of 80cm, with walls of mud-brick varying between 20 and 35cm in thickness. It had been constructed inside an older kiln of larger size, the south-west wall of which is shown in the profile drawing (pl.35) and photograph (pl.34a). The interior surfaces of the mud-bricks in the walls of both kilns had been burnt red. The more thoroughly burned bricks found loose in the fill came from the base of the walls, around the fire-pit. Through the middle of the latter was a partition, formed of a low wall half a brick wide, which originally formed a central support for the floor of the firing-chamber. This feature was also found in the similar kilns found further to the south-east in Trench E8. The kilns in Trench E9 had been built immediately over the layer of broken stone fragments which lay on the remains of the sand-bed of the First Pylon, at relative level 57. The highest preserved part of the brickwork of the kilns rose to relative level 105.

Notes on the north-west profile drawing of Trench E9 (pl.35)
This profile across the north-west end of Trench E9 covers a length of approximately 2 metres and shows an excavated depth from the ground surface of 1.38 metres. It contains two major stratigraphic phases: at the top is the surface fill, pitted in late-Ptolemaic times [a]-[b], and below lie the remains of two kilns dating from the fifth-century BC overbuilding of the Third Intermediate Period temple [e]. Just below the base of the drawn section lay the sand-bed of the First Pylon. After the demolition of the temple, the larger kiln was constructed above the ruins of the foundation. The mud-brick side of the kiln extends to the south-west beyond the edge of the trench; on the interior, the bricks were burnt during the operation of the kiln to create a band which varies from black to red. Inside the kiln near its base was some remaining ash overlying a pocket of yellow sand brought up from the pylon foundation below. Above and adjacent to this ash are mud-bricks belonging to the wall of the later kiln, built within the ruins of the first. The interior was full of black ashy grit and burned earth, with small patches of sand at the base. Another ashy layer [d] and the burned stripe [c] originally extended over the remains of both kilns and was probably created in the Thirtieth Dynasty when the upper parts of both kilns were levelled for the construction of a new temple forecourt and Building N1.

Trenches E8-E7
This linked trench, part of the continued exploration of the rear of the First Pylon towards the south-east, revealed several more pottery kilns similar to the one in Trench E9. The excavation began as a small trench just inside the position of the forecourt wall of the Thirtieth-Dynasty temple and was later extended to cut a section through the foundation of that wall. The upper fill was rather empty, except for a trace of Ptolemaic settlement activity on the north-east, consisting of parts of the lowest course of a mud-brick wall and a few fragments from Ptolemaic cooking-pots (pl.39, nos. 8-9). A destroyed pottery kiln of earlier date was encountered under the surface mud to the west of these remains, with the highest preserved portions of its mud-brick structure rising to relative level 122. The shape of the interior of the kiln was marked by a roughly rectangular red and black burned line, actually the burned inner face of its mud-brick walls (pl.36b). This part of the kiln was preserved to relative level 91 and consisted of the remains of the fire-pit, the bottom of which lay at relative level 69. The internal measurements of the fire-pit were 120 x 90cm; in its centre was a mud-brick partition like that noted in the kiln in Trench E9. The kiln was found filled with fragments of burnt lining from the higher parts of the walls, together with bits of stone and pieces of mud-brick, probably the result of the levelling of the ground above it prior to the Thirtieth-Dynasty reconstruction of the temple (pl.36a). Among the debris inside the kiln was a limestone object shaped like the cork of a bottle (Cat.**20**). This type of object, of which two similar examples were found later, seems to have had some function in the use of the kilns, perhaps as a stopper for an air-vent. A faience plug is recorded from kilns of more elaborate form at Tanis (Fougerousse 1946, 9).

Two more kilns of similar type were encountered a few metres further to the south-east in the extension of the excavation as a narrow cross-section linking Trenches E8 and E7, across the forecourt wall of the Thirtieth-Dynasty temple. These kilns are shown in the profile drawing of the north-east side of the trench in plate 38, where it can be seen how they were constructed side-by-side above the sand-bed of the First Pylon. Each has the central mud-brick division to the fire-pit, but in neither case is the brickwork preserved sufficiently high to reach the level of the floor of the firing-chamber. The internal width of the fire-pit in each case was approximately 1.15 metres and the highest remaining parts of these kilns lay at relative levels between 111 and 119. Above the ruins of the kiln on the right side of the profile was a deposit of levelled debris, including not only parts of the burnt lining of the upper walls, but also some fragments of conical handles from large siltware covers and a rough red siltware jar (pls.37a; 39, no. 7). Parallels for this vessel were found in the excavation of Building N2, dated to the Thirtieth Dynasty or early Ptolemaic Period, suggesting that the deposition of the debris over the kiln might also have occurred at this time. This would agree with the idea of a general level-ling of the site for the construction of both Buildings N1 and N2, during which the upper parts of the kiln would have been broken up. In the same dump were two more examples of limestone 'stoppers', like the one from the kiln at the north-west end of Trench E8, but these may have been dug up from the level of the kilns (Cat.**21**-**22**). Below these kilns, at a level just above the remains of the pylon founda-tion, a few fragments of fifth-century BC pottery were recovered, comprising examples of Types B.1.5 and D.1.70. The kilns themselves are typical of small updraught kilns as used at all periods from the Old Kingdom onwards. Their use here instead of more sophisticated versions suggests that the pottery manufacture was a small-scale opportunistic venture rather than a more organised industrial opera-tion. Examples of kilns of various periods have been noted at other sites and details of their operation have been published; see Holthoer 1977, 34-7 and the additional references in Spencer 1997, 63, n.11 and n.12.

The sand filling of the Thirtieth-Dynasty forecourt wall foundation appeared clearly in the cross-section of this trench (pl.38). No remains of additional kilns were found outside the forecourt, although a mass of mud-brick in the section belongs to the same chronological level. The excavation was con-tinued for another 2 metres beyond the end of the drawn profile and the width of the trench was increased (Trench E7) to allow better study of the pylon foundation. The rear edge of the foundation-pit was detected but no sand had survived above the water-table; it had been replaced by fifth-century BC fill. At a higher level the ground consisted of hard mud with some embedded mud-bricks and few sherds, chiefly from the necks of jars, some with red slipped surfaces (pl.39, nos. 10-14). At the present surface level was brickwork belonging to the mud-brick Building N2.

The kilns in these trenches are all located in the fifth-century BC stratum, which was subsequently cut by the foundation-trench of the Thirtieth-Dynasty forecourt wall. They stand on a thin layer of broken stone fragments above the great sand-bed belonging to the First Pylon of the earlier phase of the Amun-Temple, so their chronological position is sealed quite informatively between the destruc-tion of the first temple and the construction of its replacement in the Thirtieth Dynasty. The picture became more complex after the 1997 season as a result of some additional excavation of the highest level in the temple forecourt, dating after the destruction of the Thirtieth-Dynasty temple, which re-vealed two more examples of pottery kilns. These lay just to the north-east of Trenches E8-E7, immediately under the surface dust above both the ruins of Building N1, a structure in the forecourt of the Thirtieth-Dynasty temple, and the deeper remains of the First Pylon foundation from the older phase. This produces the following stratigraphic sequence for this area:

destruction of the first temple
establishment of pottery kilns on its ruins
rebuilding of the temple in the Thirtieth Dynasty with a new forecourt containing Building N1
demolition of Thirtieth-Dynasty temple forecourt and creation of fresh pottery kilns

The existence of two sets of kilns following each temple phase seemed sufficiently strange for more detailed investigation; consequently an additional section was cut from the level of the latest kilns down to that of the earlier ones (see pl.51a). Comparision of this profile with the section between

Trenches E8-E7 proved that the above sequence was indeed the correct one: there had been two separate periods of pottery-making on the site. The deepest layer shown on the profile (marked [g] on plate 51a) is the same stratum in which the earlier kilns are enveloped (see the other profile on plate 38). This layer rests on the remains of the sand filling of the foundation of the First Pylon of the earlier temple. Although partly cut by pits from above (pl.51a, [d]) this same layer was observed to have been sealed under the sand and mud foundation layer of Building N1 at the north-east end of the 1997 profile [e] - [f]. This prepared foundation has been cut away towards the southern end of the section by the introduction of fills [c] and [d]. The higher kilns are, on the other hand, situated well above this foundation and are embedded in the brickwork indicated [a] on both profiles at surface level (plates 38 and 51a), laid down above the fill which accumulated in the pitted ruins of Building N1 (pl.51a, [b]).

The persistence of small-scale pottery manufacture on this site is an interesting example of the same activity recurring at a particular spot after a long interval. The later kilns seem to belong to the late first century BC, when the presence of other features, such as rubbish-pits and light domestic walls, show that the temple forecourt had been destroyed. That other minor industrial activities were being carried out at the same period over the ruins of the temple is shown by the evidence of bronze and faience working above the remains of Building N1. The late Ptolemaic kilns and certain other post-destruction features on the site of this building are so closely linked with the problem of tracing the extent of its surviving brickwork that they have been described with the account of the excavation of the building in Chapter 3.

(f) Trenches to the north-west of the temple axis

One difference between the stratigraphy on opposite sides of the temple axis is the presence of Roman material on the north-west and its absence from the other side. This might be connected with the proximity of this side of the temple to the Roman town, which developed outside the north-west side of the Outer Enclosure. But ample evidence was found for the usual stratigraphy of fifth-century BC fill over the ruined temple of the Twenty-second to Twenty-sixth Dynasties, with some Ptolemaic deposits on the top; where Roman material occurred, it had replaced these layers. A trench cut in the 1994 season (Spencer 1996, 42, since given the reference W4) above the rear of the First Pylon foundation (although it had not then been identified as such) revealed deep Roman pits cut down to the sand-bed at a relative level of 91. Further to the south-west, the north-west side of the colonnade foundation is overlaid by a substantial pavement of Roman date, described in Spencer 1996, 41-2, and can be observed only through the ancient pits which cut the pavement, as illustrated in that volume (ibid., pls.16-17). A very small test-pit on the central section of the north-west foundation-trench of the colonnade, dug to check its alignment in an area clear of the above-mentioned pavement, revealed the top of the pre-temple ground at relative level 120 (very close to its level in front of the Second Pylon) under approximately a metre of fill containing ceramics of Ptolemaic and Roman date. The examples shown on plate 9c are part of a bowl of African Red Slip Ware (no.1), the neck of a vessel in a green marlware (no.2) and the base of a pale green glass vessel (no.3). There were also two small fragments from similar glass bases in addition to ribbed sherds from late-Roman siltware amphorae and small fragments of Egyptian Red Slip Ware bowls. A green-glazed faience figure of Bes, lacking the head, was found in the stone rubble above the sand-trench (Cat.**45**). The fill above the area in which the north-western colonnade foundation-trench joins the rear of the First Pylon sand-bed consisted of redeposited rubble and dust from the late-Roman quarrying of the temple site (see the description of Area RP2, above).

Trench W1

This excavation of 3 x 2.5 metres was located 8.65 metres from the temple axis. It eventually revealed yellow sand over the whole area but the overlying fill lacked the evidence for Ptolemaic settlement found in Trenches E1 and E2, on the opposite side of the axis. The upper fill had been disturbed to a greater extent by pitting to leave a mixture of earth, broken stone rubble and pockets of sand. At greater depth this mixture was replaced by limestone rubble over the entire area of the trench. Little pottery was found, the only piece of interest being a small red-glazed body-sherd from a Greek vessel. The sand-bed was reached at relative level 52 and was found to slope down towards the north-west.

Trench W2

This trench was situated about 3.5 metres west of Trench W1 and 14.8 metres from axis of the temple. Two small sherds from siltware jar-necks and two rims from incurved bowls of Ptolemaic date were found in the upper level, one of the bowls consisting of Memphis Black Ware. Slightly deeper, a few additional sherds of this date were recovered, including a small base from a vessel (shape as that in Spencer 1996, pl.45, 24, but in a red ware), a shallow plate and the rim of a jar (pl.32b, nos.9-10). The deeper fill consisted of hard muddy earth containing a few non-diagnostic red siltware body-sherds, and also a fine imported orange-red rim from a bowl. Near the water-level some broken stone was exposed in the north-eastern corner, but this was found to be lying above settlement fill of the first Persian Period. The latter descended well into the subsoil water and there were no remaining traces of any sand in the accessible levels.

Trench W3

This excavation was dug in 1996 above the inner end of the north-west wing of the First Pylon. It descended through refilled late-Roman pits containing pottery, fragments of fired bricks and glass, until the sand of the temple foundation was reached at relative level 54. Some Ptolemaic pottery and objects were found mixed up in the Roman fill, showing how the pits had disturbed older deposits. A fine red ware lamp of the second century BC was among the pieces found (Cat.**97**). That the purpose of the Roman activity was the quarrying of limestone was demonstrated by the presence of considerable quantities of broken limestone, some of it with traces of burning, the classic evidence for lime-preparation.

The following additional items were recovered:

Parts of two coarse siltware plates (pl.33, no. 1)
Red ware cooking-pot, (pl.33, no. 2)
Two jar-rims, Ptolemaic (same form as the example from E12 on plate 33, no.18)
Several bases from red siltware amphorae of late-Roman type
Two dishes, Ptolemaic to Roman, as in Spencer 1996, pl. 56, no.2
Incurved rim from a red-polished bowl, Ptolemaic, as in Spencer 1996, pl.51, no.27

Trench W4

This excavation was made in 1994 and has been reported in the previous volume (Spencer 1996, 42). Like the adjacent trench W3, it reached the sand of the foundation of the pylon below deep Roman pits.

(g) Excavations around the edge of the north-west wing of the First Pylon

The modern surface over the area of all these excavations consisted of very dense black mud, devoid of archaeological remains, and compacted to iron-hardness by the passage of agricultural vehicles through this part of the site. The depth of this mud which had to be removed in order to reach ancient stratified deposits varied from a few centimetres to as much as half a metre. In most of the trenches above this side of the First Pylon, the fill immediately below the mud consisted of the fifth-century BC stratum which developed above the ruins of the Third Intermediate Period temple. At a few points this fill had been cut away and replaced by material of the late-Roman Period.

Trench W5

The fill below the compact surface mud was found to be rather mixed, containing both Roman and earlier material. The bulk of the former was concentrated in the south corner of the excavation, in a pit above a brick-built lime-kiln. Intact fill of the first Persian Period was found in the centre and at the north-east side of the trench, from which came considerable quantities of pottery in a limited range of shapes, rather like the material recovered from Trench E2. This pottery consisted of the following pieces:

Fifteen plates of the range of types A.5.10 to A.5.28; with four examples of A.5.32
Twenty rims from thick siltware plates, same form as pl.32b, no.1
Twenty-five small red siltware dishes (same form as those from Trenches E1 and E2: see pl.32b, nos.2-3)
Twelve red siltware jar-rims, in range of types D.1.45 to D.1.49, and also several like the jars from elsewhere shown in pl.26, nos. 7-8 and pl.32b, nos. 4-7)
Six pointed bases from siltware jars
Fragment from a Cypriote flask-neck with handle
Body-sherds from a Phoenician amphora

Just below the surface mud part of a fine vessel of green faience with a pattern of decorative rosettes was found (Cat.**38**), as well as a fragment of a faience cylinder-bead. The fifth-century BC fill was found to rest directly on the remaining sand of the pylon foundation.

The late-Roman kiln at the south side had been cut through the Persian-Period fill down to the level of the temple sand, on the remains of which it had been constructed (pl.42a). The kiln had been roughly assembled from fired bricks measuring 22 x 11 x 8cm and 25 x 12 x 10cm. Some special bricks had been used in the walls of the kiln, presumably because they happened to be available, since they were not intended for this type of construction. These were of two kinds, the first being of rectangular shape but slightly curved, with sides of unequal length. Typical examples measured 31.5cm along the longer side and 23cm along the other. The width of these bricks was 21cm and the thickness only 7cm. Such bricks are well known in the construction of vaults (Spencer 1979, 142). The second type of special brick had been in the form of a segment of a circle, but the lack of any complete examples prevented us from determining how much of the circle was taken by each brick. It is possible that they were quadrants. The radius of specimens varied between 28 and 31cm and the greatest preserved width was 31cm, but the original width had been larger. Segmental bricks with smooth curved ends were used to create pillars in Roman buildings (Spencer 1979, 143). The kiln had originally been built with walls consisting of two rings of bricks and an internal diameter of 120cm, but this was later reduced to 94cm by the addition of an extra ring of stretchers to the interior (pl.42b). Both the original and the later interior faces show considerable vitrification through use of the kiln. The interior floor was covered by a layer of decayed limestone, buried under fallen bricks from the upper part of the structure. The base of the kiln lay at a relative level of 5 and the brickwork was preserved to a height of 70cm.

Trench W6

This small test-trench revealed fifth-century BC deposits immediately under the surface mud, at which level part of a green faience eye-amulet was found (Cat.**53**).The fifth-century BC fill descended to meet the upper surface of the pylon foundation sand, which covered the whole area of the trench. Several more examples of the common plates and jars already noted in other areas of the post-temple fill were found, together with fragments of a fine imported bowl with a red-painted interior and rim (pl.43, no. 1) and the top of a jar with a flared neck (pl.43, no. 2). From the north corner of the trench came part of the spinal column of ox, comprising four vertebrae.

Trench W7

This excavation was situated on the rear corner of the north-west wing of the First Pylon. Below the usual surface mud was compact fill of the fifth century BC, with a little Roman material at a high level on the north-west. The older material lay not only above the sand-bed of the pylon, but also occurred in pits cut into the ground beyond the edge of the foundation. This is the original pre-temple ground of the Twentieth to Twenty-first Dynasties as noted along the central axis of the temple. Two small sherds from bowls with dark and pale blue painted decoration predate the temple and must have been cut from this original ground (pl.44, nos. 2-3). Pottery fragments from the fifth-century BC fill comprised examples of type A.5 plates; jars of forms D.1.10 (1); D.1.46 (6); D.1.61 (1); D.2.15 (1), and pieces from two small vessels of the kind shown as number 1 on plate 44. Part of a mould for an amulet (Cat.**67**) and a faience model column-drum (Cat.**48**) were found at the north-west side. As excavation proceeded away from the corner of the foundation-pit into its interior, a large dump of discarded pottery was encountered, sloping down to the north-east. As mentioned in the account of the temple level (Chapter 1), this dump consisted almost entirely of broken pieces from red siltware jars of the fifth century BC with a considerable range of rim-profiles (pls.44-45a). The only other shapes found came from the upper part of the dump, comprising fragments from two small dishes, a plate and a small cup. Two pottery counters were also present (Cat.**76, 77**). From a separate, smaller, pit in the north-west part of the excavation came the top of a Phoenician amphora and a small piece from the rim of a Cypriote juglet. As for the jars, these were represented by many duplicates, the most common shapes being numbers 6-10 and 14 on plate 44, with more than 50 examples of each. A few shapes were represented only by single examples: number 11 on plate 44 (the only marlware vessel noted in the dump) and number 1 on plate 45a. The remaining foundation sand in this excavation was tested well below the subsoil water-level in the hope of finding a foundation deposit, but in vain. The sand was found to be contaminated with material from the lower slope of the dump, indicating that some of the sand had been removed in antiquity and subsequently dumped back into the hole. Ceramics at the very lowest level of the dump to be reached are illustrated on plate 45b, nos. 1-4. One example, number 4 on the plate, has an appearance characteristic of the late Third Intermediate Period, but the dump was an open context and this sherd was doubtless a residual piece, thrown in with the later material.

Trench W8

A small test-pit at the north-west edge of the pylon foundation, Trench W8 revealed fifth-century BC fill above the temple level, extensively cut by pits of Ptolemaic to late-Roman date. From the pitted areas came several Ptolemaic and early-Roman sherds from small vessels, chiefly bowls and dishes (pl.43, nos. 4-8). The bowl shown as item 8 had an external red slip. Also found were some small fragments of late-Roman bowls in African and Egyptian Red Slip Wares, together with ribbed body-sherds from coarseware amphorae. A block of sandstone measuring approximately 60 x 30 x 30cm also lay in a pit. It probably once belonged to the masonry of the pylon and had been abandoned since limestone was the prime target of the stone-robbers. The fifth-century BC fill along the north-west side of the trench had accumulated over the edge of the pylon foundation.

Trench W9

The trench W9 was located at the front corner of the north-west wing of the First Pylon. Under a surface layer of very hard mud, devoid of archaeological material, fill of the first Persian Period appeared. This was found to descend right into the water-table, but some remaining sand of the pylon foundation was observed just below the water along the north-west side. Part of a faience situla was recovered from the fill at the west corner of the excavation (Cat.**37**) and the following pottery was distributed more widely in the higher part of the fill:

Three dishes as pl.32b, nos. 2-3
Fragments from plates, as Type A.5.19-32

Jar-rims of Types D.1.15; D.2.15; D.2.18 and D.2.30.
Two pottery counters (Cat.**79**, **80**).

Additional fragments from deeper levels, close to the subsoil water:

Platter of type A.1.32
Jar of type D.1.15
Phoenecian amphora shoulder, like E.1.15 but with a slightly steeper shoulder
Small sherd with a handle from an Upper-Egyptian marl jar of the late Third Intermediate Period
Part of a cooking-pot, with a pink slip on the exterior and inside the rim (pl.43, no. 9)
Red siltware situla base (pl.43, no. 10)
Bowl-rim of fine siltware (pl.43, no. 11)
Shallow plain-rim bowl of hard red siltware (pl.43, no. 12)
Two cylindrical necks from siltware jars (pl.43, nos. 13-14)

From outside the limit of the pylon foundation, but still in fifth-century BC fill, came a coarse red siltware platter with a central division (pl.103, no. 3). In the 1997 season this excavation area was extended to cover an additional 7.5 square metres in front of the pylon, revealing an upper fill of empty mud covering pit-fill of the Persian Period. At the base of the latter, almost at subsoil water-level, a jar-rim of Type C.1.5 was recovered, indicating the presence of an older level of the late Third Intermediate Period (pl.43, no. 15). The north-west side of the trench contained some pre-temple fill beyond the end of the pylon foundation; this was investigated further in 1998 and found to be part of an extensive settlement area of the twelfth to mid-tenth centuries BC. The mud-brick wall of a grain-silo in this fill had been cut by the foundation-pit of the pylon; around the silo were pottery fragments of similar types to those found further to the north-east in the continuation of the settlement area around the remains of the New-Kingdom temple enclosure wall. For these ceramics, see Chapter 4.

3. Structures dependent on the Thirtieth-Dynasty Temple

(a) Introduction

The most substantial remains of the second phase of construction in Temple A consisted of the foundation trench of the forecourt wall, described and illustrated in the previous volume. Around the south-eastern side of the forecourt were three substantial buildings of mud-brick construction, one built along the interior of the court and the other two outside the temple. The interior building was discovered in the 1997 season, when it was excavated and designated Building N1. This had been the substructure of a long terraced platform against the inner face of the courtyard wall. The two external buildings were visible as distinct surface traces when the expedition began its work at the site, and they have been given the identifications N2 and N3 (see plate 4). It seems likely that all three buildings were contemporary and that they possessed religious or administrative functions related to the temple. Evidence from the excavations indicates that they were built either as part of the Thirtieth-Dynasty reconstruction of the temple or as early-Ptolemaic additions, but were destroyed by the end of the Ptolemaic Period, by which time the temple forecourt itself had ceased to function.

On the opposite side of the temple lie the remains of the sand-filled foundation-pit for another dependent structure, in this case probably constructed of stone on this carefully prepared substructure. The date of this building is shown by stratigraphic evidence to be later than the fifth century BC; its position just in front of the temple forecourt and to the left of the entrance is also close to the cross-axis leading from the north-west gate in the Outer Enclosure Wall to the subsidiary temple of Nekhtnebef (Temple B), all of which makes it a likely candidate for identification as the mammisi of the Thirtieth-Dynasty complex. The remains of the foundation are described at the end of this chapter, after the descriptions of Buildings N1 and N2.

Building N1 in the forecourt

(a) General condition and foundation preparation

The position of Building N1 was discovered in 1997 after an area within the rear south-eastern side of the Late-Period forecourt of the temple was investigated (see plates 2 and 4). Attention had been drawn to the region because of surface discolouration, caused by the presence of powdered mud-brick from the structure below. The ruins of the building were found to have been extensively mined for *sebakh* and the interior, particularly at the south-west end, filled with loose black dust from this activity. As this was removed, numerous stone fragments and objects which had been dumped on the site began to appear, including the lower stone from a limestone olive-press (Cat.**7**) and several examples of rectangular millstones of a type known from Greek sites (Cat.**8**, **9**, **10**). This material, however, all belonged to a period following the destruction of the building; indeed all the finds found above or within the structure were either later objects or older items from levels under its foundation. The preservation of the walls followed the present contours of the ground: best at the south-west with some 1.1 metres of brickwork surviving above the foundation-level, but becoming poorer towards the north-east, where the walls had been eroded away to the last few courses of bricks, or even completely. Most of the bricks were formed of hard black mud and measured 38 x 18-19 x 11-12cm, but some sandy bricks had also been used, with dimensions of 36 x 18 x 12cm. An overall plan of the remains is given in plate 46, with details on plates 49-50, where it will be seen that the main feature of the building is a massive wall of mud-brick around three sides, with the fourth side composed of the stone wall of the temple forecourt. The latter has, of course, completely vanished, but the sand-bed of its foundation remains to indicate its position. This was known from excavations in 1994, but an additional part was cleared beside the south-west end of Building N1 to study the relationship between the building and the forecourt wall. This study showed that the building was constructed immediately or very soon after the completion of the stone wall of the temple, to which it was attached. The whole area of Building N1 seems to have been prepared for construction by the laying down of a layer of rammed black mud, above which was a thin layer of clean sand. The thickness of the mud was about 40cm with around 10cm of sand above it, but the salt content of the ground had caused the mud layer to crumble from the top, so generally we found the sand mixed with small fragments of the black mud. A similar type of rammed mud foundation was noted in the Excavation Location 2 of 1994 (Spencer 1996, 70 and pls. 1, 43a, 44). Remains of the horizontal layer of mud and sand were revealed at numerous points under Building N1, sufficient to deduce that it had been laid down deliberately as a foundation for the structure. At greater depth were remains of occupation-levels ranging in date from the end of the New Kingdom to the Persian Period, which had been levelled for the building of the Thirtieth-Dynasty temple forecourt and Building N1.

The level of the top of the prepared mud and sand foundation-layer varied according to the extent to which it had been damaged by pitting from above; its original relative level in the south-west part of the building seems to have ranged between 120 and 130, but at the north-east end it was found at relative levels of 108 and 101. This is not much of a difference spread over the 46 metre length of the building, and it reflects the present slope of the ground. The large external walls of the building did not all rest directly on the sand. In some areas there was a stratum of compressed wind-blown dust between the top of the prepared foundation and the base of the walls, varying in thickness from a couple of centimetres to about ten centimetres. The greatest thicknesses were noted at the south-west end of the building, which is the part of the temple forecourt which would have collected most airborne dust from the prevailing wind. The time required for up to ten centimetres of dust to accumulate in the rear corner of the forecourt would be very short indeed, to judge by modern conditions. A few weeks of the usual windy weather, or even a single stormy day such as we experienced in our 1997 season, would have been sufficient. The stratum under the walls is then almost certainly just material which blew into the site during the interval between the completion of the mud and sand foundation-bed along the inner side of the stone forecourt wall and the construction of the brick walls of Building N1.

(b) The south-western and central part of the building

The opposite ends of this long building were revealed initially in two separate areas of excavation, one covering the structure from its south-western limit to the approximate centre, and the other at the north-eastern end. These two areas are shown in the detailed plans on plates 49-50, where it will be seen that the north-eastern portion was also the site of some pottery kilns. The section of the building between the two excavated parts had been almost totally eroded away but just sufficient of the main walls remained to confirm the connection. The features of the building and its contents are described following the pattern of excavation, beginning with the south-western portion (pl.49). The main brick wall enclosed the structure on the north-west and south-west, the latter side being the connection across the end of the building to link onto the interior face of the stone wall of the temple courtyard. This wall survived to a maximum height of ten courses of bricks and was 5.45 metres thick, whilst the front (north-west) wall measured 5.30 metres across and had eight courses remaining in this area. The great thicknesses suggest that they were retaining walls for a terrace platform, built to support an elevated structure. The mass of mud-brick used in the main walls had attracted the attention of *sebakh*-diggers, who had cut large pits through the thicknesses of the walls, in some cases right down to below their foundations. In such cases the pits proved to be useful sources of information on the stratigraphy, as several of them extended through the black mud and sand foundation layer of the building, allowing its presence to be detected at various points. The pit in the middle of the main south-west wall had cut away all the courses of brick just down to the level of the sand layer of the foundation, providing good evidence for the presence of this feature below the main walls. Other, deeper pits revealed the late

New-Kingdom stratum under the south-west part of the building.

Owing to the massive nature of the outer walls, excavation across their thicknesses was limited to sufficient clearance to be sure of their dimensions and the main excavation was concentrated on the interior of the building. Levels for the present tops of the walls and for their foundations are indicated on the plan (pl.49). Inside the south-west end of Building N1 were two compartments (1 and 2), measuring 3.35 x 1.9m and 3.35 x 3.2m respectively, separated by a mud-brick wall about 75 - 80cm in thickness. The majority of this cross-wall had been destroyed during the removal of *sebakh*, all but its north-eastern end having been cut down to no more than one or two courses of bricks. This wall, together with the other internal wall which formed the north-east side of Chambers 1 and 2, had been founded some 25 to 30cm higher than the bases of the main external walls, over a layer of levelled dust with limestone fragments. Three courses of bricks remained in the wall separating Chambers 2 and 3, the lowest being of bricks laid on edge, set directly on the rubble layer. The chambers were filled with loose brick-dust, in the top of which were the discarded olive-press and granite millstones, mentioned above (pls.47a-b). From the same dusty fill came a faience eye-amulet (Cat.**51**) and a small limestone figure of a falcon (Cat.**16**). At a slightly deeper level a broken block of limestone with two lines of hieroglyphic text was encountered in the north corner of Chamber 1 (Cat.**3**). The inscription contains the name of the god Amun, and the style of the deeply cut hieroglyphs suggests that it derived originally from the Third Intermediate Period temple (pls.48a, 84). In the west interior angle of the main wall of the building was a deep pit which had been cut right through the black mud and sand foundation layer at relative level 124 into older accumulated fill containing pottery of the late New Kingdom, a stratigraphic sequence noted also further north in the building.

Like the main south-west exterior wall, the cross-wall which runs transversely through the building between Chambers 1-2 and 3 was found to end abruptly at the south-east, right on the edge of the sand-filled foundation-trench of the stone forecourt wall of the temple. This is further evidence to show that the rear of Building N1 was closed by the temple wall itself, against which all the transverse walls abutted. The later removal of all the stonework of the temple wall has carried off the back of the building.

Material from the brick-dust in chambers 1 and 2:

Lower stone of an olive-press (Cat.**7**)
Broken upper millstone of granite, with a flat, lower stone of the same material (Cat.**8**)
Limestone slab with hieroglyphic inscription (Cat.**3**)
Faience eye-amulet (Cat.**51**)
Small limestone figure of a falcon (Cat.**16**)
Fragment of a pottery crucible, stained with green copper corrosion
Pottery fritting-pan (pls.54b, no. 4; 103, 1)
Base of coarse siltware bowl (pl.54b, no. 3)

From surface dust above the south-west outer wall:

Two upper millstones of tufa (Cat.**9-10**)
Pottery brazier (Cat.**96**)

From surface dust above the north-west outer wall:

Fragment of a faience amuletic figure of Isis (Cat.**46**)
Pottery lid (pl.54b, no. 6)

Moving to the north-east along the building, on the other side of the transverse wall was a small chamber (3) with a higher-level floor (R.L. 187), which had been the location of some minor industrial activities after the building had ceased to operate in its original function. There was considerable evidence for post-destruction activity inside the framework of the massive outer wall, with new areas of brickwork being added to adapt the configuration of the space to suit secular activity. The floor of Chamber 3 was built up with packed brick and the occasional re-used slab of limestone (pl.48b), a door approached by a few steps was introduced at the north-west end and the brick wall on the north-east side was extended with some roughly laid brickwork, built over the large limestone slab which appears in the floor. Within the enclosed space of 1.25 x 2.80 metres, bronze-working and glass preparation were carried out, as shown by fragments of crucibles and fritting-pans like the more complete example noted above from Chamber 2 (pl.54b, no. 4), together with many fragments of bronze waste embedded in accumulated dirt on the floor. Below this layer was a stratum of compact fill with limestone fragments, in which part of a pottery jar was embedded, of the same type as some examples from Building N2 (pl.62, nos. 2 and 4). A rough cross-wall was made at the south-east end of the room, consisting of three courses of mud-bricks laid over some large fragments of limestone. In the corner of the room by this wall was a rough block of basalt, perhaps used as a hard working surface. The introduction of the blocking-wall at this end of Chamber 3 suggests that the temple courtyard wall had been removed by the time of this re-use, an event which seems from other evidence to have occurred late in the first century BC (pl.52a). From the loose fill above the blocking-wall came the pottery mould, Catalogue **62**.

The location of the door at the north-west end of Chamber 3 was marked by a surviving limestone pivot-block against the south-west wall, with two other small blocks of limestone beside it as a doorsill. In front of these stones was an area of mud-bricks laid entirely as headers, probably the remains of a few steps up to the door (pl.49). The north-west part of this brickwork had been lost in a large *sebakh*-pit, which had removed a portion of the wall between Chambers 1 and 3, and also extended for some 4 metres to the north-east into Chamber 4A, with an additional cut into the inner face of the main wall of the building. Cleaning of the edges of this pit revealed some stratigraphic details: Chamber 4A contained three courses of mud-brick over brown dusty fill, below which the top of the black mud and sand foundation layer appeared at relative level 119. The *sebakh*-pit had cut through this into layers which pre-dated the building. On investigation, these proved to contain parts of older mud-brick walls and a quantity of pottery fragments which appear to date from the end of the New Kingdom to the early Third Intermediate Period (pl.55a). These remains come from a relative level of 42.

Chambers 4A and 4B, so designated for ease of reference although they are not really separate chambers at all but only part of a single long space divided by our own excavation baulk (later removed), occupy the area between the main external north-west wall of Building N1 and a long thinner wall which extends at right angles from the side of Chamber 3 and runs along the length of the building, parallel to the outer wall but just over 3 metres distant from it. This wall is 90cm thick and was founded at relative level 157, but the brickwork survives to a maximum height of only 38cm at the south-west end and gradually falls towards the north-east due to severe erosion. After a distance of about 9 metres the depth of the brickwork is reduced to only 3 or 4cm, just before the trace of the wall vanishes in an old *sebakh*-pit. Under the foundation of the wall are many fragments of limestone, perhaps derived from earlier temple buildings. Area 4B contained a single course of roughly laid limestone slabs of small size, extending across the space from the inner face of the main outer wall. There was no evidence as to the purpose of these slabs, and it seems probable that they were not part of the original structure. Another intrusive feature is the square pit beside the inner face of the main wall. This was lined with four courses of fired bricks arranged as shown in the detail plan on plate 51b. The base of this brick lining lay a relative level 111 and the highest preserved part reached level 150; the bricks themselves measured 27 x 13 x 7cm. The enclosed pit measured 63 x 52cm and it was filled with nothing more than ordinary brown mud. Close to the south-east side of this structure a number of pottery objects of uncertain function were found (Cat.**72**).

A small section was cut on the south-east of the brick pit to investigate the stratigraphy. The upper part of the pit had been cut through muddy fill, from which part of a Ptolemaic red-slipped incurved bowl was recovered (pl.54b, no. 1); lower down the pit had cut into the top of the black mud and sand layer noted everywhere under Building N1; some of the sand had been dragged up during the sinking of the pit to relative level 130 but the original level had been about 10cm deeper (pl.52b). Below this stratum was fill containing an ash-pit and other combustion products, together with a few sherds (pl.55b, nos.1-3), which belong to the earlier level of occupation-debris also observed below the foundations of Chamber 4A. This stratum is of the Twentieth to Twenty-first Dynasties, like the deposits to the north of the temple described in Chapter 4, where similar pottery was found (compare plates 55b, no. 3 and pl.73, no. 15). At the north-east end of Area 4B the remains of the building disappeared, owing to erosion of the brickwork to foundation level. The inner face of the main external wall became impossible to trace at a point some 17 metres along its length from the south-west end of the building, the bricks having completely vanished to expose part of the sand layer above the black mud of the prepared foundation. This foundation layer was detected again some 6 metres further to the north-east, but any bricks of the wall itself had been either removed by erosion or cut away by later constructions. Fortunately, the interior face of the wall reappeared at a greater distance to the north-east, in a separate area of excavation at the other end of the building, described below in section (c).

To return to the excavation of the south-west half of the building, the area shown on the plan as Chamber 5 consisted of a long, narrow space between the stone wall of the temple courtyard and the mud-brick wall which divided Chamber 5 from 4A-4B. The whole of this space had been severely pitted and contained little of interest. There were remains of three cross-walls in the south-west end of the space, one with a preserved length of 1.5 metres, almost sufficient to reach the line of the wall of the temple forecourt, but the others had been truncated by pits to leave only minor traces. None of this brickwork survived to heights of more than one or two courses.

Material from Areas 4A and 4B and 5:

Limestone loom-weight made from a relief fragment with a falcon (Cat.**17**)
Group of pottery bars and plaques, probably used in weaving (Cat.**72**)
Circular pottery counter (Cat.**78**)
Fragment of mottled blue-black glass inlay (Cat.**50**)
Part of a pottery mould (Cat.**63**)
Two small pottery objects (pl.54b, nos. 8-9, cf. an example from Building N2, pl.61, no. 5)
Ptolemaic bowl (pl.54b, no. 1)
Rim of a bowl with horizontal applied handle, diameter uncertain (pl.54b, no. 2)
Fragment of iron

(c) The north-eastern part of the building

The central portion of Building N1 was very difficult to trace owing to the effects of erosion and later overbuilding, as previously mentioned. The remains of the north-west wall were detected again after an interval of some 10 metres, still on the same alignment and with its impressive thickness of over 5 metres. The height of the wall, however, had been reduced by the erosion of the site to no more than two or three courses of bricks, and numerous pits had been cut through the brickwork. It was possible to follow the remains as far as the north corner of the building, and then along the north-east wall as it turned south-east towards the location of the temple forecourt wall in order to form the limit of the structure (pl.50). The thickness of this wall was 5.3 metres and it was founded on the same sand and black mud layer as noted elsewhere, but here at the slightly deeper relative level of 101. Up to five courses of bricks remained in place in this wall. Parts of the core of the brickwork had been cut out to create some later chambers associated with some kind of vat (see below). The interior corner of the building was partly obscured by other secondary features, particularly some small pottery kilns and associated brickwork which had been built on the site after the destruction of both Building N1 and the temple forecourt. Pottery kilns had also been discovered in the same area, but at a deeper level, in the 1996 season and it eventually became clear that there had been two phases of pottery-making, one pre-dating and the other post-dating the Thirtieth-Dynasty temple. This sequence is considered in more detail in the description of the kilns and other post-destruction features, below.

Little remained of this part of Building N1 apart from sections of the main external walls on the north-west and north-east. Any internal walls similar to those at the opposite end of the building had been eroded away or removed by the construction of the later pottery kilns. As there was only the external wall to work with, the space between this excavation and the previously excavated portion at the south-west was investigated in an attempt to see whether a connection could be traced through the missing section in the central part of the building. The faces of the wall in this region had been extensively damaged by later disturbance but a few preserved portions were traced on the correct line. Much of the core of the wall remained in place, however, but reduced to just a few courses of bricks, extensively cut and overbuilt by other mud-brick walls of later date. The extent of this brickwork and the alignment of the surviving parts of the faces of the wall were sufficient to show that it had originally run unbroken for a length of 46 metres to form the complete north-west side of the building (pls.4 and 46). Associated with the overbuilding above this part of the wall was a fine decorated Ptolemaic pottery jar and cover (pl.54b, nos. 8 and 5) and part of a coarse siltware jar (type as no. 4 on pl.32a). The decorated jar was made of silt clay covered by an exterior red slip, on which bands of black and white paint had been applied.

(d) Later features cut into the north-east wall of Building N1

The north-east exterior wall of Building N1 had been cut through by a large pit, which had subsequently been adapted to create two small chambers by trimming the sides to a more square form and inserting a thin wall of mud-brick through the middle (pls.50, 56, 57a). This must have been done when the remains of the main wall were still standing to some considerable height, so that the re-cut brickwork would function as the sides of useful chambers. Subsequent erosion has reduced the brickwork to a maximum height of five courses. In the north-east chamber was the base of a vat covering an area of 1.5 x 0.8 metres, built with fired-brick sides and a plaster floor at relative level 152. The brick size was 23-24 x 12 x 6cm and the plaster floor thickness was 2cm. A maximum of three courses of bricks remained in place in the walls, and many bricks of the upper course were found displaced, lying on the plaster floor. The north-east side of the vat lay close to the cut edge of the mud bricks of the wall of Building N1. Across the front of the chambers a number of rough pieces of masonry were distributed as shown in the detail plan (pl.56). The wall between the two rooms had obviously been built to divide up the original rough pit. It was 40cm thick and extended for a distance of just under 2 metres, with a finished end to the south-west side of the vat. In the course of removing the surface dust from this area the neck of a pottery amphora was found (pl.103, no. 2). The great thickness of the main walls of Building N1 made them an ideal target for pitting for various purposes once the official use of the building had ceased: recutting them for adaptation, as in this case, or for re-use of bricks, or the acquisition of clay for pottery-making or fertiliser.

(e) Ptolemaic pottery kilns above the north corner of the building

The interior northern corner of Building N1 had been overbuilt by pottery kilns with some associated brick and stone features. These remains lay at the level of the present surface of the ground and could be defined clearly by the removal of only a few centimetres of dry dust. The presence of the kilns had been noted at the end of the 1996 season and excavation commenced the following year as a separate project from the initial work on the south-west end of Building N1, some 40 metres distant. The fact that the north-east end of the building extended into the area below the kilns was discovered some time later.

The reduction of the ground-level through wind and rain erosion has left the remaining brickwork of the main walls around the northern angle of Building N1 and the later pottery kilns at approximately the same absolute level, between 155 and 160 relative to datum. Excavation of the kilns was carried out in an area of 7.5 x 6.0 metres, from which work was subsequently extended to reveal the thicknesses of the north-west and north-east walls of Building N1. Two kilns had been constructed within the north corner of the ruined building, the location perhaps chosen for shelter from strong winds. As noted above in the description of the hollowed-out chambers in the thickness of the north-east wall of Building N1, these walls must have been standing to some reasonably useful height at the time when the later adaptations were made, and the present-day planed-off surface has been produced by erosion over the centuries. The position of the kilns relative to the walls of the building is shown in plate 50. The western kiln (No. 1) was very simple, consisting of an approximately circular structure with a maximum diameter of about a metre (pl.41a). Unfortunately, the levelling of the ground has left only the lowest portions of the kilns remaining, just the fire-pit below the firing-chamber for the pottery. The circular kiln was built of mud-bricks, the inner faces of which have been burnt red during use. It was surrounded by an area of mud-brick paving, the extent of which is indicated on plate 50. The brickwork was two courses thick, but in the angle formed by the walls of Building N1 its place was taken by a pavement of limestone blocks, evidently re-used from one of the phases of temple building (pls.41a-b). The level of this pavement is far too deep to have been part of the original structure of Building N1 and it must belong to the same period of construction as the kilns. All along the inner face of the north-east wall of Building N1 is an additional coat of brickwork of which a maximum of five courses remained, founded at relative level 111. This brickwork turned to the south-west at the south-east end of the excavation, but then disappeared in a heavily pitted area.

The limestone pavement in the angle of the wall of Building N1 was investigated in more detail in 1998, when the blocks were lifted and replaced to check for re-used material. Several proved to have worked surfaces and some had dressing marks like those observed on masonry from the forecourt wall of the Thirtieth-Dynasty temple. The spaces between the blocks were filled with chunks of limestone, some of which again had worked surfaces but no preserved decoration. Also between some of the blocks and under the largest at the north end was pink bedding plaster, though this was not used consistently and may have occurred simply because it was already attached to the blocks which were being reused in the paving. Only one block bore any surviving decoration, consisting of a few low-relief hieroglyphs and a register line above a blue painted band (Cat.**12**). Below the paving blocks originally excavated in 1997 was a second course of smaller blocks as a foundation layer. From the north-east end of the paving came a small fragment of deep blue glass.

The second kiln was a square box-like structure about one metre wide, facing to the west (colourplate 4c). Again, only the fire-pit was preserved, with a length of 78cm and a width which narrowed from 56cm at the rear to 54cm at the front. The walls stood 28cm high, but broken fragments of the floor of the firing-chamber survived in the debris around the brickwork of the kiln. This floor had been made of a sheet of fired clay, perforated by triangular holes 11cm high by 9.5cm wide, to allow the hot gases to pass through. It was supported on a brick pillar inside the fire-pit, with another brick at the front, approximately centred in the open airway. The dimensions of the pillar were 32 x 30cm, with a gap of only 7cm between it and the rear wall of the kiln. The front brick measured 30 x 18cm, leaving a space of approximately 18cm on either side for the entry of air. All the structure had been formed of mud-bricks, but the surfaces of those exposed to heat had become fired red during the operation of the kiln. The fire-pit still contained a considerable quantity of charcoal fuel, derived from both palm-tree and true timber. Embedded in this, under the ceramic floor fragments at the front of the kiln, was a broken pottery bowl of Ptolemaic style with a ring-base and flared rim (pl.54b, no. 7) and fragments from what had clearly been a tripod separator or 'fire-dog', used to support a vessel during firing. Curiously, there was no accumulation of broken pottery fragments or spoiled vessels in the vicinity of the kilns, perhaps because such remains would have been at a higher level which has since disappeared.

The Excavation of Building N2

(a) Introduction

In the 1995 season the smaller of the structures outside the temple (Building N2) was selected for excavation (pl.58a). It covered an area of approximately 17 x 15 metres. Stratification against the south-east wall of the temple forecourt suggests that the building was constructed a short time after the temple wall, since there was a build-up of fill against the latter, on which the brickwork of the building rests. The building consisted of a series of chambers on the south-east, belonging to brick foundations, and an open court at a lower level on the north-west, adjacent to the side of Temple A. Indeed, the evidence strongly suggests that the stone temple wall was utilised as one side of this courtyard. The bricks of the building were 34 x 17 x 12cm in size. There is some evidence for re-use of parts of the structure by squatters after its abandonment for official purposes.

(b) The fill between this building and Building N3 to the south-west

The excavation was begun at the southern corner of the building, with enough overlap to reach the northern side of the adjacent Building N3 so that the intervening deposits could be sectioned. In the south-east end of this street, which was only 1.15 metres in width, were a few displaced fragments of limestone pavement. The compact mud fill between the two structures contained the following material:

Limestone *ex-voto* with a royal face in relief on each side (Cat.**13**)
Fragment of another limestone ex-voto carving of a royal head (Cat.**14**)
Part of a broken phallic figure in limestone (Cat.**19**)
Fragments from two crucibles with bronze staining
A handle from a large lid of coarse pottery
Rim from a fine red ware cooking-pot (pl.62, no. 1)
Top of a coarse red siltware jar (pl.62, no. 2)
Top of a fine red ware jar with a cylindrical neck (pl.62, no. 3)
Jar of coarse red siltware, lacking the neck (pl.62, no. 4)
A base sherd from a small fine pottery vase, with red pigment inside and blue outside.

Further along the street to the south-west, part of the dump was encountered which runs under the wall from the west corner of Chamber 1. This was full of bits of broken limestone and coarse red siltware potsherds, and the following items of interest:

Two shoulder bones of goats, with other small bone fragments
Pottery mould for a diamond-shaped inlay (Cat.**64**)
Fragment from the base of small faience vase
Small piece of decayed faience from the rim of a bowl
Pottery dish of fine red ware, shape as in Spencer 1996, pl.51,19
Three pottery jars of the same form as item number 4 on plate 62
Hand-made pottery dish of gritty yellow fabric, with traces of exterior white plaster coating (pl.62, no. 5), plus fragments of two others, similar
Pottery bowl of medium fine red ware (pl.62, no. 6)
Coarse red siltware dish (pl.62, no. 7)
Part of a bowl of coarse red siltware, diameter uncertain (pl.62, no. 8)
Pottery bowl of coarse red siltware (pl.62, no. 9)
Base of a bowl in coarse red siltware (pl.62, no. 10)
Rim from a vase of medium fine red pottery (pl.62, no. 11)
Rim sherds from two coarse red siltware jars (pl.62, nos. 12-13)
Coarse siltware bowl of large diameter, blackened by smoke (pl.62, no. 14)

(c) Excavation of the internal chambers

The area of work was expanded progressively to bring the entire building under excavation. It soon became clear that only the foundations had survived and further excavation was limited to the delineation of the plan of the foundation walls, with a few probe-trenches to examine the deeper stratigraphy. The site was covered by much powdery surface dust, below which the individual compartments within the foundation were gradually revealed, as illustrated in the plan on plate 60.

Chamber 1

The south-west side of this large chamber of approximately 7.0 x 4.5 metres was excavated to a greater depth than the remainder, to reach the base of the wall on that side at relative level 139, giving about 60cm of surviving wall depth (pl.58b). This wall was 1.75 metres wide. The south-eastern wall of this chamber had been built directly on top of an earlier mud-brick feature. The foundation of the west corner of Chamber 1 had been cut through a rubbish-dump, containing a quantity of broken pottery, faience fragments and a few objects (pl.59b). This dump extended under the adjacent Chamber 3 and into the street between the building and its southern counterpart. From the dump in the western corner of Chamber 1 came the following items:

Several rough fragments of worked limestone
Half of a bowl of yellow faience (pl.61, no. 12)
Two green faience bases of 7-8cm diameter (pl.61, no. 13)
Fragments from four crushed faience vessels, three green and one yellow
Parts of two small amulets: a broken figure of a god and a broken red crown
Sherds from two imported amphorae, probably of the type Dressel 1B
Three small pottery objects of uncertain function, one complete. Gritty beige fabric. (One drawn, pl.61, no. 5)
Small pottery dish of coarse red siltware (pl.61, no. 6)
Part of a fine red ware pottery bowl (pl.61, no. 7)
Rim and shoulder from a siltware vase, the exterior eroded (pl.61, no. 8)
Pottery rim and shoulder from a vase of fine red ware (pl.61, no. 9)
Rough red pottery rim from a large jar, burnt black on the surface (pl.61, no. 10)
Pottery base of fine red ware, pl.61, no. 11
Coarse red siltware potstand

Further away from the corner, the fill in the south-western part of Chamber 1 consisted of compact mud, from which the following pieces were recovered:

Pottery mould for a Bes-figure (Cat.**65**)
Limestone shadow-clock or gnomon (Cat.**11**)
Base of a pottery dish in a grey marl fabric (pl.61, no. 2)
Coarse red siltware pottery dish (pl.61, no. 3)
Lower half of a pottery brazier in coarse red siltware (pl.61, no. 4)
Base of a pottery vase like that shown in pl.61, no. 11
Handle from an imported vase (shape as that in Spencer 1996, pl.52, 17)
Small fragment from a jar-rim of fine red ware (too small to draw)

From a slightly greater depth:

Part of the base of a Memphis Black Ware bowl
Fragments from a vessel of green faience.

Some burnt deposits were noted at a high level in the north-eastern part of the chamber. From the surface dust in this area came two amphora handles, one of type Dressel 1B and one Rhodian with an illegible stamp. A pottery situla-base was also found here (pl.61, no. 1). From the extreme north-east end of room came part of a red ware bowl with an incurved rim, a small rim of black pottery, body-sherds of imported amphorae and many non-diagnostic sherds of coarse red siltware.

Chamber 2

This chamber, measuring 4.1 x 2.3 metres, was covered by loose dust above more compact mud fill, with some high-level burnt earth at the south-east side. The great thickness of the brickwork, over 4 metres, between this chamber and no.1 is typical of the foundations of Late Period and Ptolemaic mud-brick buildings. From the fill in this chamber came a small amount of pottery, listed below.

Red pottery body-sherds from an Egyptian amphora
Handle from an amphora, resembling those of the Dressel 1B form, but made of Nile silt
Fragment of a small handle and neck from a fineware vase, with a white slip on the handle and inside the rim
Part of a coarse red pottery cooking-vessel (pl.61, no. 14)
Rims from two red siltware jars (pl.61, nos. 15-16)

Chamber 3
This small room of 2.6 x 2.9 metres lay in the west corner of the foundation. Near the surface was the usual dust and empty mud fill, but at a slightly lower level, part of the underlying dump extending below the wall from Chamber 1 was revealed. In this were the following pieces:

Small fragment from a limestone shadow-clock (gnomon), like Cat.**11** from Chamber 1
Bronze nail (Cat.**32**)
Upper part of a green faience vase, mostly decayed to dull white (pl.61, no. 17)
Fragmentary base of a faience vessel
Several pieces of a coarse pottery tray of circular shape

Chamber 4
This chamber contained a great amount of carbon and other combustion products, around the remains of an oven. A piece of a large siltware lid was found in the west corner.

Chamber 5
The south-west end of the room was occupied by an oven full of grey ash, built beside the remains of another. The oven lay at relative level 172, and was probably added to the building during secondary occupation. Around the oven was a quantity of burned earth, but it did not go under the walls, except under the rough wall on the north-east. This consisted of only two courses of poorly assembled bricks and was probably a later addition, like the oven. The thickness of this brickwork was 80cm. Another rough wall of exactly the same kind of construction had been placed in the north-eastern part of the room. From this chamber came a quantity of non-diagnostic siltware sherds, and the following other material:

Fine red pottery bowl with an incurved rim, the upper part of the exterior red-slipped (pl.61, no. 18, cf. the bowl in Spencer 1996, pl.51, 28)
Coarse red pottery handle from a large jar
Pottery jar-stopper

(d) The courtyard between the foundation of Building N2 and the temple forecourt wall

Enclosed between the brick foundations described above and the south-east wall of the Thirtieth-Dynasty temple forecourt was an open area, set at a lower level than the remainder of the building and entered by a door at the south-west (pl.59a). One side of this doorway had been built in mud-brick at the end of the south-west wall of the building, but the opposite jamb must have abutted onto the exterior face of the temple wall, if the presence of the stone wall itself was not considered sufficient to form this side of the entrance. This indicates that the temple wall was standing at the time of the construction of the brick building, and was used as the north-western limit of the rectangular space under discussion. The temple wall, however, did not survive to the end of the Ptolemaic Period, since minor brick features, rubbish-pits and pottery deposits spread across the line of the wall into the temple forecourt. These remains seem to belong to the same phase as the intrusive mud-brick elements and ovens which lie over the foundation of the brick building. A roughly built brick wall from the same re-occupation, situated at the north corner of the open courtyard between the temple and the building foundation, was found to have extended across into the temple forecourt, showing that the stone temple-wall had been removed by this stage (pl.60). This minor brick wall was subsequently cut by the robbing out of the stone foundations or the temple wall in the Roman Period.

The size of the courtyard was about 14 x 4 metres; the presence of a low-lying courtyard beside buildings elevated on higher foundations of brickwork is a feature which still occurs in Egyptian houses of the Delta. All along the edge of the stone-robbers' trench above the line of the temple forecourt wall was a conspicuous deposit of limestone fragments. The remainder of the surface within the courtyard belonging to Building N2 was covered by a layer of loose powdery dust, from which came following sherds:

Imported amphora base, from the south-west end of the courtyard
Bowl fragment similar to that published in Spencer 1996, pl.51, 16
Red ware base as in Spencer 1996, pl.54, 11

Around the door at the south-west was a large amount of broken limestone, but little pottery or other material. A short distance into the court from this entrance more occupation-debris was encountered, consisting of faience fragments, a pottery mould for some kind of implement (Cat.**66**), a plaque of burnt limestone with incised decoration (Cat.**15**) and the rim of a cooking-pot (pl.63, no. 16). Among the faience fragments was a larger piece from the shoulder and rim of a yellow-glazed vase (pl.63, no. 17).

The fill under the dust in the courtyard was composed of dense mud, cut by many pits and overlaid by some burnt patches from cooking fires. All of these remains probably date from the squatters' re-occupation phase. Some pits had cut the brickwork of the main north-western wall of the building foundation, which formed one side of the courtyard. In particular, two large pits beside the south-western end of this wall were cut some distance into its face; they contained a quantity of pottery which is listed below:

Fragments of two vessels like that shown in pl.62, no. 5
Small round-based dish in red siltware (pl.63, no. 8)
Dish of medium fine red pottery with a low ring-base (pl.63, no. 9)
Rim of a fine red ware cooking-vessel (pl.63, no. 10)
Jar-rim in medium fine red ware (pl.63, no. 11)
Top of a jar of coarse red siltware (pl.63, no. 12)
Red siltware jar-neck (pl.63, no.13)
Broken fine pottery vase of alabastron shape (pl.63, no. 14)
Neck of a vase with handles. Fine red fabric with a pale cream exterior (pl.63, no. 15)
Rim of a coarse red siltware dish like that published in Spencer 1996, pl.51, 18
Base of a red siltware incurved bowl like that published in Spencer 1996, pl.51, 30
Shallow dish of fine red ware like that published in Spencer 1996, pl.54, 8

To the north of these rubbish pits were some areas of burnt earth from cooking-fires and a small pit full of broken limestone. A nearby circular pit filled with hard mud may have been a well-shaft. The fill in the area between the burnt traces and the mud-pit contained some pottery, of the following kinds:

Complete small bowl of coarse red siltware (pl.63, no. 1)
Jar-neck of red siltware, diameter uncertain, between 19 and 24cm (pl.63, no. 2)
Small red siltware dish (pl.63, no. 4)
Red siltware bowl, broken at the base (pl.63, no. 5)
Rim of a red pottery shouldered vase with remains of handles (pl.63, no. 6)
Two red siltware necks from storage-jars (pl.63, nos. 3 and 7)
Rim-fragments from two red pottery plates (form as that published in Spencer 1996, pl.51, 1)
Two handles from cooking-pots

The lack of any preserved parts of Buildings N1, N2 and N3 above floor-level makes it difficult to form definite conclusions about the buildings except that all structures were built originally for official purposes connected with the temple. They may have been built very soon after the completion of the forecourt as part of a process of adding the necessary administrative and support departments to the refurbished temple. Building N1 on the inside of the court must have been an integral part of the temple, probably a chapel or series of shrines on top of a terrace platform retained by the massive mud-brick wall. The scale of this wall is such that no other function seems appropriate. By the first century BC, however, all the brick buildings and the temple forecourt were in ruins and were being used for temporary secular occupation and for the disposal of refuse in deep pits.

A sand-filled foundation north of the temple

(a) Introduction

The discovery of this foundation for a small religious structure was made in 1998, during the excavation of an enclosure wall of New-Kingdom date to the north of Temple A. The foundation-pit lies on the exterior of this wall and was cut some distance into its north-western face. The earlier wall had, of course, been levelled long before the preparation of the foundation, which was cut through the older deposits and features from a considerably higher level, now removed by erosion. Immediately adjacent to the south-west side of this foundation was another, earlier one, also filled with sand. This is described in Chapter 4 with details of the New-Kingdom enclosure wall and other early remains in the area.

(b) Structure of the foundation-pit

This foundation had been lined with a thick retaining wall of mud-brick on all sides except the south-east, where it had been cut into the New-Kingdom enclosure wall. This cut had taken a little over 5 metres from the side of the older wall, no trace of which would have been visible above the ground surface at the time of construction. The bricks surrounding the foundation measured 38-40 x 18-20 x 10cm. The pit had been dug sufficiently large to allow the lining to be constructed from the inside, founded on the base of the foundation. Since the brick lining did not reach the actual limit of the cutting in the ground, a foundation-trench was left which was visible in sections along the south-western side. This trench was about 60cm wide; in the area adjacent to the older foundation on the south-west it occupied all the space between the brickwork around the two foundations. The average thickness of the brick retaining wall was 3.3 metres, except on the south east, where only some 60cm of brickwork had been used to straighten up the cut in the New-Kingdom wall. A section across the south-west side of the foundation showed that stratified layers of settlement material with some conspicuous burned stripes had been cut by the foundation-trench of the sand-box brickwork. Pits sealed under these layers were found to contain sherds of the fifth century BC, including some pieces from a Phoenician amphora, so the foundation has to belong to a subsequent period. The Thirtieth Dynasty would seem to be the most likely date for its construction, as part of the redevelopment of the temple complex under Nekhtnebef, although a Ptolemaic date cannot be excluded. The rectangular shape of this building and its location suggest that it might have been the mammisi of the complex (see p.45).

The enclosed area of the sand-filled foundation is a simple rectangle measuring 16.1 x 31.7 metres. The present levels of the tops of the walls around the pit are shown on the plan in plate 66. Comparison of these with the levels inside the corners, each of which was excavated, shows the shallowness of the foundation, little more than half a metre. Close inside the angles the ground had not even been dug out to this depth, but had been left as a sloping surface which fell in level away from the corner. The brick retaining walls were adjusted to accommodate this slope by increasing the number of courses as the ground-level fell, but even at the full depth of the pit there were only four or five courses of bricks remaining (pls.77a-b). Much of the sand filling had been removed and its place taken by water-laid mud, but a thin layer of sand survived in the corners. This was excavated in a search for foundation deposits but none were present. The sand layer was only about 20cm thick and was soon passed as the base of the foundation was reached. In the two corners at the north-west side the bottom of the foundation consisted of older occupation fill, but on the south-east bricks belonging to the cut-down part of the New-Kingdom enclosure wall were found under the last of the sand.

The shallowness of this foundation is probably the result of erosion of its upper structure rather than original design. The whole of the area to the north-west of Temple A as far as the enclosure walls of the Twenty-sixth and Thirtieth Dynasties is low-lying and it forms a natural channel for storm water from higher parts of the site, with severe scouring of the surface. The foundation was probably considerably deeper and the building which it supported would have been at a much higher level, closer to the elevation noted in the north-west gate of the Outer Enclosure Wall (see below).

The north-west gate in the Outer Enclosure Wall

(a) Introduction

A more distant structure connected with the Thirtieth-Dynasty temple is the Outer Enclosure Wall, a description of which was given in the previous report (Spencer 1996, 32-5). During the 1996 season the gate in the north-west wall of the enclosure was excavated. This gate lies on the axis of Temple B, a monument dated by foundation deposits of Nekhtnebef (Spencer 1996, 43-5, 84, pl. 90), and its presence is a good additional indicator for the dating of the Outer Enclosure Wall to the reconstruction of the temple complex which took place under this king.

The fill above the gate was excavated sufficiently to establish its dimensions and to search for the original floor-level of the passage. The deep layer of surface dust from the erosion of the brickwork of the wall was removed to expose the jambs of the gate, which were then cleaned to study the brickwork. Deep excavation was restricted to the first 6 metres of the interior end of the passage and a two-metre wide cut along the full length of the south-western jamb, together with a 5 x 5 metre trench on the exterior angle of the opposite jamb, as shown on plates 64a and 65.

(b) Description of the gate

The jambs of the gate consist of the same kind of bricks as used throughout the Outer Enclosure Wall, composed of hard black mud and measuring 38-40 x 19-20 x 12cm. The bonding along the jambs consisted of alternate layers of headers and stretchers, mortared with mud (pl.64b-c). At the exterior face there was a rebate in the corner of each jamb: the one on the south-west was 0.85 metres in depth and extended 1.15 metres from the angle, whilst the opposite rebate was 0.75 metres deep by 1.45 metres long. There was no trace of there having been any stone masonry in these recesses, nor was there any surviving plaster. Apart from these exterior rebates, the jambs of the gate were perfectly straight through the thickness of the wall with a space of 6.55 metres between them, widening slightly to 6.70 at the inner end. The erosion pattern of the area has cut the top of the wall on this side of the enclosure into a steep slope, which falls from the outer face towards the interior, so the jambs were preserved highest at the outer face of the wall where the brickwork rose to relative levels of 398 on the south-west and 420 on the north-east. The steady fall in level through the wall places the top of the bricks at the interior end of the gate at relative levels of 212 (south-west) and 224 (north-east). The foundation level of the gate lies at 172, so only some 40 centimetres of brick has survived at the inner end of the gate, compared with 2.40 metres at the outer face. Study of the sections of the fill inside the passage suggested that the floor-level of the gate had been at a relative level of about 340, so much of the original brickwork at the inner end has been eroded below this into the foundation. Even the maximum height of the brickwork at the exterior of the north-east jamb, noted above as rising 2.40 metres above the base of the wall, is actually only 80cm above this floor-level, showing how little of the above-ground structure of the gate has survived. The ancient floor was marked only by a variation in the rather homogenous fill of the passage; there were no traces of any masonry or plaster paving. The upper fill in the passage consisted of brick dust from the erosion and collapse of the wall, below which, under the old floor-level, there was a limited quantity of Late-Dynastic domestic pottery of coarse siltware. This was embedded in the ground which had accumulated on the site outside the earlier Inner Enclosure Wall, the exterior face of which at this point lay just 2.45 metres inside the Outer Wall. As indicated on the plan in plate 65, the earlier wall runs right across without any gate, but at such a low level that its ruins would have not have been visible above ground in the Thirtieth Dynasty. This is clear evidence to show that the purpose of the gate in the Outer Enclosure was to provide an entrance on the axis of Temple B of Nekhtnebef, presumably with a processional way leading to that temple past the probable location of the mammisi (see Chapter 6).

The thicknesses of the jambs of the gate were 17.9 metres, rather less than the thicknesses obtained at other points along this side of the Outer Enclosure Wall (Spencer 1996, 32). Whether the difference was achieved by a gradual narrowing or by steps in the alignment of the faces cannot be established without further excavation along the length of the enclosure. Across the outer end of the passage was a thin wall at a high level, extending from close to the angle of the south-western jamb into unexcavated fill and built of mud-bricks measuring 34 x 17 x 12cm. This wall was only a single brick in thickness and had been founded on accumulated fill at relative level 341, that is, approximately on the original floor of the passage (pls.64b, 65). The surviving height of the wall was 50cm and its thickness 35cm. Beyond this wall towards the north-west was a deep fill of broken bricks with a few sherds from Ptolemaic jars. Further in this direction lie many house remains in fired brick from the extensive Roman town which developed beyond the ridge created by the Outer Enclosure Wall.

4. A New-Kingdom Enclosure Wall and adjacent features to the north-west of the Main Temple

(a) Introduction

Excavation in the 1998 season was concentrated in an area to the north-west of the temple of Amun, where a small test-trench cut in 1993 had revealed some mud-brick features covered by fill which contained pottery dating from the early Third Intermediate Period. A domestic area was expected, but the extensive later excavation resulted instead in the identification of part of an enclosure wall of New-Kingdom date, buried in fill containing pottery which ranged in date from the Ramesside Period into the Twenty-first Dynasty. This settlement fill extended along the west side of the temple and was noted around the foundation-pit of the First Pylon in Trench W9. Other finds of similar pottery were made in parts of the pre-temple ground between the foundation-trenches in the heart of the temple, but in lower density than in the north-west sector, suggesting a widespread area of late New-Kingdom occupation had been cleared for redevelopment in the Twenty-second Dynasty.

Parts of the north-western side of the brick wall had been cut by the foundation-pits of two small religious buildings, which on stratigraphic and topographical evidence date from the Twenty-second and Thirtieth Dynasties respectively. The portions of the enclosure wall revealed by excavation included the north corner and parts of the north-west and north-east sides; the latter continues in a south-easterly direction towards the axis of the later Amun-Temple (pl.66). Within the angle of the wall were several grain-silos, embedded in the fill mentioned above, and cut into the external edge of the corner of the wall was a brick-built tomb-chamber containing the partly robbed burial of a man named Iken, evidently a Lower-Egyptian Vizier from the reign of Osorkon I. The individual structures and associated fills are described below in chronological order.

(b) The New-Kingdom enclosure wall

This massive mud-brick wall with a thickness of 11.6 metres is the earliest feature so far discovered on the temple site. It is founded at a deep level below the present water-table, and some of the pottery from the fill against its inner face is characteristic of the Twentieth Dynasty, so it is probable that the wall is considerably earlier. The ceramics from the upper levels of this fill continue the chronological sequence into the Twenty-first Dynasty, by which time some eroded portions of the wall were becoming buried in the accumulated deposits. Surprisingly, much of the brickwork was found to be well preserved at a depth of only a few centimetres under the surface mud, in a part of the site which suffers more than most from erosion by rainwater. From the corner at the north the length of the north-western portion of the wall is 46.4 metres, ending at a finished jamb belonging to one side of a gate, the opposite side of which has not yet been located. The north-eastern side of the enclosure has so far been traced for a distance of 15.2 metres from the interior of the corner. For the first 10 metres of this length the top of the wall is preserved at a relative level of around 130, not very deep under the surface mud, but then the level of the surviving bricks dropped as the wall reached the more disturbed and pitted ground in front of the later temple of Amun. Sherds of Ptolemaic date were found in the pit-fill above the early wall at this point (pl.76b, nos. 3-6). The bricks of the wall vary in size: the majority are in the range of 37-40 x 18-20 x 10cm, but a few are larger, particularly in the north-east section, measuring 44 x 21 x 12 cm. The quality of the bricks also differs at individual points; the core of the north-western side of the enclosure consists of very hard mud-bricks, with occasional sandy bricks here and there, whilst the bricks along parts of the north-western and north-eastern faces are considerably softer. This difference has resulted in the soft areas being eroded to greater depths, as shown by the relative levels on the plan (pl.66). Through the core of the wall the majority of the bricks are laid as headers, the usual pattern for thick masses of brickwork, although as always there are numerous irregularities. The faces were bonded as alternate layers of headers and stretchers. The position of this enclosure and the direction taken by the walls as they extend from the corner can leave no doubt as to its function as an enclosure for a temple which preceded the Third Intermediate Period temple of Amun on approximately the same spot.

(c) The grain-silos and accumulated fill inside the enclosure wall

The corner of the enclosure had come to be occupied by a cluster of grain-silos, embedded in fill which contained pottery fragments of the late New Kingdom and early Third Intermediate Period, together with remains of hearths and many fallen mud-bricks. The disposition of the highest level of silos is shown in plates 67-68; at the south-west side of the cluster was a small structure with walls on three sides, but only a single course of brick remained of these walls. The majority of the silos shown in the plan were founded at high levels in the fill, with their walls surviving to heights of between 10 and 30cm. The diameters of the silos ranged from 1.75 to 2.80 metres, apart from the more solidly constructed Silo 4, which was over 3 metres across. This silo was built at a deeper level than the others and possessed walls consisting of two rings of brick instead of only one. That there had been older silos at deeper levels was confirmed by the discovery of Silo 16 in the section-trench beside the enclosure wall, described below. Some of the fill which covered Silo 4 sloped down to pass beneath Silos 5 and 11, and the fill beside number 11 went below number 5, establishing a relative sequence. Silo 6 stood at a similar level to number 5, but Silo 12 was built later, on a slightly higher deposit of fill. Silo 15, however, was earlier than number 12 and also pre-dated the construction of the small building to its south-west. After the destruction of the various silos they had all been covered by fill containing dumped broken pottery of the early Third Intermediate Period.

There was no remaining fill of similar date outside the corner of the enclosure wall; instead the ground contained sherds of the Late to Ptolemaic Periods, the latter coming from several very deep rubbish-pits (pl.76b, nos. 1-2 and 7-8). Among these fragments was part of a cooking-pot with a red-slipped interior and rim (pl.76b, no. 1), a bowl of Memphis Black Ware (pl.76b, no. 2) and a red siltware vessel which certainly possessed only a single handle (pl.76b, no. 7).

(d) Contents of the silos

A quantity of pottery and other material was recovered from inside some of the silos. The ceramics were no different from those found at the same level in the fill outside, much of the deposit having been dumped over the silos after they had been abandoned. The test-trench of the 1993 season in the area had been located above part of Silo 4 and the pottery from the surface fill at this point is shown separately from the more recently excavated material, on plate 71a, although both collections consist of similar material. The ceramics from the earlier test are here listed first.

From fill above Silo 4 (found 1993)
Silt bowl with internal rim and interior spiral thin pink slip (pl.71a, no. 1)
Carinated bowl of red siltware with a faint exterior pnk slip (pl.71a, no. 2)
Part of a siltware jar (pl.71a, no. 3)
Rim from a siltware vessel of very large diameter, with an external pink slip (pl.71a, no.4)
Rim and shoulder of a siltware jar with an external pale cream slip (pl.71a, no. 5)
Neck from a siltware jar with an external cream slip (pl.71a, no. 6)
Neck from a siltware jar with a pink-cream external slip, extending onto the interior (pl.71a, no. 7)
Body-sherd, the exterior white-slipped and decorated with red bands (pl.71a, no. 8)

Silo 4
Silt plate or cover (pl.72, no. 7)
Siltware jar-rim, uncoated (form as no. 5 on pl.75)
Pointed red siltware base with a cream exterior slip (pl.75, no.11)
Two joining sherds from a large pink-cream slipped jar or neck. Nile Silt B (form as no. 2 on pl.74)

Silo 5
Carinated bowl of uncoated red siltware (form as no. 2 on pl.73)
Part of a siltware bowl with an internal rim (form as no. 9 on pl.72)
Siltware neck from a jar (form as no. 6 on pl.71a)

Silo 6
Rims from siltware bowls (forms as nos. 2 and 4 on pl.72)
Fragments from at least six siltware bowls with internal rims (forms as no. 1 on pl.71a and nos. 8-9 on pl.72)
Top from a siltware jar (form as no. 9 on pl.75)
Three body-sherds from a Levantine flask, cream-slipped with red-painted circular decoration
Siltware necks from two jars, one with an external yellow slip (form as no. 6 on pl.71a)

Silo 11
Flint sickle-blade (Cat.**25**)
Two pottery counters (Cat.**91, 92**)
Siltware plates (form as no. 1 on pl.70)
Rounded siltware bowl with a red-painted band around the rim (pl.72, no. 4)
Fragments from numerous red siltware bowls with internal rims (forms as no. 1 on pl.71a and nos. 8-9 on pl.72)
Complete siltware bowl with internal rim, and fragment of another (pl.72, no.10)
Rim and neck of a jar with an external pink-orange slip, extending over the inside of the mouth. Only one handle preserved, but the rim was not complete, so there could have been another. Perhaps an import (pl.75, no. 14). Cf. Aston 1996, fig.196 (h)
Neck-fragments from siltware jars (forms as no. 6 on pl.71a and nos 9, 13 on pl.73)
Carinated bowl of uncoated red siltware (form as no. 2 on pl.73)
Red siltware cup with thin sides and a flared rim (pl.73, no. 3)
Top of a siltware jar (form as no. 7 on pl.74)
Coarse siltware base of a bread-mould (pl.75, no. 18)
Large red siltware jar-rim with a thin pink slip on the exterior and inside the rim (pl.73, no. 17)
Siltware handle from a storage jar
Foot from a red siltware chalice (form as no. 7 on pl.73)

Silo 12
Pieces from two very large platters of coarse red siltware (Nile Silt C). Diameters were about 80cm.
Coarse red siltware bowl with an external pink slip (pl.73, no. 1)
Part of a carinated siltware bowl with a thin red slip on the exterior and on the inside of the rim (pl.73, no. 2)
Very coarse siltware cup (pl.73, no. 4)
Chalice of coarse red siltware (pl.73, no. 8)
Upper part of a large jar of red siltware with a streaky pale red external slip (pl.74, no. 1)
Neck from a jar of uncoated red siltware (form as no. 9 on pl.73)

Silo 15
Fragments from siltware plates, some with red paint on the rim (forms as no. 1 on pl.70 and no. 1 on pl.72)
Parts of siltware bowls with internal rims (forms as nos. 8-9 on pl.72)

Part of a red siltware chalice (pl.73, no. 7)
Foot from a chalice like the foregoing example
Large diameter rim from a coarse siltware jar with an external pale greenish slip, which extends over the inside of the rim (pl.74, no. 3)
Upper part of a jar of coarse red siltware (pl.75, no. 9)
Part of a quartzite saddle quern

Silo 16
See description below

(e) The accumulated deposits under the upper-level silos

The deeper stratigraphy was tested by a section-trench, cut between the inner face of the enclosure wall and Silo 6 and cutting the edge of the brick bin [9] to show the stratigraphy under it. This test descended for 1.1 metres to a relative level of 45, at which point the ground became too wet to continue. A quantity of pottery was recovered and is noted below. This test also revealed part of the curved wall of the earlier Silo 16, rising to relative level 126 and founded approximately at relative level 65. The base of this silo was filled with collapsed bricks from its upper structure, mixed with additional collapse from the enclosure wall (see the profile on plate 69). The fill over the ruins of this low-level silo consisted of hard mud containing many sherds and brick fragments, a composition found to be typical of the whole area of the silos. The substantial wall of Silo 4, at the north-east end of the excavation, is also founded deeper than the smaller silos and the base level was not reached in the time available. Another silo at a low level occurs to the south-west of the main excavated area, in Trench W9, next to the foundation-pit of the First Pylon of Temple A. This silo was embedded in fill of the same character as that from the site of the other silos, indicating that the area occupied by this kind of material was quite large and also that silos were constructed repeatedly over the ruins of older ones as the level of the ground rose with the accumulation of occupation-debris. The north-west end of the foundation of the First Pylon in Trench W9 had been cut into the eleventh- to tenth-century BC fill, and had truncated the wall of this silo in the process. Pottery from this early fill in Trench W9, shown on plate 70, included the following forms, most of which are well represented among the ceramics from around the group of silos situated further to the north-east:

Many fragments of plain-rimmed siltware bowls (Nile Silt B), a few with red-painted bands around the exterior rim, running over to the interior of the vessel (pl.70, nos. 1-3)
Bowl of brown siltware wih an internal rim (pl.70, no. 4)
Rims from siltware jars (pl.70, nos. 5-7); also examples as no. 4 on plate 75
Small siltware dish or cover (pl.70, no. 8; cf. the similar but larger vessel from Qantir in Aston 1996, fig. 36, no. 8 and fig. 190 (h) in Phase I; also Aston 1998, 177 [503] and the example in Bourriau and Aston 1985, pl.35, no. 37).
Siltware jar necks with external cream or pink slips (as pl.73, nos. 12-13)
Bread moulds with hand-trimmed exteriors, perforated in middle of the base by a hole about 18-20 mm diameter (pl.70, nos. 9-10)
Cream-washed body-sherds
Handle from a Silt B pink-slipped amphora

Remains of the silo wall in Trench W9 rose to relative level 75 and the base of the structure lay in the subsoil water. The deeper silos appear to have been more solidly built than those created above them. The distance between the main group of silos in the angle of the early enclosure wall and the one revealed in Trench W9 is approximately 35 metres, but the extent of the late New-Kingdom and Twenty-first Dynasty occupation was even larger, since similar pottery was found in the fill in front of the north-west end of the Second Pylon of Temple A and also on the opposite side of the temple axis, in levels below the foundation of the late-Dynastic Building N1 (see plate 55a-b). The few sherds noted in the pre-temple ground in the heart of the temple also seem to have belonged to the eleventh to tenth century BC stratum (pl.71b).

Material from the stratigraphic section in the Silo Area

Top stratum (to a depth of 10cm)
Flint sickle-blade (Cat.**26**)
Fragment of large platter in coarse red siltware
Small plain rims from plates and bowls (forms as nos. 1-3 on pl.70 and 1, 3 and 5 on pl.72)
Top from a siltware jar (form as no. 7 on pl.74)
Upper part of a siltware jar, the surface blackened by burning (pl.75, no. 5)
Body-sherds with thin cream and pink slips
Toe bone of a goat

Second stratum (to 20cm)
Fragments of a large flat platter of coarse red siltware
Siltware bowl (pl.72, no. 2)
Siltware bowl with an all-over orange slip and a red-painted band on the rim (pl.72, no. 3)
Numerous fragments from siltware bowls with internal rims (forms as no. 4 on pl.70 and nos. 8-10 on pl.72)
Fragment from a carinated bowl of uncoated siltware (form as no. 2 on pl.73)
Large jar-neck with a pale cream wash (form as no. 16 on pl.73)
Marlware jar-neck (pl.73, no. 10)
Siltware jar-neck with a pink slip on the exterior and a cream slip on the inside of the rim (pl.75, no. 13)

Third stratum (to 30cm)
More examples of siltware plates and bowls (forms as nos. 1-3 on pl.70 and 1, 4 and 5 on pl.72)
Additional fragments from siltware bowls with internal rims (forms as no. 4 on pl.70; no. 1 on pl.71a and nos. 8-10 on pl.72)
Parts of the rims from siltware jars (forms as no. 12 on pl.73 and nos. 3-5 on pl.75)
Lower part of a coarse red siltware bread-mould (pl.75, no. 17)

Fourth stratum (to 40cm)
Fragments of bone and pottery occurred at the eastern end, with broken brick fill on the west. From this level and below, most of the pottery was situated inside the remains of Silo 16.
Fragments of a coarse siltware platter
Parts of two red siltware bowls with red-painted bands inside and outside the rim (pl.72, no. 1)
Part of a siltware bowl with an internal rim (form as no. 9 on pl.72)
Fragment of a carinated bowl in uncoated red siltware (form as no. 2 on pl.71a)
Coarse siltware bowl (pl.72, no. 11)
Upper half of a siltware jar with slightly ribbed sides (pl.75, no. 6)
Two cylindrical necks from siltware jars with a cream-pink slip on the exterior and over the inside of the rim (pl.73, no. 13)
Part of a small jar of coarse red siltware (pl.73, no. 5)
Upper part of a jar of red siltware, with a pink slip on the exterior and over the inside of the rim (pl.73, no. 6)
Two handles, probably from storage-jars of the type shown on pl.74, no. 2
Shoulder blade of a goat

Fifth stratum (to 50cm)
More examples of the common siltware plates and bowls with plain or internal rims (forms as nos. 1-4 on pl.70; no. 1 on pl.71a and nos. 1-2, 4-5, 8-10 on pl.72)

Two fragments from the upper part of a storage-jar. Nile Silt B with an external thin cream-pink slip (pl.74, no.2)
Top from a short-necked jar of uncoated siltware (pl.75, no. 4)
Very coarse siltware vessel of unusual form (pl.75, no. 10)

Sixth stratum (to 70cm)
Part of a pottery figure of a horse (Cat.**68**)
Fragments of several very large platters in coarse siltware (Nile Silt C)
Red siltware bowl (form as pl.70, no. 3, from W9)
Siltware bowl or cover (pl.72, no. 6)
Fragment of a siltware bowl with an internal rim (form as no. 9 on pl.72)
Sherds from two carinated bowls (form as no. 2 on pl.73)
Several large pink- or cream-slipped body-sherds from big storage-jars at the west end in fallen brick fill
From east end:
Pieces of two large uncoated siltware jars (pl.73, no. 15)
Coarse siltware neck from a jar with an internal and external red slip (form as pl.73, no. 12)
Base of a siltware chalice (form as pl.73, no. 7)

(f) Minor features in the area of the silos

Close to the inner face of the early enclosure wall were some smaller brick circles which seem to have been simple storage bins, possibly for animal fodder, rather than grain-silos. These are the features numbered 1-3, 9-10 and 14 on the plan (pl.68). Between the brick circles 9/10 and Silo 6 was a hearth full of black carbon, enclosed in its own ring of mud-bricks. All these elements were buried in the same kind of fill as the silos, characterised by fallen mud-brick and sherds characteristic of the eleventh to early tenth centuries BC. The brick structure at the south-west end of the excavation contained similar sherds, but as these came from the level of the base course of bricks they must pre-date the building. Very few objects were found in the fill and those that were recovered were very simple: some pottery gaming-pieces cut from sherds, a few flint sickle-blades, two rough clay beads and the part of a terracotta animal figure noted above. Drawings of the forms of pottery from all parts of the upper-level fill within the angle of the enclosure wall, with that from inside the silos, are included in plates 72-75, and a list of these ceramics is given below:

Pottery from the fill around the silos and against the inner face of the enclosure wall
Fragments from numerous shallow plates of red siltware, some with red paint around the rim (forms similar to no. 1 on pl.70)
Rounded siltware bowl with a plain rim (pl.72, no. 5)
Pieces from siltware bowls with internal rims (pl.72, nos. 8-9)
Carinated bowl of coarse red siltware with a small ring-base (pl.72, no. 12)
Small siltware vessel with a convex base and vertical sides (form as no.8 on pl.70)
Wide-mouthed siltware jar with a short neck, with a pale pink slip on exterior and over the inside of the rim (pl.74, no. 4)
Wide-mouthed siltware jar with a short neck, with a thin cream exterior slip, extending over the inside of the rim (pl.74, no. 5)
Wide-mouthed coarse siltware jar with a short neck, with two streaks of red paint on the outside of the rim (pl.74, no. 6)
Short-necked siltware jar with an exterior red slip, which extends to the inside of the rim (pl.75, no. 1)
Short-necked siltware jar with an exterior pink slip, which extends to the inside of the rim (pl.75, no. 2)
Short-necked jar of uncoated siltware (pl.74, no. 7)
Part of two short-necked jars of uncoated siltware (pl.75, nos. 3-4)

Siltware jar-neck of cylindrical shape, with a pale red interior and exterior slip (pl.73, no. 9)

Tall, slightly flared, siltware jar-neck with an external pink slip, which extends over the inside of the rim (pl.73, no. 12)

Upper part of a cylindrical jar-neck of coarse siltware, with an external thin red slip containing clear streaks of more solid colour. This slip continues for a short distance over the inside of the rim (pl.73, no. 14)

Siltware jar-neck with a flared rim and and bands of an external red slip, streaks of which continue on the inside of the rim (pl.73, no. 16)

Uncoated siltware jar with a contracted mouth and slightly ribbed sides (pl.75, no. 7)

Uncoated siltware jar with a contracted mouth and slightly undulating sides. From upper fill on the outside of Silo 4 (pl.75, no. 8)

Uncoated siltware jar with a contracted mouth (pl.75, no. 9)

Flared rim from a siltware jar, with a red-painted band inside the rim (pl.75, no. 12)

Small rim from a siltware vessel, with an external pink slip (pl.75, no. 15)

Part of a two-handled flask in a hard pink fabric (pl.75, no. 16). Cf. Aston 1998, 681 [2796]

Fragment of a coarse red siltware bread-mould with a hole in the base (pl.75, no. 19)

Pottery from the upper fill around the small building to the south-west of the silos

Fragments of shallow plates of red siltware (forms similar to no. 1 on pl.70)

Siltware bowls with internal rims (forms as no. 4 on pl.70; no. 1 on pl.71a and nos. 8-10 on pl.72)

Carinated bowl in uncoated red siltware (form as no. 2 on pl.73)

Cylindrical jar-necks of red siltware (forms as nos. 6-7 on pl.71a and no. 9 on pl.73)

Short-necked jar-rims, mostly with thin pink or cream external slips (forms as nos. 4-5 on pl.74 and nos. 1-2 on pl.75)

Top of a jar of uncoated siltware, with a contracted mouth (form as no. 6 on pl.75)

Neck from a jar of fine siltware (form similar to no. 13 on pl.75)

(g) The fill around the exterior of the corner of the enclosure wall

In the investigation of the north corner of the early enclosure wall, fill of exactly the same character as that around the silos was encountered above the eroded parts of the wall itself, showing that the outside of the wall was already in a state of decay by the early part of the Third Intermediate Period. The damage, however, cannot have extended right across the thickness of the wall, because in the interior of the corner was the base of a pottery jar which had obviously been placed against extant brickwork. Naturally, the outside of a corner would have been the most vulnerable point for collapse to begin. A clay oven was found to have been constructed above part of the wall in this region, and was later cut by the building of the tomb-chamber of Iken (for an account of this tomb, see below). The surviving part of the oven was preserved to a height of 39cm, at which point its diameter was 80cm (pl.79b). This narrowed to 60cm at the base. In the north side was a hole 9cm in diameter, situated at a height of 26cm. The strata above the cut-down parts of the corner of the wall showed two distinct layers of sherds separated by an empty band of fill. The deeper layer of pottery was at the same level as the oven and contained sherds of the same kinds as found in the area of the silos, whilst the higher stratum produced later ceramics, dating from around the end of the Third Intermediate Period and commencement of the Twenty-sixth Dynasty. This layer extended above the remains of the tomb of Iken, and some sherds of mid-seventh century BC date were found in the fill in the top of the chamber, but the lower stratum containing the earlier pottery had, like the oven in the same level, been cut by the construction of the tomb. About 6 metres to the east of the tomb were traces of some mud-bricks on a similar orientation to that of the tomb's longer axis, associated with a small area of clean sand filling. These features could have been remnants from a second tomb, almost completely eroded away. The mid-seventh century BC material in the area was very similar to some of the pottery found in previous seasons in the excavation of the settlement-deposits which were cut by the construction of Temple C under Psamtik I (Spencer 1996, 63ff.). The presence of ceramics of this age over the tomb of Iken shows that the tomb had been destroyed and partly robbed by this time. The two phases of pottery noted in this area included the following items:

Lower stratum above the eroded enclosure wall but cut by the tomb of Iken
Siltware bowl with an internal rim, from north of the tomb (form as no. 8 on pl.72)
Siltware bowl with an internal rim, from the level of oven (form as no. 9 on pl.72)
Siltware jar-neck (pl.73, no. 11)
Red siltware jar-neck (pl.76a, no. 1). Compare Spencer 1996, pl.69, type D.1.61
Red siltware jar-neck (pl.76a, no. 2). See Aston 1996, fig. 63, no. 16 and fig. 200 (b); id. 1998, 695 and pl.X [2820]
Part of a siltware jar with a contracted mouth (form as no. 7 on pl.75)
Siltware body-sherds with pale pink or cream exterior slips, probably from large storage-jars
Stump from the foot of a red siltware chalice
Two pottery counters (Cat.**93-94**)

Upper stratum of mid-seventh century BC material
Small dish or lid (pl.76a, no. 7)
Small hand-made siltware platters (Spencer 1996, pl.61, type A.1.32)
Foot and part of the body from a red siltware chalice (pl.76a, no. 6)
Rim and side from a Type C.1.6 jar (see Spencer 1996, pl.64)
(For sherds from the disturbed upper fill in the tomb of Iken, see the description of the tomb below)

From the pit above the enclosure wall
Pink ware jar-neck, probably from a Phoenician amphora, with a fragment of another (pl.76a, no. 3)
Two red siltware jar-necks (pl.76a, nos. 4-5)
Pottery disk with 2 holes (Cat.**95**)

(h) Notes on the late New-Kingdom to Twenty-first Dynasty pottery

Details of the provenances of the ceramics from the various levels of fill in the angle of the New-Kingdom enclosure wall and from similar deposits on the north-west side of Trench W9 have been given above. The pottery includes certain products typical of the Ramesside Period, particularly some large storage-jars with pale cream or pink exterior slips, but the majority appear to date from the Twenty-first Dynasty. Drawings of the shapes are given on plates 70-75 and the various principal types represented are described below. The presence or absence of parallels for the rare types of pottery, usually represented by single specimens, has been noted in the lists of provenances above. Unless stated to the contrary, all forms consisted of silt fabrics.

1. Plain-rimmed bowls and plates (pls.70, nos. 1-3; 72, nos. 1-5)

These varieties of simple vessels changed relatively little in shape from the New Kingdom to the Late Period. The examples from this assemblage consist chiefly of uncoated Nile Silt B, with sometimes a band of red paint along the rim. The very shallow form of plate from the extension of Trench W9 (pl.70, no. 1) was also noted in the upper fill around the silos and inside Silos 11 and 15, all contexts which suggest a date at the later end of the sequence. Some of the more rounded shapes (pls.70, nos. 2-3; 72, nos. 2-5) were distributed more regularly throughout the various levels of the fill, from the bottom of the cross-section (pl.69) to the surface fill and interiors of some of the upper-level silos, indicating that they had been longer-lived types.

Parallels: Aston 1996, fig. 36, no. 6 from Qantir [for our pl.72, 5]; ibid., fig. 187 (j) [for our pl.70, 2]. Many bowls of similar form are illustrated in Aston 1998 and as Type X in Nagel 1938, pls.vii-viii.

2. Shallow bowls or covers (pl.72, nos. 6-7)

Only one example of each of these shapes was recovered, one from Silo 4 and the other at the bottom of the cross-section trench. This agrees with the observed stratigraphy of the silos, since Silo 4 is known to pre-date the group of smaller silos and would, therefore, be closer in date to the deeper layers of the fill.

Parallels: Aston 1996, fig. 63, no. 550, from Memphis [for our pl.72, 6]; ibid., fig. 36, no. 2 from Qantir [for our pl.72, 7]. The latter piece is also paralled from Saqqara (Aston 1991, pl.47, no. 6).

3. Large-diameter bowls with internal rims (pls.70, no.4; 71a, no. 1 and 72, nos. 8-10)

These were found at all levels in the fill around the Ramesside enclosure wall and examples were also found in the pre-temple fill in Trench W9. The diameters of the vessels can be as large as 40cm and, perhaps surprisingly, the fabric is a fairly weak siltware, so breakages must have been frequent. Many examples bear surface treatment in the form of a thin slip or wash of pale pink or cream colour. The complete vessel from inside Silo 11 shows the form of the ring-foot. Two examples of bowls of this class were excavated in 1993 from deep in a trench behind the temple of Psamtik I (Spencer 1996, pl.41, nos. 5-6).

Parallels: Lopez-Grande *et al.* 1995, pls.xviii, h; xxii, c; Aston 1996, fig. 40, no. 4; id., 1998, 343 [1178-1182], 459 [1650-1652], 527 [2128-2134], 467 [1703-1716]. These examples from Qantir are in various fabrics. The absence of this type of bowl from the pottery found in the New-Kingdom tombs of Saqqara and Deir el-Medina suggests that the form came into use in the late Twentieth Dynasty.

4. Biconvex bowls (pls.71a, no. 2; 72, no. 12; 73, nos. 1-2)

The shapes include both rounded and ring-bases, and the height of the carination varies. Most examples came from contexts inside and around the upper-level silos, suggesting a Twenty-first Dynasty date, but one fragment of a bowl was noted near the base of the cross-section trench. The lack of more examples from early contexts is probably only an effect of the limited scope of deep excavation in the fill. The complete shape shown on plate 72 (no. 12) is a single example from the surface fill.

Parallels: An example was found in the fill behind the temple of Psamtik I in 1993 (Spencer 1996, pl.41, no. 4). Others are noted from Qantir, Memphis and Tanis, although perhaps dated too late at the latter site: Aston 1998, 589 [2422]; id., 1996, fig. 68, no. 7 and fig. 29, no. 205; see also ibid., fig. 89, no. 123 from El-Hibeh [for our pl.73, 2] and Holthoer 1977, pl.40, RB1 [for our pl.73, 1].

5. Plain-rimmed cups (pl.73, nos. 3-4)

These two forms were noted only as single examples, from Silos 11 and 12 respectively. A similar vessel to number 4 on plate 73 has been published in Aston 1997, 88 and pl.115, type 95, although with a red slip which our vessel lacks.

6. Chalice cups (pl.73, nos. 7-8)

Fragments of footed cups of this type were not plentiful, but those that were found were distributed at high and low levels, suggesting that the type was in use over the period of time it took for the fill to build up against the enclosure wall. Small chalices were used in the late New Kingdom (Nagel 1938, pl.xvii, final two examples of his Type XXV; see also Aston 1998, 175 [488-490]) and their presence around the silos shows that a rough versions continued to be made in the Twenty-first Dynasty. Better-made chalices appeared in subsequent stages of the Third Intermediate Period.

7. Small jars with cylindrical or flared necks (pls.71a, no. 6; 73, nos. 9-10, 12-14)

The slipped neck (pl.73, no. 9) was found in the upper fill and within Silos 11 and 12. It is not dissimilar from a slightly larger jar-neck found in the 1993 test of the surface above Silo 4 (pl.71a, no. 6). The neck shown as number 10 on plate 73 is a single rare specimen from a marlware jar, found high up in the cross-section trench and so effectively in the surface fill. The flared shapes with cream to pink slips (pl.73, nos. 12-13) came from rather deeper levels in the cross-section beside the enclosure wall and in Trench W9. These are probably from globular jars, as published in Aston 1998, 605 [2484]. (The neck on our plate 73, no. 11 is from a different context). Number 14 on plate 73 is a jar-neck from the surface fill around the silos. See Aston 1996, fig. 196 (f).

8. Large jars with cylindrical or flared necks (pls.71a, no. 7; 73, nos. 15-17; 74, nos. 1-2)

These are all parts of large storage-jars made in Nile Silt B fabric, often with the addition of exterior pale pink or cream slips. The jar shown as number 15 on plate 73 came from the lowest level of the cross-section trench, and pieces of the handled vessel (pl.74, no. 2) were present in the stratum immediately above. This would place these two forms in the earlier part of the sequence in the accumulation of the eleventh- to tenth-century BC fill and suggest a date in the Twentieth Dynasty. Parallels for the shapes tend to confirm this view; a slightly smaller version of the jar-neck (pl.73, no. 15) occurred in graves at Tell el-Yahudiya, dated to between the reigns of Ramesses III and VI (Aston 1996, fig. 5, nos. 3-4; see also ibid., fig. 20, a-c; Hope 1989, fig. 5, no. 3; pl. 6c). Another similar neck was found at Balamun in the level below Building N1 (see plate 55b, no. 3). In addition to being present in the deeper strata of the cross-section trench, pieces of the longer-necked storage-jar with handles (pl.74, no. 2) were found in Silo 4, which, as noted in the description of the site is an older context than the adjacent smaller silos. Again, the parallels for this shape concur with a Ramesside date. The form is noted at Qantir and Memphis in a variety of fabrics (Aston 1998, 609 [2487], 615 [2498], 619 [2513]; id., 1996, fig. 39, no. 1; fig. 61, no. 397 and cf. fig. 204a of Phase I) and also at Tell el-Yahudiya (Hope 1989, fig. 3, no. 1; pl.6a). Examples of jars of very similar form were found in the tomb of Tia at Saqqara, but made in marl clay, the appearance of which the pale slip on the silt fabric of the Balamun vessels was designed to imitate (Aston 1997, 92 and pl.120, type 162). Similar vessels also occurred in the tomb of Iurudef (Aston 1991, pls.50, no. 56; 51, nos. 57-58).

The remaining types of jars in this group were all noted in the upper fill or inside the later silos. Only one example of the long-necked jar (pl.74, no. 1) was found, inside Silo 12. This shape is known from Memphis and has been re-dated by Aston to the Twentieth Dynasty (Aston 1996, fig. 61, no. 398; cf. fig. 199 of Phase I). Like the two-handled storage-jar cited above, this vessel consists of silt fabric covered by a thin external slip, in this case coloured pale red.

Parallels: Aston 1996, fig. 165 C6, from Medinet Habu and dated to the Twenty-first Dynasty [for our pl.73, 17].

9. Short-necked jars with modelled rims (pls.71a, no. 5; 74, nos. 3-7; 75, nos. 1-2)

Examples of the large-diameter rim (pl.74, no. 3) were recovered inside Silo 15, one of the latest silos to be built, and in the surface mud above Silo 4. One other vessel of this group (pl.74, no. 7) was found in the top of Silo 11 and all the others were recovered from the upper-level fill around the grain-silos and the small building to their south-west. The lack of examples from the deeper levels might suggest that this type of vessel was a product whose development dates from the beginning of the Third Intermediate Period rather than the end of the New Kingdom. The limited testing of deep strata, noted in the discussion of the Biconvex Bowls, above, makes such conclusions very tentative.

Parallels: Aston 1996, fig. 18, no. 6 from the tomb of Ramesses VI in marl clay [for our pl.74, 4]; ibid., fig. 39, no. 2 from Qantir [for our pl.74, 6].

10. Short-necked plain-rimmed jars (pls.70, nos. 5-7; 71a, no. 3; 73, nos. 5-6; 75, nos. 3-9)

This rather varied group consists of jars which consist of uncoated siltware, lacking the thin, streaky slips noted so frequently on the other types of jars and bowls. Fragments of these simple jars were found to be distributed throughout the depth of the fill around the silos, suggesting that they belonged to a long-lived type of vessel. The plain appearance would indicate that they were standard utilitarian products, probably the least likely to be affected by changing fashions. The most common style among the group was that represented by the shapes drawn as number 3 on plate 71a and numbers 5-9 on plate 75, with a plain, slightly flared rim and convex sides in which a slight ribbed effect was often apparent, perhaps the result of the coiling method of manufacture. As mentioned above, they occurred at all levels and examples were noted inside Silos 4, 6 and 15. The vessels resemble the so-called beer-jars of the New Kingdom (see Aston 1996, fig. 194a and 198a; id., 1997 pl.115, type 103; id., 1998, 185-7 [523-529]; 273 [904-910]). A similar jar-neck with a more pronounced flared rim was recorded from the fill in Trench W9 (pl.70, no. 5).

Certain other vessels in this group have more vertical sides and thicker rims of various styles (pls.70, nos. 6-7; 73, nos. 5-6). The two examples from the north-west side of Trench W9 on plate 70 were each represented by single specimens from the small area excavated. Both were of uncoated siltware. Forms 5 and 6 on plate 73 were found inside Silo 16 within the cross-section trench, a relatively early context in the fill around the New-Kingdom enclosure wall. One of these pieces (pl.73, no. 6) was red-slipped on its exterior and on the inside of the rim.

Examples of the plain jar-rims shown on plate 75, numbers 3 and 4, came from the surface fill around the silos and from depths of between 30 and 50cm in the cross-section trench beside the enclosure wall. They are of a style encountered in some areas of the pre-temple ground inside the Amun-temple, two fragments having been recovered in Trench A2 (pl.71b, nos. 8-9) and one from the fill beneath the marked axis-stone of the temple in Trench A1 (pl.71b, no. 10). A similar jar-rim was extracted from the pre-temple ground in front of the Second Pylon (pl.71b, no. 7). All these pieces consisted of uncoated brown siltware. A jar-neck of the same type has been published from Saqqara (Bourriau and Aston 1985, pl.35, no. 39).

11. Bread-moulds (pls.70. nos. 9-10; 75, nos. 17-19)

Numerous fragments of bread-moulds in coarse red siltware were found, but no complete specimen was recovered. The moulds are very easily recognised from the characteristic scraped planes on the sides, as indicated on the drawn pieces. Most examples had a hole in the centre of the base. This style of bread-mould does not seem to have been noted elsewhere and might be a local variant. The only example of similar appearance which has been found in the literature is a bread-mould from Heracleopolis but this has been dated to the ninth century BC (Aston 1996, fig. 88). A base which might have come from a similar vessel is known from Saqqara (Bourriau and Aston 1985, pl. 36, no. 82).

Note: Numerous additional parallels for the above ceramics are now available from Qantir (Aston 1998). This source came into my hands too late to be able to include more than a few of the more obvious references in the foregoing account.

Later features cut into the New-Kingdom enclosure wall

(a) Introduction

The part of the New-Kingdom enclosure wall so far revealed by excavation had survived in reasonably good condition at no great depth below the modern ground surface, but had not entirely escaped damage from later building activities. The north-west exterior face of the wall had been cut into by two successive foundation-pits for small religious buildings dependent on the temple of Amun at different periods. The effect of this was to remove some of the brickwork from the face of the wall, making it difficult to discover the original thickness during the excavation. The older of these two foundations probably dates from the Twenty-second Dynasty, and is described below in section (d). The other foundation-pit probably dates from the Thirtieth Dynasty and the description of it is given in Chapter 3 with the other features of the same period.

The enclosure wall had also been cut by a mud-brick tomb-chamber containing the burial of an official named Iken, built on the north corner. The ground-level at the time of the construction of the tomb was considerably higher than its modern level, and the preserved part of the tomb consists only of the lower courses of the chamber walls, for which a foundation-trench had been cut through the vanished surface fill into the brickwork of the enclosure wall, as described below.

(b) The tomb of Iken on the north corner of the enclosure wall

The tomb-chamber of Iken had interior dimensions of 2.10 x 3.45 metres and was enclosed by thick walls of mud-brick (pls.78a-b, 79a). The wall thicknesses were 1.50m (N), 1.30m (S), 1.12m (W) and 1.50m (E), giving external dimensions for the tomb of 4.70 x 6.25 metres. The structure had been founded at relative level 31, cut through some areas of early Third Intermediate Period occupation-fill and into the underlying eroded corner of the New-Kingdom enclosure wall. In the stratum of fill was the pottery oven at relative level 96, mentioned above, which had been cut through by the foundation-trench of the eastern wall of the tomb. The walls of the tomb itself were preserved to relative levels between 104 and 117, whilst the base of the chamber, under the burial, was at relative level 69. The floor of the tomb had been covered by a thin layer of greenish-coloured sand, which extended under the burial on the eastern side. Remains of crushed brick along the edges of the walls suggest that there was a vaulted roof, but nothing remained of the superstructure. The reconstruction shown in plate 104b is based on the assumption that the burial was situated at a moderate depth, as usual in the Delta. The vault probably rose some 2 metres above the level of the interment, which would give about 2.5 metres of superstructure above the Twenty-second Dynasty ground-level. No doubt the visible part of the tomb took the form of a simple mastaba, concealing the internal vault.

The bricks of the tomb walls measured 36 x 18 x 8.5cm. At the same level as the present tops of the walls was a stratum of fill with sherds of the mid-seventh century BC, some of which had spilled into the chamber during ancient plundering. These pottery fragments comprised parts of plates of Types A.5.15 and A.5.28, pieces of hand-made platters within the range of variation of Type A.1.32 and one or two jar-rims of Type D.1.70 (see Spencer 1996, pls.61, 63 and 69). In the fill above the burial was a small red siltware lid (pl.76a, no. 8). The outline of a pit dug into the interior of the chamber and partly through the floor survived as evidence of this disturbance, later confirmed by the disarray of the burial. The northern end of the tomb had suffered most; a quantity of seventh-century pottery fragments were found to be mixed with the fill and of the lower legs of the burial there remained only scattered fragments of bone. The disturbance continued along the west side of the chamber, where a calcite vessel (Cat.29) from the original funerary equipment was found out of place in the fill of a pit in the floor, 50cm distant from the west wall. A fragment of gilded cartonnage was also found in this pit. The vase has been rolled forwards from the southern end of the tomb, where two similar vessels remained in position against the south wall (Cat.28, 30), directly under a group of faience shabti-figures (Cat.58). These had been placed in a standing position against the south wall, but had fallen forwards and become embedded in compact mud, probably from the base of the vaulted roof (pls.79c, 80a). The shabtis were inscribed with the name of the owner, variously written as Iken or Iuken. They are described in the Catalogue of Finds.

The remains of the burial were found on the east side of the chamber. The body was extended on its back with the head to the south and the arms crossed over the chest (pl.80b). The ancient tomb-robbers had broken and displaced many bones: the skull had been pushed over to the right and crushed, numerous ribs broken or dislocated, but no signs of ante-mortem fractures were detected. The condition of the bones had suffered additionally through having lain at a level close to the ground surface, in mud which has been alternately saturated by rainwater and then dried. The burial also lay directly under a track used by agricultural vehicles to cross the site. Joyce Filer contributes the following note on the stature of the human remains:

> 'Most methods for estimating the probable living stature of an individual are based upon the correlation between body height and the length of limb bones. As research has indicated that there is considerable variation between different populations with regard to limb-bone length/ stature ratio it is necessary to use population specific formulae. Currently, the negro stature regression equations proposed by Trotter (1970, table 28) are the most appropriate for ancient Egyptian and Nubian individuals.
>
> The stature of Iken was calculated from the length of the intact left femur. Taking into consideration the recommendations of Buikstra and Ubelaker (1994, 70) that the measurement of fragmented or distorted bones should be used with extreme caution, and given that the skeletal elements of this male individual were in poor condition, the femoral measurement was taken *in situ*, prior to the removal of the skeleton. Thus, the ensuing calculation must be viewed purely as an estimate.
>
> Using a femoral measurement of 46cm and applying the appropriate formula for male individuals, the stature for Iken is 167.41cm +/- 3.94cm. This result concurs with other research findings into stature. For example, in a study of the stature of skeletons from predynastic Naqada, Robins and Shute (1986, 324) suggested an average male stature of 170cm (with 157.5cm for females) which, although from an earlier epoch than Iken, gives a general indication of the probable trend of ancient Egyptian stature.'

Examination of the remaining teeth showed them to be worn down to expose the dentine, indicating that Iken was at least of mature adult age at his death. The body was surrounded by a layer of soft brown organic matter, saturated with moisture from the mud, which was all that remained of a wooden coffin. This had been equipped with bronze-framed inlaid eyes of obsidian and limestone (Cat.**34**), which were found in the head region, with remains of gold foil from the face-mask adhering to the edges of the bronze. More gold foil from the surface of the mask or other parts of the coffin was discovered in contact with the brown layer. A separate layer of soft white material between the brown traces of the coffin and the actual skeleton also proved to have been gilded on both surfaces, and was probably the remains of cartonnage with gold foil decoration. Some pieces of this cartonnage were decorated additionally with a fine check pattern of blue-painted squares on a white background. The gold was not restricted to the head area but was found distributed over much of the body, some of it being *in situ* since it was still attached to traces of the wood or cartonnage. There had clearly been some gold foil on the hands. Other pieces of the gilding had been moved by the plunderers, in particular a considerable quantity found bunched up on the right side of the abdomen. After washing and straightening, the gold foil was found to consist of a combination of long, thin strips, larger irregular pieces and many small fragments. Suggestions as to how it was applied to the coffin are given in the Catalogue.

Along the length of the body and particularly around the sides was a compressed grey-white deposit which consisted of thousands of small faience beads, chiefly disks with some cylinders. The vast majority were coloured white, although they could well have been blue-green originally and decayed to white; there were also a few which were black or red glazed. The great quantity and wide distribution of these beads suggests they might have belonged to a bead net on the body, torn apart by the plunderers in search of valuable objects. This would explain the distribution of the beads down the sides of the body.

Just to the south of the head were some fragments from a thin, flat bronze object, the shape of which recalls that of the plate to cover the embalming incision (Cat.**36**). If it is indeed such an object, then it had clearly been moved during the plundering. Another object found a considerable distance from its expected position was the granite heart-scarab (Cat.**31**), which was recovered from deep down in the mud beside the right side of the spine in the region of the abdomen. The scarab might have been set into a pectoral of gold which had been taken by the tomb-robbers, and the heavy scarab had either been dumped or had fallen out. Scattered across the waist just below the base of the ribcage were several amulets in the form of small figures of deities: Horus, Osiris, Anhur, Hathor and Isis with Harpocrates (Cat.**40-44**). These were all made of faience except for the figure of Horus, which was of Egyptian Blue. As the burial was gradually excavated the thin layer of sand across the floor of the chamber could be seen below it, covering the mud-bricks of the floor.

List of material from the tomb
Three calcite vases (Cat.**28-30**)
Large quantity of faience shabti-figures inscribed for I(u)ken (Cat.**58**)
Fragmentary bronze plate, probably an embalming incision cover (Cat.**36**)
Granite heart-scarab inscribed with the name of Iken, preceded by a title which is almost certainly a writing of 'Vizier'. The name of Iken's mother, Iyu, also appears in the text, and the cartouches of Osorkon I have been added at the top and bottom (Cat.**31**)
Amuletic figures of Horus, Osiris, Anhur, Hathor and Isis with Harpocrates (Cat.**40-44**)
A great quantity of faience beads, mostly coloured white, but originally perhaps blue-green (Cat.**57**)
Bronze-framed inlaid eyes with one bronze eyebrow and fragments of the other (Cat.**34**)
Decayed wood from the coffin, found in contact with areas of gold foil
Fragments of plaster from cartonnage, some painted blue and some with gold foil attached
Gold foil strips and fragments from the decoration of the coffin and cartonnage (Cat.**35**)

The discovery of the tomb of Iken was unexpected, since no other clearly funerary objects or structures had been encountered during the work on the temple site. The presence of the cartouche of Osorkon I on the heart-scarab is a most welcome piece of absolute dating, which provides a fixed point at the top of the stratigraphic build-up of fill around the enclosure wall. The position of the tomb is of great interest in view of its proximity to the Amun-Temple and the fact that it was placed above the crumbling remains of an enclosure wall. Just how visible the wall would have been at the commencement of the Twenty-second Dynasty is unclear; the exterior of the corner and of the face of the north-east side of the enclosure had suffered from robbing of the bricks and was already hidden by the accumulation of fill, but the interior was in much better condition and remained at a higher level. It is most likely that the line of the wall had come to be marked by an elevated ridge, part brickwork and part overlying fill, in the same manner as unexcavated massive walls at other archaeological sites create such raised embankments. In modern times in the Delta, at least, such raised areas are often used for the building of tombs in order to avoid the damp and the same practice might have occurred in antiquity. If so, the location of the tomb might have been determined by a combination of factors: the choice of an elevated piece of ground and proximity to the temple, as was common for the burials of important persons from the Third Intermediate Period onwards. Parallels for the latter custom are to be found at Memphis (*PM* III, 846-7, with references), Medinet Habu (*PM* II, 476-80), and, of course, in the royal cemetery of Tanis (Montet 1947, 1951, 1960). For comments on the identity of Iken, see Chapter 6.

(c) Foundations of the two subsidiary chapels to the north-west of the enclosure wall

Establishing the true thickness of the New-Kingdom wall was not straightforward, owing to the brickwork of its north-west face having been cut back by later foundation-pits for these two small religious buildings. The suggested functions for these two monuments are as a barque-station dependent on the Twenty-second Dynasty temple and the mammisi of the Thirtieth-Dynasty temple respectively, as shown on plate 2. The dating depends on the position of the buildings and the stratigraphy of the site, since no foundation deposits were found despite an extensive search. The two foundations are located side by side, with a distance of only 5 metres between them, through which a cross-section was cut. The profiles of this trench showed that the original ground had consisted of empty mud, cut by some pits containing pottery of the fifth century BC, sealed by a thin layer of carbon. The north-east foundation had cut the Persian pit-fill, placing the date of this monument at some subsequent period, of which the Thirtieth Dynasty seems the most probable. The pits and overlying black stratum did not extend to the side of the south-west foundation-pit, which was cut into a higher level of original mud, so the profile did not help to date this monument. It must post-date the New-Kingdom enclosure wall, into which it is cut, and, if it was indeed a barque-station dependent on the Twenty-second Dynasty temple then it should belong to that period. The position of the monument also supports the view that the part of the temple of Amun in front of the Second Pylon of Sheshonq III was added in the Twenty-sixth Dynasty, since the processional approach to this barque-station was obstructed by the First Pylon.

A description of the earlier of these two foundations is given below, but details of the more northerly sand-bed are included with the Thirtieth-Dynasty additions to the temple complex, in Chapter 3.

(d) Details of the south-western foundation

Less than half of the original extent of this foundation has survived, the remainder having been destroyed by deep pitting in the late-Roman Period, perhaps connected with the dumping of refuse from the Roman town on the ridge to the north-west. The archaeological deposits in this area have a depth of only about 70cm above the subsoil water-table and the ground surface is regularly flooded by rainwater. The surviving part of the foundation consists of approximately half the estimated length of the facade, with the north-east end of the pylon and some 16.5 metres of the north-east side. The shape follows the classic design of an Egyptian temple: wide at the front for the pylon and narrower at the rear, so it is not difficult to estimate the original dimensions and reconstruct the plan as a small temple with a facade of 26 metres (50 cubits) and a length of around 35 to 40 metres (pl.2). The actual remains are shown in the drawing on plate 66. The edge of the foundation was retained by a lining of black bricks, the thickness of which varied at different points between 50 and 100cm. The interior had been entirely filled with clean sand but of this filling only a small part remained in place along the north-east side, particularly in the end of the pylon. At this point the sand was found to be overlaid by a considerable quantity of broken limestone, which had been covered by rain-washed mud. The stone almost certainly came from the destruction of the monument, but the lack of any inscribed fragments suggests it was the remains of the temple-platform rather than parts of the upper walls. From amongst this debris came a few fragments of Ptolemaic pottery including the inturned rim of a bowl (form as in Spencer, 1996, pl.53, no.9). The clean sand was removed to a depth of 1.70m below the present top of the foundation, equivalent to a relative level of -79, but no foundation deposits were found, nor was the bottom of the sand filling reached, despite the use of a motor pump to remove the subsoil water. From the sand came only a few widely scattered sherds from the neck of a marlware pottery jar with faint red-painted decoration, which looks like a product of the late New Kingdom (pl.104a, no. 2).

The north-east side of the foundation was traced to the rear of the pylon for 16.5 metres, at which point the brick lining vanished in a heavily pitted region. Tests cut further along the projected line of the edge failed to reveal anything but redeposited fill with late-Roman sherds, covered by thick layers of water-laid mud. The same kind of deposits had replaced all the original sand in the interior of the foundation apart from a small quantity along the edge, immediately against the black brick lining. Further investigation across the suspected location of the south-west side of the temple revealed no surviving traces of sand or of the edge of the pit. The brick lining was followed along the front for just over 13 metres before it vanished in late-Roman cutting like the north-eastern side. The destruction was so complete that it suggests the sand of the foundation was systematically quarried for use in Roman buildings, probably for mortar production. It appeared that the hollow left by the removal of the sand had been used to some extent for rubbish disposal, but a great part had filled up progressively with water-laid mud washed down into the area from the high settlement mounds, as still occurs in every winter rainstorm. The older mud deposits possessed a distinct red tinge, probably from contamination by red-brick dust eroded from the buildings of the nearby late-Roman town.

5. Catalogue of Finds

This catalogue contains material entered in the register of the Egyptian Supreme Council for Antiquities and some additional fragmentary pieces which were not registered. A difference between this catalogue and that published in *Excavations at Tell el-Balamun 1991-1994* is that the category for Jewellery has been excluded from this volume, and the examples of beads appear instead under their materials, or as part of foundation deposit groups.

I. Stone objects

1 The lower half of a quartzite triad depicting Ramesses II between two divinities, one of whom is almost certainly Amun, and the other probably the goddess Mut. All the figures are broken off at waist level, and no trace was found of the upper portion of the sculpture. The surface of the stone has suffered considerably from erosion and from deliberate damage, the latter caused by the grinding away of stone powder for magico-medicinal purposes. This damage shows that the figure must have been exposed on the surface for a considerable length of time before being dumped into a pit and buried in mud, from which it was excavated.

The figures are shown seated, with their feet resting on a thick base-plinth. The feet and legs of all the figures are in poor condition. The king wears the short royal kilt and his hands rest on his knees. The figure of Amun on his right is badly damaged, having lost all of the right arm and most of the left arm also; the fronts of the legs are eroded and have a deep gash below the knees. Like that of the king, this figure wore the short kilt. To the king's left is a goddess wearing a long dress. Almost all parts of the arms of this figure have been lost, and the corner of the base-plinth in front of the goddess is also missing. On the front of the throne between the figures are cartouches of Ramesses II, as shown in the drawing on plate 83.

The sides of the sculpture show differing amounts of damage, the left side next to the goddess having suffered more erosion and deliberate cutting than the other end, beside Amun, where the inscriptions are much more visible (pl.81). This indicates that the sculpture lay at some time with one end protruding from the ground and, therefore, vulnerable to damage. On the damaged side only a part of a cartouche with the royal prenomen remains visible, but the opposite side still bears three clear cartouches with remains of titles and epithets. In the latter the king is described as being 'beloved of Amun-of-Ramesses in Sma-Behdet'. A deep cut in this side contained traces of white plaster, suggesting that some damage may have occurred whilst the sculpture was still in use in the temple and attempts were made to conceal it.

The most extensive inscriptions survive on the back of the group, which is broken at the top and eroded near the base. Between these areas of damage, parts of six vertical columns of hieroglyphs remain, containing the nomen of the king followed by either 'beloved of [Amun]-of-Ramesses in (*m*) Sma-Behdet', or '...who resides in (*ḥrt-ib*) Sma-Behdet'. The name of the divinity in each case was Amun-of-Ramesses, as in the text on the side of the statue, and traces of the final *n* of Amun were visible above the cartouches (pl.82). For the findspot of the sculpture to the south-east of the gate of Temple A, see plates 22 and 24a. Height of group 116cm., Width 143cm., Depth 98cm. Height of throne 52cm. (1995/19), pls.81-83.

2 Upper part of the back-pillar from a limestone statue, with an inscription written in a vertical line of hieroglyphs, cut in sunk relief. The text consists of an offering-formula invoking a goddess Nebet-Tjau, requesting food-offerings on behalf of the owner, whose name must have been on the missing lower portion. The top of the back-pillar is flat. From stone rubble above the axis of Temple A, just in front of the Second Pylon. Height 39.7cm., Width 16.0cm., Depth 15.0cm. (1997/1), pls.84, 85.

3 Block of limestone, broken in two joining pieces, with an inscription in two horizontal lines on one face, carved in deeply cut hieroglyphs. The upper line consists only of three groups contaning the signs for *n* and *stp* (or *nw*). Below is a second line of inscription, reading from right to left, containing the name of the god Amun. The style of the inscription suggests that the block belonged to the temple of the Twenty-second Dynasty. From pit-fill in chamber 1 of Building N1. Height 55.0cm., Length 137.0cm., Thickness 17.0cm. See plates 48a, 84.

4 Piece of limestone worked on two faces, probably from a door-jamb, with remains of an inscription on one surface. The remaining portion shows only part of a register-line with four hieroglyphs in a vertical column to the right. From a layer of broken stone under the suface mud in the east corner of Trench A2. Height 20.4cm., Width 21.5cm., Depth 10.3cm., pl.85.

5 Fragment of limestone with traces of a relief, including part of the hieroglyph for the Sed-festival. From under the Roman bedding plaster in Area RP1. Height 13.8cm., Width 16.5cm., Depth 10.2cm., pl.85.

6 Flat fragment of white marble wall-facing with a trace of a Latin inscription. From redeposited fill above the temple level in Area RP1. Height 10.1cm., Width 12.1cm., Thickness 2.4cm., pl.85.

7 Limestone lower stone from an olive-press, consisting of a thick square block with a slightly concave upper surface, around the edge of which is cut a circular channel, which drains to a single run-off point. From surface dust in Chamber 1 of Building N1. Size 71.0 x 71.0 x 21.5cm., pls.47a-b, 84.

8 Red granite mill consisting of a flat lower stone slab with incised grooves in a herringbone pattern and an upper stone with a central slot. The upper stone was found broken into two halves; its underside bears grooves similar to those in the lower stone, against which it was operated. The object is a kind of mill well attested at Greek sites and also recorded from Graeco-Roman contexts in Egypt. The ends of the upper stone show drilled holes into which iron staples have been set, by fusing the iron into the holes with molten lead. These iron attachments served to hold in place a long wooden beam for operating the mill by hand, engaged in the slots in the edge as described below in the text following catalogue entry **10**. Adjacent to the holes at each end of the stone is a groove 22cm in length, into which additional iron rods had been set to hold together the two broken pieces of this millstone (pl.86). From surface dust over the south-west end of Chamber 1 in Building N1; found under the olive-press (**7**). Upper stone: Length 46.0cm., Width 34.3cm., Thickness 15.5cm. Lower stone: Length 56.0cm., Width 44.0cm., Thickness 7.5 to 9.0cm. Lower stone found in the surface dust a short distance to the east of the upper stone, above Chamber 2. See plates 47a-b, 86.

9 Another example of a millstone of similar type to the foregoing, consisting of the upper stone only, but made from dark grey-black tufa. A hole filled with lead corrosion in either end marks the position of the attachment of iron staples. On either side of the hole at one end only there are two more shallow drilled holes, clean of any metal residues (pl.86). Squared slots are cut at the middle of all four edges on the front, for engagement with an original wooden handle. The underside bears longitudinal grooves. From the surface dust above the south-west wall of Building N1. Length 54.0cm., Width 42.0cm., Thickness 11.0cm., pl.86.

10 Smaller example of a millstone like **9**, made in dark grey tufa. There is a single hole in each end, containing remains of lead, and slots for the handle in the front edges of the shorter sides. The lower surface is cut with grooves in a herringbone pattern. Provenance as last. Length 47.5cm., Width 38.5cm., Thickness 11.0cm., pl.86.

The foregoing catalogue items **8-10** are of a type which has been described as the 'Theban Mill', a device adequate for grinding sufficient grain to provide for the needs of a household for a day. Use of these mills has been described by Robinson and Graham 1936, 326ff., where many examples are published. The form of the upper stones in these three examples from Balamun are typical, with the top shaped into a kind of hopper for the grain, the sides sloping down to the slot, through which the grain fell to be ground between the grooved surfaces of the upper and lower stones. The latter consisted of flat slabs with incised grooves. The upper stones were moved back and forth by means of a long wooden bar attached to the stone, engaged in the square recesses in the edges and held down by the iron staples fixed at each end. The method of operation is shown in an ancient illustration on a bowl in the Louvre (Rostovtzeff 1937, 87, 90 and fig.1). Examples in Greece have been dated as early as the fifth century BC, but many may well be later, and these examples at Balamun are most probably late Ptolemaic. Similar mills have also been found at Karanis (Gazda 1983, 28-9, fig.50), Nebesha (Petrie 1888, 27, pl.vii, 21) and Koptos (Petrie 1896, 25). Most of the Greek examples are made from tufa and the two examples in this material catalogued here must have been imported. Some millstones have been recovered from ancient shipwrecks and may have travelled as ballast or cargo (Baatz 1994, 97ff.). Many such mills were made at Thera, and it has been suggested that the name 'Theban Mill' is an error for 'Theran Mill' (Robinson and Graham, op. cit., 330, n.14). The example in red granite (**8**) is without doubt an Egyptian copy.

11 A small gnomon of limestone, lacking the raised section at the end. From Building N2, fill in the south-west half of Chamber 1. Height 6.0cm., Length 8.3cm., Width 3.3cm. (1995/5), pl.87. A fragment from a similar object was found in Chamber 3 of the same building. Similar objects of sandstone and basalt are in the Egyptian Museum, Cairo (JdE 42927 and 67342).

12 Limestone block of narrow, rectangular shape with remains of hieroglyphs on one face. The only surviving visible signs comprise three complete hieroglyphs for the letter '*t*' and a trace of a fourth, together with the feet of two bird-signs above. Found re-used in the pavement on the ruins of the north corner of Building N1. Height 16.8cm., Length 58.4cm., Thickness 17.5cm., pl.85.

13 Limestone trial-piece with the head of a king in sunk relief on both sides. In front of the face on one side are traces of a roughly incised vertical line of inscription which is insufficiently clear to be legible. From fill against the exterior south-west side of Building N2. Height 11.0cm., Width 8.4cm., Thickness 1.7cm. (1995/6), pl.88.

14 Fragment of a limestone trial-piece with part of the head of a king in low relief on one side. Provenance as last. Height 5.7cm., Width 6.3cm., Thickness 1.4cm. (1995/7), pl.88.

15 Trial-piece of burnt limestone with sunk-relief carvings of flowers. From the fill in the south-west end of the courtyard belonging to Building N2. Height 3.9cm., Width 3.9cm., Thickness 1.2cm., pl.87.

16 Small figure of a falcon, roughly carved in soft limestone. Little detail is shown; the beak has been broken off. From the fill in Chamber 2 of Building N1. Height 3.5cm., Width 1.8cm., Length 3.6cm. (1997/3), pl.88.

17 Limestone loom-weight made from a fragment of temple relief, with a figure of a falcon on one face. The piece has been cut to a roughly circular shape around the falcon image, and a hole drilled through the edge for suspension. The reverse is flat with incised line, perhaps a crude attempt to draw a bird. From fill in Chamber 4B of Building N1. Height 9.3cm., Width 9.7cm., Thickness 2.8cm. (1997/2), pl.88.

18 Cuboid basalt weight. From Trench E1 in the forecourt of Temple A, upper level. Height 5.8cm., Width 4.6cm., Length 5.0cm. (1995/14). Not illustrated.

19 Fragmentary erotic figure in limestone, showing a man with a large phallus. The head of the figure is missing. From fill against the exterior south-west side of Building N2. Height 3.5cm., Width 2.2cm., Depth 4.0cm., pl.88.

20 Limestone bung with a roughly rounded head and tapering shaft, broken at the tip. The working of the object has left distinct, flat planes. The end of the shaft shows traces of burning. From fill close to the kiln in Trench E8. Length 7.0cm., Diameter of head 4.6cm., of shaft 2.5cm. tapering to 2.3cm. (1996/5, part), pl.89, centre.

21 Limestone bung similar to last, but of larger size. As with the foregoing example, clear dressing planes are visible on the object, with 14 such smooth surfaces along the tapering shaft. The tip is missing and the shaft has been burned. From the section between Trenches E7 and Trench E8, among the fragments of kiln lining. Length 7.7cm., Diameter of head 5.0cm., of shaft 2.7cm. tapering to 2.5cm. (1996/5, part), pl.89, right.

22 Limestone bung similar to the last two entries, with a rather more flat head. Tip broken and lower part of shaft burned. Provenance as last. Length 6.7cm., Diameter of head 5.0cm., of shaft 2.7cm. tapering to 2.5cm. (1996/5, part), pl.89, left.

23 Fragment from the side and plain rim of a limestone bowl, of simple hemispherical form. From fill in Trench E9. Height 12.4cm., Maximum diameter 24.4cm., pl. 87.

24 Flint sickle-blade with a serrated cutting edge. From fill south-west of Silo 14. Length 3.6cm., Width 2.7cm., Thickness 0.6cm. Early Third Intermediate Period. (1998/16), pl.87.

25 Flint sickle-blade with serrated edge. One side consists of cortex. From inside Silo 11. Length 5.9cm., Width 4.0cm, Thickness 1.1cm. Early Third Intermediate Period. (1998/17), pl.87.

26 Flint sickle-blade with serrated edge. From the top level of the section-trench beside Silo 6. Length 5.2cm., Width 3.4cm., Thickness 0.8cm. Early Third Intermediate Period. (1998/18), pl.87.

27 Flint sickle-blade with a serrated edge, much polished from use. From fill in the silo area. Length 6.1cm., Width 3.0cm., Thickness 0.6cm. Early Third Intermediate Period. (1998/32), pl.87.

28 Calcite vessel with a rounded base, convex sides and raised, plain rim. There is a perforated handle at each side. The rim surface is partly decayed. From the tomb of Iken, found *in situ* below the shabtis. Height 21.2cm., Width across handles 28.5cm., Diameter at rim 15.8cm. (1998/24), pls.80a, 87, 89.

29 Calcite vessel with a rounded base, convex sides and raised rim. There was a perforated handle at each side, but both are missing. The rim surface is partly decayed. One side of the vessel was cracked and has been repaired. From the tomb of Iken, loose in the top of the pit, west of the burial. Height 18.8cm., Width across handles 26.8cm., Diameter at rim 15.7cm. (1998/25), pl.87.

30 Calcite vessel with a flat base, convex sides and raised rim. There is a perforated handle at each side. The rim surface is slightly damaged. From the tomb of Iken, found *in situ* below the shabtis. Height 19.2cm., Width across handles 30.8cm., Diameter at rim 18.2cm. (1998/26), pls.80a, 87, 89.

31 Grey granite heart-scarab of Iken, found out of position on the right side of the spine at the level of the abdomen. Details of the back are limited to the modelling of the head. An inscription in five lines of incised hieroglyphs is cut on the underside, separated by horizontal register-lines. The text differs from the regular formula of Chapter 30B of the Book of the Dead, and refers instead to Anubis restoring the heart. It also contains the name of the deceased and that of his mother, Iyu. The group of three signs in front of the name of Iken seem to be a writing of the title 'Vizier', with the use of the wrong bird-hieroglyph. Above and below the text are the cartouches of Osorkon I, which were inscribed less carefully than the remainder of the text as if added at a later stage. Height 3.0cm., Length 6.9cm., Width 4.6cm. (1998/27), pls.89, 99.

II. Metal

32 Copper or bronze nail of square section. From Chamber 3 in Building N2. Length 7.8cm., Width 0.4cm., Thickness 0.4cm. (1995/13), pl.91.

33 Copper or bronze nail, cleaned of corrosion. From fill above the sand-bed of Temple A in area RP 1 at the rear of the First Pylon. Length 5.0cm., Diameter of head 1.1cm., pl.91.

34 Two bronze-framed inlaid eyes from the coffin of Iken, with inlays of limestone and obsidian. Gold foil from the gilding of the face-mask adheres to the edges. Heights 2.3 and 2.6cm., Lengths 7.3 and 7.0cm. Also a bronze eyebrow from the same coffin, 7.5cm long, together with fragments of another. From the tomb of Iken. (1998/20), pl.92.

35 Pieces of gold foil, the remains of the gilding which decorated the wooden coffin and cartonnage mask of the burial of Iken. Some large pieces of two thicknesses. The thinner foil came from the coffin, while the thicker foil may have belonged to amulets, although no pieces were found to retain any recognisable shapes. There are also many strips, varying in width from 0.6 to 1.1cm, which almost certainly were used in the decoration of the wig of the coffin. Some of these strips had traces of blue paint along their edges, suggesting the usual decorative headdress of alternate gold and blue bands. An excellent parallel from the same period is the head-piece of the body-case for Hekakheperre Shoshenq in the Cairo Museum (Montet 1951, pl.21; Yoyotte 1968, 181). The combined length of these strips amounts to over 6 metres. The ancient disturbance of the burial had shifted much of the gilding from its original position; many of the strips from the wig were found bunched up on the right side of the waist. The weight of all the gold foil from the tomb was 45.2g. (1998/34), pl.90.

36 Fragmentary remains of a thin bronze object, possibly an embalming cover-plate. Height 7.3cm., Width 11.8cm., Thickness 0.2cm. Found displaced near the head in the burial of Iken, pl.99.

III. Faience and glass

37 Part of a model situla in pale green-glazed faience. The rim is perforated by a small hole, made post-firing, probably as a replacement suspension-point for the original loop-handle which had been broken. From redeposited fill under the surface mud in Trench W9. Height 9.0cm., Diameter at rim 3.4cm., pl.91.

38 Fragment from a faience flask, decorated with a floral pattern around the sides. Pale green glaze, varying to yellow in places. From the surface mud in Trench W5. Height 6.0cm., Thickness 0.6cm., pl.91.

39 Five fragments of a pale green-glazed faience vessel, probably a situla-shaped vase. The glaze has decayed to dull beige. Two of the fragments bear remains of decoration or inscriptions in black, but insufficiently preserved for identification. From the tomb of Iken. Lengths of fragments range from 4.1 to 6.5cm. (1998/22), pl.90.

40 Amuletic figure of Horus made of Egyptian Blue. The figure is shown wearing the Double Crown and there is a perforation the the top of the back-pillar. Front of the plinth broken. From the burial of Iken. Height 4.5cm., Width 1.1cm., Depth 1.1cm. (1998/21), pl.92.

41 Faience amuletic figure of the goddess Hathor, standing with her arms at her sides. The headdress is missing. Glaze decayed to white. From the burial of Iken. Height 3.8cm., Width 1.2cm., Depth 1.5cm. (1998/28), pl.92.

42 Faience amuletic figure of Isis and Harpocrates, the figure of the latter largely missing. The surface is not well preserved, the glaze has decayed to white and the face of the goddess has lost its features. Her headdress is missing. From the burial of Iken. Height 3.5cm., Width 1.3cm., Depth 1.8cm. (1998/29), pl.92.

43 Faience amuletic figure of the god Anhur, standing, holding the udjat-eye and wearing the lunar disk headdress. The front corner of the plinth is missing. Found in three pieces and restored. From the burial of Iken. Height 4.5cm., Width 1.0cm., Depth 1.6cm. (1998/30), pl.92.

44 Faience amuletic figure of the god Osiris, glazed dull white, shown wearing the Atef headdress and holding the crook and flail. From the burial of Iken. Height 4.9cm., Width 1.3cm., Depth 1.6cm. (1998/31), pl.92.

45 Blue-green glazed faience amuletic figure of Bes, lacking the head. From fill above the north-west sand-trench of the colonnade foundation in Temple A. Height 4.4cm., Width 3.0cm., Depth 1.6cm. (1995/17), pl.91.

46 Part of the body of a faience amuletic figure of a goddess, probably Isis. From pit-fill above the exterior edge of the north-west wall of Building N1. Height 2.6cm., Width 2.7cm., Depth 1.7cm. (1997/13), pl.91.

47 Part of a model column-drum, made in green glassy faience. The object had a central perforation which was square in section. From stone rubble over the south-east sand-trench of the colonnade, just in front of the Second Pylon. Height 3.9cm., Width of fragment 1.8cm. The original diameter must have been around 5.0cm. , pl.91.

48 Incomplete model column-drum in pale yellowish-green glassy faience, with a square perforation like that of the preceding example. From pit-fill in the north corner of Trench W7. Height 3.9cm., Diameter 3.8cm., pl.91.

49 Six fragments of inlays in red, blue and green glass. Probably from the ornamentation of a piece of temple furniture: the plano-convex form and rounded ends of some of the pieces recall decoration in the style of vulture or falcon-wings. From a rubble layer just above the pre-temple ground in front of the Second Pylon of Sheshonq III. Preserved lengths range from 0.9 to 3.5cm., pl.92

50 Fragment of mottled blue-black glass inlay, with one convex surface. From pit-fill in Chamber 4B of Building N1. Height 2.0cm., Width 1.7cm., Thickness 0.3cm., pl.91.

51 Faience eye-amulet of very abbreviated form. Glaze lost. Perforated loop at the top for attachment. From dusty fill in Chamber 2 of Building N1. Height 1.4cm., Width 1.7cm., Thickness 0.7cm. (1997/5), pl.91.

52 Composite amulet of the sacred eye of Horus with an attached papyrus-column, half missing. Originally green, but the glaze has largely decayed to white. From a rubble layer just above the pre-temple ground in front of the Second Pylon of Sheshonq III. Height 1.2cm., Thickness 0.5cm. (1997/6), pl.91.

53 Part of a large eye-amulet in green-glazed faience with black details. Perforated lengthways. From just under the surface mud in the north corner of Trench W6. Height 3.9cm., Length 4.5cm., Thickness 0.5cm., pl.91.

54 Five cylinder beads of green-glazed faience. From a rubble layer just above the pre-temple ground in front of the Second Pylon. Lengths 1.1-1.6cm., Diameters 0.7-0.8cm. (1997/7), pl.91.

55 Part of a green-glazed faience spacer-bead with black decoration on both sides. Pierced twice, but one perforation broken. From Persian-Period fill above the destroyed earlier temple level in Trench TG2. Height 2.4cm., Width 2.8cm., Thickness 0.5cm., pl.91.

56 Faience cylinder bead, glaze decayed to dull white. From fill at the front of the north-west gate in the Outer Enclosure Wall. Length 1.9cm., Diameter 0.45cm., pl.91.

57 Several hundred small disk beads, with some cylinder beads and a few double beads, apparently from a bead-net which covered the body in the burial of Iken. The majority of these faience beads were originally glazed green, now decayed to dull white. A few are glazed red or black. Diameters of ring beads 0.3cm., Lengths of cylinders 0.8cm. (1998/23). Types shown on plate 91.

58 Group of faience shabti-figures from the tomb of Iken, found *in situ* above the calcite vessels at the south-west end of the chamber (pls.79c, 80a). Only four were found to be intact; the remainder had been cracked into two or more fragments as a consequence of the pressure on the mud in which they were embedded, caused by the passage of vehicles along the track which ran over the tomb. The original total number present was around 130, established through a count of all the preserved heads and parts of heads, but complete accuracy was not possible because some of the figures had been completely crushed to powder. All the preserved examples were glazed pale green with details shown in black. Of the facial features only the eyes and eyebrows were shown. Each of the 'worker' figures originally had a head-band with two ribbons over their long wigs, and held two hoes and a basket, but the smaller number of overseers hold whips or sceptres and lack the basket. They also differ from the ordinary figures in having a short wig indicated in black paint on top of the long wig, which was moulded in relief.

Eleven variant forms of the inscription were noted on 42 figures, and they are shown on plate 95. The fragmentary and decayed condition of the majority of the figures prevented the identification of additional examples. Height 10.6 (all)., Width 3.0-3.4 (max)., Depth 2.0-2.6cm. (1998/33), pls.93-95.

IV. Pottery objects

59 Pottery loom-weight. From the fill above the sand at the gate of Temple A. Length 4.0cm., Width 2.1cm. (1995/11), pl.97.

60 Pottery mould for an eye-amulet. From section-trench E4 across the forecourt wall of Temple A: fill into which the trench was cut. Height 4.8cm., Width 4.8cm. (1995/8), pl.97.

61 Pottery mould for an eye-amulet. From the sand in the rear angle of the foundation of the north-west wing of the First Pylon in Temple A. Diameter 4.2cm., Thickness 1.6cm. (1997/4), pl.97.

62 Pottery mould for the manufacture of a faience or glass inlay of long, thin shape. From high-level fill at the south-east end of Chamber 3 in Building N1. Length 7.8cm., Width 2.8cm., Thickness 1.9cm. (1997/10), pl.96.

63 Pottery mould, probably to reproduce the form of a foot of a figure of Bes or an animal-figure. From a pit in the internal wall between Chambers 4B and 5 of Building N1. Length 7.9cm., Width 5.2cm., Thickness 2.0cm. (1997/9), pl.96.

64 Pottery mould for an inlay of diamond-shape. From the dump between Buildings N2 and N3. Length 4.5cm., Width 2.0cm, Thickness 1.2cm. (1995/10), pl.97.

65 Rectangular mould of pale red pottery for a Bes-figure. The internal detail in the mould is very eroded and unclear. From Building N2; fill in the south-western half of Chamber 1. Height 1.9cm., Width 1.7cm., Thickness 0.6cm. (1995/9), pl.97.

66 Pottery mould for casting some kind of implement or fitting, probably in bronze. The fragmentary object is double-sided, with a mould for a plain flat blade on one side and an object of more complex shape on the other. From fill in the south-west end of the courtyard belonging to Building N2. Length 7.4cm., Width 6.7cm., Thickness 1.5cm., pl.97.

67 Part of a pottery mould for a faience amulet, with only a headdress of sun-disk and horns preserved. From pit-fill in the north corner of Trench W7. Height 2.6cm., Width 3.3cm., Depth 2.3cm., pl.97.

68 Front part of a red pottery figure of an animal, almost certainly a horse since a mane is indicated. Eyes and ears shown in relief and line of mouth incised. Forelegs lost. From fill inside Silo 16. Height 5.6cm., Length 6.8cm., Width 3.0cm. Early Third Intermediate Period. (1998/19), pl.96.

69 Part of the back of a terracotta figure, possibly of a goddess or an image of Bes. A portion of the characteristic hole, so common in the back of terracotta figures, is preserved. From fill in the south corner of Trench E5. Height 8.4cm., Width 4.4cm., Thickness 1.1cm., pl.97.

70 Part of the base of a hollow pedestal from a terracotta figure, made of coarse brown siltware. Traces of red paint survive on the exterior. From dumped fill above the sand-foundation of the First Pylon of Temple A in Trench E11. Height 6.1cm., Width 4.5cm., Depth 4.0cm., pl.97.

71 Hollow pedestal from a terracotta, sufficiently preserved at the top to include part of the foot of the figure. Made in coarse brown silt pottery with some traces of blue paint remaining. Possibly part of the same figure as the previous entry, although the fragments do not join. From Trench E11. Height 8.0cm., Width 5.0cm., Depth 2.9cm., pl.97.

72 Group of objects of uncertain use, perhaps spacers used with a loom, formed of hard marl pottery with a green surface and reddish core. The fabric is full of crushed ceramic temper. This group consists of two complete rectangular-section bars (one broken in two and now repaired) and parts of two others, together with two thin, oblong plaques. Three of the bars have triple incised lines across one narrow face, close to one end; the absence of similar marks on the remaining fragment indicates that it comes from the opposite end of the object. One of the complete bars and both fragments have been considerably blackened by burning. The edges of one of the thin plaques are stained with patches of red pigment. From fill in Chamber 4B of Building N1, close to the square brick-lined pit. Dimensions of the complete bars are 14.3 x 2.8 x 1.4cm and 14.8 x 2.3 x 1.4cm; the fragmentary ones measure 5.8 x 2.8 x 1.5cm for the marked example and 7.8 x 2.6 x 1.3cm for the plain fragment. Dimensions of the two thin plaques are 5.9 x 4.9 x 0.5cm and 6.1 x 4.9 x 0.8cm. (1997/11), pls.96-97.

73 Circular counter or gaming-piece of red silt pottery. From stone rubble above the north-west sand-trench of the colonnade, in front of the Second Pylon. Diameter 3.3cm., Thickness 0.7cm.(1997/12, part), pl.97.

74 Circular counter or gaming-piece of red silt pottery. From Ptolemaic fill in front of the Second Pylon. Diameter 3.2cm., Thickness 0.7cm. (1997/12, part), pl.97.

75 Circular counter or gaming-piece of pink silt pottery. Provenance as last. Diameter 3.2cm., Thickness 0.7cm. (1997/12, part), pl.97.

76 Circular counter or gaming-piece of red silt pottery. From the dump of Persian pottery in Trench W7. Diameter 3.5cm., Thickness 0.5cm. (1997/12, part), pl.97.

77 Circular counter or gaming-piece of red silt pottery. Provenance as last. Diameter 3.3cm., Thickness 1.1cm. (1997/12, part), pl.97.

78 Circular counter or gaming-piece of red silt pottery, with a small round depression drilled into one side. From fill in Chamber 4B of Building N1, just east of the square red-brick pit (see pl.52b). Diameter 2.7cm., Thickness 0.5cm. (1997/12, part), pl.97.

79 Circular pottery counter or gaming-piece of red silt pottery. From fill at the north-west side of Trench W9, above the foundation of the First Pylon of Temple A. Diameter 3.9cm., Thickness 0.8cm., pl.99.

80 Circular pottery counter or gaming-piece of highly micaceous red silt pottery. From surface fill in Trench W9. Diameter 3.7cm., Thickness 0.9cm., pl.99.

81 Circular pottery counter or gaming-piece, cut from a sherd of red silt pottery with a cream slip on the exterior side of the original vessel. From high-level fill in area of silos. Diameter 3.8cm., Thickness 0.8cm. (1998/3), pl.98, row 1, no.4.

82 Circular pottery counter or gaming-piece of red silt pottery. From high-level fill in area of silos. Maximum diameter 3.5cm., Thickness 0.7cm. (1998/4), pl.98, row 1, no.1.

83 Irregularly shaped red silt pottery counter or gaming-piece. From high-level fill in area of silos. Maximum diameter 4.2cm., Thickness 0.8cm. (1998/5), pl.98, row 1, no.2.

84 Circular pottery counter or gaming-piece of red silt pottery. From area of silos. Maximum diameter 3.2cm., Thickness 0.8cm. (1998/6), pl.98, row 2, no.2.

85 Circular pottery counter or gaming-piece of red silt pottery. From high-level fill in area of silos. Maximum diameter 3.5cm., Thickness 0.6cm. (1998/7), pl.98, row 2, no.4.

86 Circular pottery counter or gaming-piece of red silt pottery, missing a small part. From high-level fill in area of silos. Maximum diameter 3.8cm., Thickness 0.9cm. (1998/8), pl.98, row 1, no.3.

87 Irregularly shaped pottery counter or gaming-piece of red siltware with a thin orange slip on one side. From high-level fill in area of silos. Maximum diameter 3.2cm., Thickness 0.8cm. (1998/9), pl.98, row 2, no.3.

88 Circular pottery counter or gaming-piece of red silt pottery. From area of silos. Maximum diameter 2.8cm., Thickness 0.8cm. (1998/10), pl.98, row 3, no.4.

89 Circular pottery counter or gaming-piece of red silt pottery. Part of interior surface of the sherd lost. From area of silos. Maximum diameter 3.1cm., Thickness 0.6cm. (1998/11), pl.98, row 3, no.1.

90 Circular pottery counter or gaming-piece of red silt pottery. From area of silos. Maximum diameter 2.3cm., Thickness 1.0cm. (1998/12), pl.98, row 3, no.2.

91 Circular pottery counter or gaming-piece of red silt pottery. From Silo 11. Maximum diameter 3.1cm., Thickness 0.7cm. (1998/13), pl.98, row 2, no.1.

92 Irregularly shaped red silt pottery counter or gaming-piece. From Silo 11. Maximum diameter 3.1cm., Thickness 0.7cm. (1998/14), pl.98, row 3, no.3.

93 Circular pottery counter or gaming-piece of red silt pottery. Found in fill above the north corner of the tomb of Iken. Maximum diameter 3.3cm., Thickness 0.65cm., pl.99.

94 Circular pottery counter or gaming-piece of red silt pottery. Found in fill above the north corner of the tomb of Iken. Maximum diameter 3.0cm., Thickness 0.8cm., pl.99.

95 Small circular object of red siltware pottery, perforated by two holes. Probably used in weaving. From fill above the eroded exterior face of the New-Kingdom enclosure. Maximum diameter 2.8cm., Thickness 1.0cm., pl.99.

96 Coarse red siltware brazier, of tall, circular shape, with tripod stand at the upper part. One portion of this stand is missing. Lower down the body are three air-holes and a semicircular opening near the base for access to the fuel. From surface fill above the south-west wall of Building N1. Height 26.5cm., Diameter of base 23.0cm. Ptolemaic, pl.98.

97 Lamp of fine brown pottery with a red surface slip. Possesses a low base-ring, long narrow spout and vestigial handle. Pattern on upper surface of radiating lines from a central filling-hole. From the broken stone layer above the temple foundation sand in Trench W3. Height 3.3cm., Length 9.8cm., Width 6.6cm. Ptolemaic. (1996/3), pl.98.

98 Two pieces from a lamp of fine pale beige pottery, made in upper and lower sections. Part of spout and base-ring preserved. From pit-fill in Trench W8. Larger fragment measures 4.8 x 4.0cm. Second century AD, pl.98.

99 Part of an amphora-handle with a Greek stamp, probably Rhodian. From fill in Trench E11. Length 8.9cm., Width 4.0cm. (1996/4), pl.96.

100 Loom-weight of soft-fired silt clay. The object is oval with a groove around it for attachment. From just west of Silo 6. Dimensions 5.0 x 3.5.x 2.3cm. Early Third Intermediate Period. (1998/1), pl.99.

101 Rough barrel-bead of red siltware pottery. From just west of Silo 6. Length 2.6cm., Diameter 1.9cm. Early Third Intermediate Period. (1998/2), pl.99.

102 Rough pottery bead similar to last, slightly broken at the ends. From fill beside the inner face of the north-west wall of the New-Kingdom enclosure. Length 2.8cm., Diameter 2.0cm. Early Third Intermediate Period. (1998/15), pl.99.

V. Foundation Deposits

103 Pieces found with a disturbed foundation deposit of the Third Intermediate Period, with inscriptions of a priest of Amun named Hor (see Chapter 6). From the rear corner of the north-west side of the Second Pylon (1995/3). The first item is probably later in date and was given the excavation number 1995/4.

1. Limestone model mortar with a flat base and roughly dressed sides. No handles are present. Interior only slightly hollowed. From the rubble fill in the pits, and probably not part of the foundation deposit of Hor, but displaced from a later deposit. It resembles the model mortars from the deposits of Psamtik I in Temple C (See Spencer 1996, pl.91). Height 6.0., Diameter 5.9cm., pl.99.

2. Fragmentary plaque of green malachite (found in two pieces in the rubble). Height 2.2cm., Width 1.6cm., Thickness 0.4cm.

3. Calcite hemi-disk inscribed for the priest of Amun, Hor. The text on this example is a shortened version of that on the plaques of this priest from the deposits described below. Height 4.1cm., Width 3.1cm., Thickness 0.5cm., pl.99.

4. Corroded silver plaque, incomplete, text lost. Dimensions 2.2 x 1.6 x 0.25cm.

5. Sherds from the rims of four red siltware pottery cups and one small dish.

104 Complete foundation deposit of the Third Intermediate Period, with inscriptions of the priest of Amun of *P₃-iw*, Hor. From the front corner of the north-west side of the Second Pylon. (1995/1). See plates 10a-b, 11a-b, 100 and colourplate 1b-c.

1. A thin brick of dense, black mud, measuring 38 x 28 x 6cm.

2. Small plaque of thin gold foil over an organic core, probably wood, with faint traces on one face of the same inscription as nos. 3, 4 and 5 below. Dimensions 2.7 x 1.3 x 0.3cm.

3. Silver plaque, corroded, with part of an inscription of the priest of Amun of *P₃-iw*, Hor. The complete text was the same as that on nos. 4-5 below. Dimensions 3.0 x 1.7 x 0.25cm.

4. Calcite hemi-disk with inscription of the priest Hor. On this example, the simple stroke determinative after the name has been omitted. Dimensions 4.7 x 3.1 x 0.5cm.

5. Bronze plaque, covered with green corrosion when found, now cleaned to reveal an inscription of the priest Hor. Dimensions 7.0 x 2.5 x 0.3cm.

6a-b. Fragmentary plaque of green malachite, uninscribed. Original dimensions 3.3 x 1.8 x 0.35cm.

7. Group of faience beads, consisting of the following types and quantities:

   Ring-beads from 0.6 - 0.8cm in diameter. Pale green glazed or white. (10)
   Ring-beads from 0.2 - 0.3cm in diameter. Most white; a few pale green. (27)
   Cylinders, from 0.3 - 0.8cm in length. White, pale green and a few bright blue. (23)
   Double rings, about 0.3cm in width. White. (5)
   Small fragments of faience, unpierced. White and pale green. (19)

8. Roughly shaped piece of hard, crystalline limestone. Dimensions 4.5 x 4.0 x 1.8cm.

9. Two rough pieces of black granodiorite, measuring 7.2 x 5.7 x 3.1cm and 6.4 x 3.5.x 1.8cm.

10-13. Four conical cups of red siltware pottery, restored from fragments. Average height 9.3cm., Diameter 12.0cm (pl.100).

14-16. Three low dishes of red siltware pottery. Average height 2.2cm., Diameter 10.0cm. (pl.100).

17. Rectangular plaque of pale green-glazed faience with no surviving inscription. Dimensions 7.1 x 3.3 x 1.1cm.

18. Rectangular plaque of pale green-glazed faience, with flat sides and back, but a slightly convex front surface. This bears the remains of an illegible text in black paint, carelessly applied and now partly effaced. It probably once contained a royal name and titles. Dimensions 4.4 x 2.5 x 1.4cm.

The numbers of the above list refer to the drawings on plate 11a, which show the location of each item in this deposit.

105 Complete foundation deposit of the Third Intermediate Period, with inscriptions of the priest of Amun, Hor. From the rear corner of the south-east side of the Second Pylon. (1995/2). See plates 12a-b, 101 and colourplate 2a-b.

1. Brick of black mud, containing no chopped straw, and measuring approximately 40 x 22 x 7cm.

2. Calcite hemi-disk inscribed for the priest of Amun, Hor. Dimensions 4.6 x 3.3 x 0.4cm.

3. Plaque of decayed organic material, probably wood, with a thin gilded surface. This was originally inscribed on one face with the same text as the previous entry, but only faint traces survive as parts of the gilded surface have flaked off. Dimensions 2.7 x 1.3 x 0.3cm.

4. Two pieces of a corroded silver plaque, no text remaining, but probably once inscribed as nos. 2-3 above. The silver plaque from the front of the north-west side of the pylon was inscribed. Dimensions 3.2 x 1.7 x 0.2cm.

5. Malachite plaque without inscription. Dimensions 3.2 x 1.4 x 0.3cm.

6. Bronze plaque with an inscription of the priest, Hor. Found heavily corroded and split into two pieces. Dimensions 6.4 x 2.7 x 0.4cm.

7. Faience plaque, originally glazed pale green, but most of the glaze has decayed to off-white. Both the large surfaces are slightly convex and one bears traces of black paint, but no text is now recognisable. Broken in two pieces: Combined dimensions 5.6 x 2.4 x 1.0cm.

8. Green-glazed faience plaque, inscribed on one side in black paint with the cartouche of a king Sheshonq, probably Sheshonq III. For a discussion of the dating of this plaque, see Chapter 6. The name is preceded by the title 'Son of Ra, Lord of Diadems'. Dimensions 6.0 x 2.8 x 0.9cm. See the detail photograph on plate 101.

9. Green-glazed faience plaque with flat surfaces, but lacking any inscription. Parts of the glaze have gone white. Dimensions 5.0 x 2.1 x 0.5cm.

10. Two rough pieces of granodiorite measuring 8.0 x 6.0 x 4.1cm and 8.3 x 6.7 x 2.8cm.

11. Model of a limestone mortar of very simple type, broken in two fragments with part missing. The surviving portion of the object measures 2.7cm high, 6.5cm wide and 8.3cm long.

12. Fragment of corroded iron, about 2.3cm in length.

13. Group of faience beads, comprising the types and sizes listed below, with approximate quantities in parentheses:

> Cylinders, from 0.6 - 1.5cm in length. White, pale green and dark blue. (60+)
> Simple small ring-beads, 0.3 - 0.5cm in diameter. Pale green or white. (20+)
> Double-rings, from 0.4 - 0.5cm in width. Most were white, a few pale green. (20+)

The conditions under which this deposit was excavated from below the water-table means that not all the beads may have been recovered.

14. Eight red pottery cups, restored from fragments. Each approximately 10.0cm high and 12.5cm in diameter. See plate 101.

The positions of the above items in the deposit are shown in the drawing on plate 12a. At a higher level in the rubble which lay in the pits in this corner of the pylon, a rough piece of quartzite was found, probably a sample of material disturbed from this foundation deposit, although it is also possible that it was introduced from elsewhere. It measured 4.7 x 2.2 x 3.5cm.

106 Complete foundation deposit of Nekhtnebef. From the rear southern angle of the naos area of Temple A. (1995/16). See plates 101-102 and colourplate 3a-c.

1. Model limestone mortar, in the form of a cylindrical vessel, with a flat base and two vestigial lug-handles shown in relief at the sides. Height 5.4cm., Diameter 4.0cm.

2. Model quartzite grindstone of crescent shape, the upper stone belonging to item 3, below. Length 8.4cm., Width 2.5cm., Thickness 3.5cm.

3. Model quartzite quern, the lower grindstone of the group with no.2, consisting of a rectangular piece with a concave top. Height 3.8cm., Width 5.6cm., Length 8.6cm.

4. Two blue-glazed faience cups, both fragmentary. Each has a flat base and vertical straight sides, rising to a plain rim. Under the rim was a slight groove. Some of the blue glaze has scaled off. Height of each 3.0cm., Diameters distorted, approximately 4.5 and 5.0cm.

5. Large green-glazed faience plaque inscribed: 'The King of Upper and Lower Egypt, Kheperkara' on one side and: 'The Son of Ra, Nekhtnebef' on the other. Much of the glaze has gone white. Dimensions 6.7 x 3.6 x 0.8cm. See the photographs on plate 101.

6. Hollow gold plaque, inscribed: 'The King of Upper and Lower Egypt, Lord of the Two Lands, Kheperkara' on one side, and: 'The Son of Ra, Nekhtnebef' on the other. Dimensions 2.1 x 0.95 x 0.25cm.

7. Silver plaque, inscribed: 'The Lord of the Two Lands, Kheperkara' on one side, and: 'The Son of Ra, Nekhtnebef' on the other. Dimensions 2.0 x 0.85 x 0.2cm.

8. Chalcedony plaque, inscribed with the titles 'The Good God, Lord of the Two Lands' on one side and with the prenomen: 'Kheperkara' on the other. Dimensions 1.3 x 0.7 x 0.4cm.

9. Green felspar plaque, inscribed on one side only: 'The Good God, Lord of the Two Lands, Kheperkara Nekhtnebef.' Dimensions 1.6 x 0.85 x 0.25cm.

10. Red jasper plaque, inscribed: 'The Lord of the Two Lands, Kheperkara' on one side and with the nomen: 'Nekhtnebef' on the other. Dimensions 1.5 x 0.9 x 0.25cm.

11. Green malachite plaque, uninscribed. Dimensions 1.4 x 0.7 x 0.25cm.

12. Blue glass plaque, inscribed on one face only with a text reading: 'The Lord of the Two Lands, Kheperkara, Son of Ra, Nekhtnebef, (may he) live forever.' The glass is banded to imitate lapis-lazuli. Dimensions 8.5 x 1.3 x 0.5cm.

13. Remains of a decayed metal plaque, perhaps of lead, measuring 4.3 x 2.6cm.

14. Corroded bronze plaque, inscribed with traces of a text which read: 'The Lord of the Two Lands, Kheperkara' on one side, and: '[The Son of Ra ?] Nekhtnebef' on the other. Dimensions 2.9 x 1.4 x 0.35cm.

15. Three fragments of iron corrosion from between one and three plaques. The fragments measure 2.5 x 2.0; 2.7 x 1.9 and 3.0 x 1.8cm respectively.

16. Piece of black bitumen measuring 2.0 x 1.7 x 1.5cm.

17. Four fragments from two model mud-bricks. The sizes of the fragments are 2.8 x 2.3cm with 3.1 x 2.8cm from one model brick, and 3.4 x 2.4cm with 2.4 x 1.6cm from the other, so each brick was just under 6cm in length.

18. Corroded white material, probably from a decayed plaque of metal. It now consists of a mass of powder measuring 6.2 x 4.0cm, embedded in a lump of concreted sand.

6. Commentary

(a) Introduction

Historians frequently have unrealistic expectations from the excavation of Egyptian temples, assuming that decorated walls or gates adorned with sculptures will be revealed from the accumulated earth. The kind of information which can be recovered from a temple, however, is governed more than anything by the position of the original floor-level of the monument relative to the modern level of the uppermost intact archaeological strata, ignoring any mounds of redeposited dump on the ground surface. It should be obvious that any site where the ground-level has been reduced since the construction of the monument to a depth below that of the original floor (even though it might have become deeply buried subsequently) will never yield *in-situ* masonry of the walls of the temple. Such features usually only survive in those monuments whose ruins became rapidly buried in later material - most often by becoming enveloped in later settlements - with the upper parts of the ancient walls protruding from the accumulated fill, or incorporated into more recent structures. The majority of the surviving temples of Upper Egypt were preserved in this way, aided by the key factor that they were constructed of sandstone and consequently escaped the lime industry which was responsible for the destruction of the limestone temples of Middle and Lower Egypt.

That excavations in the Delta have not revealed much in the way of surviving temple buildings is related directly to the matter of floor-level described above. At most Lower Egyptian sites where the location of the temple has been identified, it is quite clear that the ground has been cut down below the level of the floor of the building as a result of the exploitation of the ruins as quarries. This activity was not limited to the above-ground portions of the monuments but often included the removal of stone and sand from the foundations, and the piecemeal method of working in deep pits left the sites encumbered with mounds of spoil, which can rise well above the ancient floor-level but which generally contain little except for chips of stone. It is important to bear in mind that such destruction did not occur only between the Roman Period and the nineteenth century, but happened on occasion during the Pharaonic Period. The demolition of the Amun-Temple at Tell el-Balamun in the fifth century BC was followed by the quarrying of sand from its foundations, resulting in the lowering of the ground well below the floor-level before the site began to rise again with the accumulation of rubbish deposits and fill. The Thirtieth-Dynasty temple was constructed on this mixed stratum of material but was itself quarried out at a later date.

Identifying a monument which has been dug below its original floor establishes the kind of features which can be expected to be revealed by excavation, and helps to determine how the work can best be carried out to recover information from the remaining parts of the structure. These consist of all those elements which lay below the floor, and may include not only the foundations but also any kind of material which might have been buried deliberately in antiquity, such as foundation deposits, cached temple furniture such as sculpture or *ex-votos*, and tombs within the precincts. The foundations, and how they relate to the pre- and post-temple fill, are the primary source of information on the layout and building history of the monument. Foundation deposits are the most likely type of cached material to be recovered, thanks to their positions at the corners being fairly predictable, but the discovery of buried caches of temple sculpture is far less likely and has usually been the result of chance finds. Once again, the destruction of a temple below its floor-level reduces the possibilities of such caches remaining, as any furnishings within the building would have been destroyed or removed for re-use at the same time. The high settlement mounds of Tell el-Balamun to the north-east of the temple are littered with fragments of hard stones, all of which almost certainly came from monuments in the temple which were cut up to be re-used as querns, door-pivots and similar domestic objects. The overlying dumps of debris on a temple site, mentioned above, will contain nothing in its original position and are unlikely to produce any substantial loose blocks of temple masonry if the building consisted of limestone. Other materials of no use for the production of cement, such as quartzite and granite, can sometimes remain in considerable quantities, as at Bubastis, Behbeit el-Hagar or Tanis.

The foregoing comments are not made to discourage the exploration of the Delta temple complexes, but only to introduce a degree of realism into what should be expected from such work. In fact, the details which can be extracted when working with just the foundations of a monument can provide a good picture of its form and date.

(b) The temple of Amun in the New Kingdom

The discovery in the 1998 season of part of a mud-brick enclosure wall dating from the New Kingdom shows that there must have been a temple of this age in the same general area as that later occupied by the temples of the Twenty-second and Thirtieth Dynasties. The surviving parts of the New-Kingdom wall run in directions which would take the north-eastern and south-western boundaries of the enclosure around the site of these later monuments. The survival of the north corner of the early enclosure was the result of its having been located sufficiently distant from the later monuments to have escaped being totally cut away during the redevelopment of the complex or in the later quarrying of the ruins. Whether other parts of the perimeter of the enclosure lie partly preserved below the ground surface is yet to be determined.

As described in Chapter 4, the pottery from the fill against the inner face of the wall dates from the Twentieth to Twenty-first Dynasties so the most likely date for the enclosure would seem to lie in the Ramesside Period. It could well have been constructed by that ubiquitous builder, Ramesses II, of whom a few monuments have been found at Tell el-Balamun. In addition to the quartzite triad of the king with Amun and Mut from the British Museum excavations (Cat.1), there are also some massive blocks of worn granite lying to the south-east of the Amun-Temple which were dug out by Howard Carter in 1913 and were found to bear the name of Ramesses II. Parts of a basalt statue of the king were found in fields close to the site in 1991. A temple enclosure of Ramesses II might have followed the lines of one from earlier in the New Kingdom, but is more likely to have been an enlargement of an older complex. Although no evidence for such a monument has yet been found at the site, texts from the reign of Tuthmosis III refer to the existence of a temple for Amun at Paiuenamon (Helck 1956, 1443; Gardiner 1944, 42, n. 8). Inscriptions on the statues of Nebwa attest the cult of Amun at the site under Horemheb (Legrain 1907, 269-70, 272-3; Borchardt 1930, 135, no. 883; Lefebvre 1929, 243-5; Gardiner 1944, 41, n. 3; Malek 1986, 320, n. 8, 321, n. 18). Construction of a temple for Amun-Ra, Lord of Sma-Behdet, is recorded on a stela of Ramesses II from Tell el-Hagar, close to Tell el-Balamun (Farag 1939, 127-132, pl.12). The establishment of a complete temple complex by Ramesses III in *Niwt t3-mhw*, with the name, 'The House of Ramesses Ruler in Thebes Great of Victories', is recorded in the Great Harris Papyrus and might refer to Tell el-Balamun, as understood by Brugsch, Gauthier and Yoyotte (Brugsch 1879, 289-91, 1198-99; Gauthier 1926, 81; id., 1928, 35-6; Yoyotte 1971-2, 171; id., 1985-6, 231). Others have preferred to see this foundation placed at Pi-Ramesse (Kitchen 1986, 427-8, n. 20; Grandet 1994, II, 43-45, n. 171; Malek 1986, 182). The above references have now been conveniently assembled by F. Leclère, in *Les Villes de Basse Égypte au Ière Millénaire av. J-C.* (Doctoral thesis, Université de Lille III, June 1997).

The features and fill inside the corner of the New-Kingdom enclosure seem to have begun to accumulate while the enclosure and the temple which must have once existed inside it were still in use; only the uppermost level of this stratigraphic deposit begins to encroach over portions of the wall itself. There is no reason why a temple built in the Ramesside Period should not have continued to function, probably with later additions, until the major rebuilding of the Twenty-second Dynasty; indeed, the Second Pylon of Sheshonq III might itself have been added to the front of the Ramesside temple. If this were the case, then the core of the Ramesside monument would lie in the area later occupied by the sand-bed of the Thirtieth-Dynasty temple, the excavation of which would have removed all older traces. But it is also possible that the New-Kingdom temple faced to the north-west instead of the north-east and that Sheshonq III levelled the older structure and began a new temple at right-angles to the earlier axis. The presence of the tomb of Iken on the eroded corner of the Ramesside enclosure wall indicates that there must have been a functioning temple in existence at the time of Osorkon I, because the location of the tomb was motivated by a wish to place it close to the sanctuary of Amun. There is no reason why this should not have been the Ramesside temple still in use, perhaps with some Twenty-first Dynasty additions which have not survived.

(c) The burial of Iken

Some comments on the position of the tomb of Iken have been given in Chapter 4, pointing out that this is an example of the custom which appeared in the Third Intermediate Period of building tombs in or around the enclosures of temples. With regard to historical matters, it is interesting to note that the only recorded individual with the name Iken from the Third Intermediate Period is documented on the stela of Prince Iuwelot from Karnak (Ranke 1935, 48; Legrain 1897, Erman 1897; see also the photograph in Drioton 1949, 179). The text of this stela records the purchase of land by Iuwelot from, among others, several children of a certain Iken, in order to create an estate of 556 arourae, which he left to his son, Khaemwas. These purchases are recorded as having been made in Year 10 of Osorkon I, whilst Iuwelot was still young (see Kitchen 1973, 121, 195, 311). Since the Iken of Tell el-Balamun was buried during the reign of Osorkon I, this would place Iuwelot one generation after him and, therefore, in the same generation as any children of Iken. So from the chronological point of view there is no difficulty in the Iken of Tell el-Balamun being the same as the one documented on the stela of Iuwelot. No titles are given for the Iken on the stela, but for his children to have had dealings with Iuwelot he must have been of considerable social status and would almost certainly have held some official position. For the Iken buried at Tell el-Balamun, there is the title 'Vizier' which precedes his name on the granite heart-scarab (Cat.**31**).

The next problem is geographical, in trying to determine the location of the land bought by Iuwelot. Line 2 of the stela places this north-west of the island called *Iw-nfrt* and Erman's translation (Erman 1897) restores 'Thebes' without any explanation, as noted by Gauthier (Gauthier 1925, 44). The determinative used with the word for 'island' is an example of the common confusion between the signs for *i3t* and *iw*. But the toponym *iw-nfrt* is the name of a sanctuary of Horus of Behdet (Gauthier 1925, 45). There is also an inscription from the reign of Takeloth III which refers to Amun of *P3-iw* (Gauthier 1937, 21-22; Otto, 1975), the same abbreviation of *P3-iw-n-Imn* used on the plaques from the foundation deposits at the Second Pylon. On the other hand, there is a reference to *iw-nfrt* in a Theban context (Daressy 1896, 182). The term could well have been a generic one, used for sanctuaries at different locations. Without additional evidence it is impossible to say whether the Iken of the Iuwelot stela is the one buried at Tell el-Balamun, but it is a possibility given the links between two sanctuaries of Amun, at Karnak and at Balamun. The distance between the two locations is irrelevant; Hekakheperre Sheshonq II, for example, was High-Priest of Amun in Thebes but was buried at Tanis (Montet 1951).

(d) The foundation deposits of the Second Pylon and the priest Hor

The excavation and contents of these deposits have been described in Chapters 1 and 5. In spite of there being only a single surviving plaque with a royal name, the identification of the king as Sheshonq III seems reasonably certain. Even the careless manner in which the cartouche was written can be paralleled in other inscriptions of this ruler, whose texts show frequent irregularities in writing, even in the case of inscriptions on stone (Daressy 1903, 283-4. These blocks are exhibited in the Cairo Museum but are not published in photographs or drawings). The cartouche shown in detail on plate 101 has *mry Imn* at the top and the hieroglyphs for Sheshonq below on the left. The second *s3*-sign has suffered some loss through decay of the surface and the *n* is a simple line; to the right is the epithet *s3-B3st*. The compressed and poorly executed signs at the bottom of the cartouche are a careless writing of *ntr hk3 Iwnw*, the more confused by the fact that the *q* of Sheshonq appears to have overlapped the top of this group. This epithet, and the *s3-B3st* mentioned above, were both used by Sheshonq III.

The presence of only a single royal plaque in contrast to the numerous examples inscribed with the name of Hor, priest of Amun of *P³-iw*, is unusual. Even allowing that one of the faience plaques from the front north-west corner deposit has probably lost a royal cartouche, the inscriptions of Hor are in a substantial majority. Clearly, the priest must have been given delegated authority to supervise the foundation of the pylon. To hold such a responsibility, actually deputising for the king in this official role, Hor must have been of a much higher rank than it might seem from the few titles which it was possible to fit on a foundation deposit plaque. A priest Hor of high status is documented on monuments from Thebes at this period, identified for the time being in the literature as Hor vii/viii/ix/xi, because several holders of the name once thought to have been distinct individuals are now considered one and the same (Bierbrier 1975, 73-4; Kitchen 1986, 561). Several statues from Karnak provided this Hor with ample space to enumerate his titles, which included Royal Seal-bearer, Sole courtier, Priest of Amun in Karnak, Fan-bearer on the right of the King, and Secretary of Pharaoh (Legrain 1914, nos. 42226-8; Jansen-Winkeln 1985, 136ff). This certainly was an individual who could have acted for the king, but an identification of the priest Hor of Balamun with Hor vii/viii/ix/xi can only be suggested, not proved. A little additional positive evidence comes from the hieroglyph which appears on some of the foundation deposit plaques after the title: 'priest of Amun [of] *P³-iw*' and immediately before the name. This sign was difficult to interpret on such small-scale inscriptions; the initial suggestion that it might be a writing of *imntt* 'west' seemed unsatisfactory, as it did not fit very well with the palaeography nor did it make sense. *P³-iw* is a well-attested abbreviation for *P³-iw-n-Imn*, but *p³-iw-imntt* in this context is most unlikely. Among the titles of Hor vii/viii/ix/xi is 'Fan-bearer on the right of the King', and there is a strong possibility that the problematic hieroglyph on the plaques is *ḥw*, 'fan'. If so, this might be an example of a massive abbreviation of the same title, prompted by lack of space. The suggestion that an official who held several high Theban offices should officiate at the founding of a temple in Tell el-Balamun is not as improbable as it might appear, since both centres belonged in the estate of Amun. If, on the other hand, Hor of Balamun was a separate individual from the one attested from Theban sources, he could well have belonged to a branch of the same family, in which the name appeared in different generations. The king for whom Hor acted, Sheshonq III, was in any case closely tied to the Delta, building extensively at Tanis and being buried there. It is important to remember that our evidence as to the areas of activity of officials of the period is distorted by the fact that Thebes was an important religious centre in which royal and private individuals wished to place sculptures and inscriptions, and these monuments have survived and have been excavated. But the lack of excavation in northern sites means that we do not know whether the same individuals might also have been active in the cities of Lower Egypt, particularly at a period when political power was centred in the Delta.

(e) The temple of Amun in the Twenty-second to Twenty-sixth Dynasties

Whether the rear part of the temple, behind the Second Pylon, included any elements taken over from buildings of Ramesside or Twenty-first Dynasty date cannot be determined because of the problem of the presence of the foundations of the Thirtieth Dynasty, as noted above. For the front part of the temple, however, the building history is relatively clear. The whole monument from the Second Pylon to the front gate was constructed on a site which had been levelled to a relative level of 125 ± 10. This is the level of the highest preserved parts of the pre-temple ground into which the foundation-trenches and pits for the pylons and other features were cut. The best-preserved sand filling of these foundations rises to the same height, and it seems that this was the level at which the base courses of masonry rested on the sand. The small amount of surviving masonry in front of the Second Pylon rests on the sand at relative level 121 (pls.17b, 18a).

There are problems in trying to estimate the depth of the masonry foundations above the sand, since it appears that the both the sand filling of the foundation and the surrounding ground were at the same level, rather than the sand being lower in the pits to allow space for the introduction stone blocks. The fact that the pre-temple ground along the centre of the temple has not been greatly lowered by later destruction is demonstrated by the presence of the axis-marker slab in its original position (pl.21b). So any masonry intended to have been sub-floor must have been placed on the sand and subsequently hidden by raising the floor-level throughout the temple with earth or sand brought in for the purpose. This material would have been far less compact than the deeper pre-temple ground, which would explain its disappearance during the destruction and quarrying of the monument. This is the only way in which any masonry to support the bases of the walls, columns and particularly the huge First Pylon could have been set into place, although the method would have inherent weaknesses, since the stone of the foundation would not have been contained in trenches cut in solid ground. A minimum of one metre of stone foundation above the sand would have placed the floor-level of the temple at a relative level of about 225, which is above the general level of the present-day surface. Given that the depth of foundation masonry was probably greater - 1.5 to 2.0 metres would not be exceptional - the floor could well have been higher. The demolition of the temple in the fifth century BC reduced the surface to much lower levels and left the site as an area of undulating dumps and hollows, some of which cut well down into the sand-bed. The hollows then gradually became filled with rubbish, dust and mud to create a more uniform surface, at least through the central part of the temple site, at a level which was probably some half a metre lower than that of the temple floor. This ground then seems to have remained derelict until the commencement of the Thirtieth-Dynasty rebuilding of the temple, apart from the introduction of small pottery kilns above the former position of the south-east wing of the First Pylon. The foundation-trenches for the forecourt wall of the Thirtieth-Dynasty temple were cut through the fifth-century BC fill into the remaining elements of the foundation-system of the older monument.

The dating of the colonnade and First Pylon

As mentioned in the description of the temple level (Chapter 1), there is no preserved stratigraphic link between the face of the Second Pylon and the sand-filled foundation-trenches of the colonnade. It is, however, clear that the colonnade and First Pylon were built as one project. The lack of preserved foundation deposits in the First Pylon leaves only limited evidence for its dating, based on a few sherds recovered from the sand-bed and the position of the pylon relative to other structures. The latter observation has been made in Chapter 4, where it was pointed out that a small barque-station existed in front of the Second Pylon, to the north-west of the temple axis. The position of this chapel would be ideal for it to have been built at a time when the Second Pylon of Sheshonq III formed the front of the temple, but the design was upset by the construction of the First Pylon, which blocked the axis of the barque-station. This suggests that the small chapel was redundant by the time the First Pylon was built, a situation which can only apply if the building of the First Pylon took place after the Twenty-second Dynasty, and the Twenty-sixth would seem the most likely candidate.

Of the sherd evidence, a rim of Type D.1.51 from deep within the clean foundation sand of the colonnade would appear to be of Saite date, and the fill into which the foundation of the north-west wing of the First Pylon was cut contained some sherds dating from the end of the Third Intermediate Period (Type C.1.5, see page 44).

This meagre evidence would suggest that the colonnade and First Pylon were probably added in the Twenty-sixth Dynasty to the front of the temple of Sheshonq III. Given the activity of Psamtik I in building Temple C and the Inner Enclosure Wall, it would be surprising not to find some Saite building activity in the main temple of Amun. The existence of statues of a priest of Amun in Paiuenamon during the reign of Apries is additional evidence for there having been a flourishing temple at the site in the Saite Period (Munro 1987).

The size of the First Pylon

The width across the foundation of the pylon was 78 metres, but the curvature of the corners of the pit would have limited the size of the pylon itself to a slightly smaller dimension. In any case, the masonry of the footing of a pylon was always placed a short distance away from the edge of the foundation-trench so that a pylon of a specified size could be created within a more roughly-cut foundation, by allowing the base courses to project beyond the final dressed end of the pylon. The full width of the First Pylon in the Amun-Temple at Tell el-Balamun would, therefore, have almost certainly have been designed to span 140 cubits, that is about 73.2 metres, allowing some 2.4 metres at either end for the projecting base courses and the construction gap. The size can be compared with the Ninth and Tenth

Pylons at Karnak, which were both 125 cubits across. Temple pylons in excess of 140 cubits width are rare, examples being the First and Second Pylons at Karnak or the later pylon of the temple of Edfu. The scale of the pylon at Balamun is a measure of the importance ascribed to this sanctuary of Amun in the Late Period.

(f) The temple of Amun in the Thirtieth Dynasty

Of the major rebuilding of the temple begun by Nekhtnebef only a limited amount has survived. At the rear there is only the huge foundation-pit of some 80 x 40 metres, with the remaining sand filling deeply buried under dumps of spoil from quarrying operations, whilst in the front part of the temple only the foundation-trench of the wall of the forecourt survives. As an aid to the interpretation of the site, earth from our own excavations has been piled up in a ridge along the line of the forecourt wall so that the boundary of the Thirtieth-Dynasty forecourt can now be seen once again. The use of spoil for this purpose rather than any more useful material should permit this reconstruction to last for some considerable time. An account of the excavation of the forecourt wall was given in the previous report (Spencer 1996, 38-9).

In addition to these remains of the main temple, there are also the dependent mud-brick structures N1, N2 and N3, together with the foundation-pit of what was probably the mammisi (see Chapter 3). It is not possible to be certain whether all three mud-brick buildings were constructed under the Thirtieth Dynasty or added early in the Ptolemaic Period, but the relationship of Building N1 with the temple forecourt wall suggests that it, at least, was built as soon as the forecourt wall had been completed. It is in the forecourt area where we find the evidence for the abandonment of this part of the temple by the end of the Ptolemaic Period, as the forecourt was encroached upon for small-scale industrial activities and rubbish-disposal. This phase was also evident over the ruins of Buildings N1 and N2, which had been used for similar activities.

Looking at the wider area of the Thirtieth-Dynasty temple complex, it is possible to see some of the relationships between the individual monuments in the enclosure. The figures given on plate 105 show how distances of 300 and 400 cubits were used to create a balanced layout between the temples, their separate axes and the enclosure wall. These relationships are further evidence for the attribution of the Outer Enclosure Wall to the building programme initiated under Nekhtnebef.

Bibliography and Abbreviations

AEPHE   *Annuaire de l'école pratique des Hautes Études.* Paris.

AJA   *American Journal of Archaeology.* New York.

ASAE   *Annales du Service des Antiquités de l'Égypte.* Cairo.

Aston 1991   Aston, D.A., 'The Pottery' in Raven, M.J., *The Tomb of Iurudef. A Memphite Official in the reign of Ramesses II*, 47-54. London.

Aston 1996   Aston, D.A., *Egyptian Pottery of the Late New Kingdom and Third Intermediate Period (Twelfth - Seventh Centuries BC). Tentative Footsteps in a Forbidding Terrain.* Heidelberg.

Aston 1997   Aston, D.A., 'The Pottery', in Martin, G.T., *The Tomb of Tia and Tia. A Royal Monument of the Ramesside Period in the Memphite Necropolis*, 83-102. London.

Aston 1998   Aston, D.A., *Die Keramik des Grabungplatzes QI, Teil 1. Corpus of Fabrics, Wares and Shapes. Die Grabung des Pelizaeus-Mueum Hildesheim in Qantir - Pi-Ramesse.* E Pusch and M Bietak (eds.) Mainz.

Baatz 1994   Baatz, D., 'Die Handmühlen', in Salies, G.H., et al., *Das Wrack der antike Schiffsfund von Mahdia*, Band 1. Köln.

Bierbrier 1975   Bierbrier, M.L., *The Late New Kingdom in Egypt.* Warminster.

Borchardt 1930   Borchardt, L., *Statuen und Statuetten von Königen und Privatleuten*, vol. III. *Catalogue Générale du Musée du Caire.* Berlin.

Bourriau and Aston 1985   Bourriau, J. and Aston, D.A., 'The Pottery', in Martin, G.T., *The Tomb-Chapels of Paser and Ra'ia at Saqqara*, 32-55. London.

Brugsch 1879   Brugsch, H., *Dictionnaire Géographique de l'ancienne Egypte.* Leipzig.

BSFFT   *Bulletin de la Société française des fouilles de Tanis.* Paris.

Buikstra and Ubelaker 1994   Buikstra, J.E. and Ubelaker, D., *Standards for data collection from human skeletal remains.* Arkansas Archaeological Survey Research Series, No. 44.

Daressy 1896   Daressy, G., 'Une inondation à Thebes sous la regne d'Osorkon II', in *RT* 18, 181-86.

Daressy 1903	Daressy, G., 'Rapport sur Kom el-Hisn', in *ASAE* 4, 281-85.
Drioton 1949	Drioton, E., *Encyclopédie Photographique de l'Art. Le Musée du Caire*. Editions 'Tel'. Undated.
Erman 1897	Erman, A., 'Zu den Legrain'schen Inschriften', in *ZÄS* 35, 19-29.
Farag 1939	Farag, N., 'Une stèle de Ramses II', in *ASAE* 39, 127-32.
Fougerousse 1946	Fougerousse, J.L., 'Un atelier de fours à céramique à Tanis', in *Kêmi* 8, 1-28.
Gardiner 1944	Gardiner, A.H., 'Horus the Behdetite', in *JEA* 30, 23-60.
Gauthier 1925, 1926, 1928	Gauthier, *Dictionnaire des Noms Géographiques contenus dans les Textes Hieroglyphiques*, vols. I, III and V. Cairo.
Gauthier 1937	Gauthier, H., 'Un Curieux Monument des Dynasties Boubastides à Heracleopolis Magna', in *ASAE* 37, 16-24.
Gazda 1983	Gazda, E.K. (ed), *Karanis, an Egyptian Town in Roman Times*. Ann Arbor.
Ghattas 1982	Ghattas, F.A.M., 'Tell el-Balamoun 1978', in *ASAE* 68, 5-9.
Ghattas 1983	Ghattas, F.A.M., 'Some Selected Amulets from Tell el-Balamon Abu Gallal', in *ASAE* 65, 149-55.
Grandet 1994	Grandet, P., *Le Papyrus Harris I*, 2 vols. Cairo.
Helck 1956	Helck, W., *Urkunden des Ägyptischen Altertums*, Heft 18: *Urkunden der 18 Dynastie*. Berlin.
Holthoer 1977	Holthoer, R., *New-Kingdom Pharaonic Sites: The Pottery*. Lund.
Hope 1989	Hope, C.A., *Pottery of the Egyptian New Kingdom, Three Studies*. Victoria College Archaeology Research Unit Occasional Paper No. 2. Victoria.
Jansen-Winkeln 1985	Jansen-Winkeln, K., *Ägyptische Biographen der 22. und 23. Dynastie. Ägypten und Altes Testament*, Bd. 8/1-8/2, 136ff. Wiesbaden.
JdE	*Journal d'Éntrée du Musée*. Egyptian Museum. Cairo.
JEA	*Journal of Egyptian Archaeology*. London.
Kêmi	*Kêmi. Revue de Philologie et d'Archéologie égyptiennes et Coptes*. Paris.
Kitchen 1973	Kitchen, K.A .,*The Third Intermediate Period in Egypt (1100-650 BC)*. Warminster.

Kitchen 1986

Kitchen, K.A., *The Third Intermediate Period in Egypt (1100-650 BC), Supplement*. Warminster.

LÄ

Lexikon der Ägyptologie. Wiesbaden.

Lefebvre 1929

Lefebvre, G., *Histoire des Grandes Prêtres d'Amon de Karnak*. Paris.

Legrain 1897

Legrain, G., 'Deux stèles trouvées à Karnak en février 1897', in *ZÄS* 35, 12-19.

Legrain 1907

Legrain, G., 'Notes d'Inspection', in *ASAE* 8, 248-75.

Legrain 1914

Legrain, G., *Statues et Statuettes de Rois et de Particuliers*, III, *Catalogue Générale du Musée du Caire*. Cairo.

Lopez-Grande *et al.* 1995

Lopez-Grande, M., Quesada Sanz, F. and Molinero Polo, M.A., Excavaciones en Ehnasya el Medina (Heracleopolis Magna), II. Madrid.

Malek 1985

Malek, J., 'Paiuenamun, Sambehdet, and Howard Carter's Survey of Tell el-Balamun in 1913', in *RdE* 36, 181-85.

Malek 1986

Malek, J., 'Tell el-Belamun', in *LÄ*, VI, 319-21.

Montet 1935

Montet, P., 'Études sur les constructions de Tanis', in *Kemi* 5, 58-63

Montet 1947, 1951, 1960

Montet, P., *La Nécropole Royale de Tanis*, Vols. I-III. Paris.

Munro 1987

Munro, P., 'Die Statuen des *Hrw* aus Baqliya und Tell el-Balamun', in Osing, J. and Dreyer, G., *Form und Mass, Fs. für Gerhard Fecht. Ägypten und Altes Testament*, Bd. 12, 307ff. Wiesbaden.

Nagel 1938

Nagel, G., *La céramique du Nouvel Empire à Deir el-Medineh*, I. Cairo.

Otto 1975

Otto, E., 'Amun', in *LÄ*, I, 241, n. 37.

Petrie 1888

Petrie, W.M.F., *Nebesheh (Am) and Defenneh (Tahpanhes)*, in id., *Tanis*, II. London.

Petrie 1896

Petrie, W.M.F., *Koptos*. London.

PM

Porter, B. and Moss, R.L.B., *Topographical Bibliography of Ancient Egyptian Hieroglyphic Texts, Reliefs and Paintings*, vol. II *Theban Temples*, 2nd ed., 1971; vol. III *Memphis*, part 2: *Saqqara to Dahshur*, 2nd. ed. revised by J. Malek, 1981. Oxford.

Ranke 1935

Ranke, H., *Die ägyptische Personnennamen*, I: *Verzeichnis der Namen*. Glückstadt.

RdE

Revue d'Égyptologie. Louvain.

Ricke 1960

Ricke, H., *Die Tempel Nektanebos II in Elephantine und ihre Erweiterungen. Beiträge zur Ägyptischen Bauforschung und Altertumskunde*, 6. Cairo.

Robins and Shute 1986

Robins, G. and Shute, C.C.D., 'Predynastic Egyptian stature and physical proportions', in *Human Evolution* 1, 14, 313-24.

Robinson and Graham 1936

Robinson, D.M., and Graham, J.W., *Excavations at Olynthus,* VIII: *The Hellenic House.* Baltimore and Oxford.

Rostovtzeff 1937

Rostovtzeff, M., 'Two Homeric Bowls in the Louvre', in *AJA* 41, 86-96.

RT

Recueil de Travaux relatifs à la philologie et à l'archéologie égyptiennes et assyriennes. 1870-1923. Paris.

Spencer 1996

Spencer, A.J., *Excavations at Tell el-Balamun 1991-1994.* London.

Spencer 1997

Spencer, A.J., 'Egyptian Dynastic Pottery', in Freestone, I.J. and Gaimster, P (eds.), *Pottery in the Making*, 62-67. London.

Trotter 1970

Trotter, M., 'Estimation of Stature from Intact Limb Bones', in Stewart, T.D., (ed.), *Personal Identification in Mass Disasters,* 71-83. Washington.

Yoyotte 1968

Yoyotte, J., *Treasures of the Pharaohs.* Geneva.

Yoyotte 1971-2

Yoyotte, J., 'Récherches sur la géographie historique et réligieuse de la Basse Égypte', in *AEPHE* 79, 167-73.

Yoyotte 1985-6

Yoyotte, J., 'Sites et cultes de Basse Égypte orientale, de Sile à Tanis', in *AEPHE* 94, 231-35.

Yoyotte 1992

Yoyotte, J., 'Le Tell de San el-Hagar. Une montagne d'origine humaine', in *BSFFT* 6, 103-21.

ZÄS

Zeitschrift für Ägyptische Sprache und Altertumskunde. Berlin and Leipzig.

PLATES

(a) Pottery jar in a pit above the foundation of the north-west wing of the Second Pylon

(b) Foundation deposit at the front north-west corner of the Second Pylon

(c) Plaques, material samples and examples of beads from the
foundation deposit at the north-west corner of the Second Pylon

(a) Plaques, material samples and examples of beads from the
foundation deposit at the south-east corner of the Second Pylon

(b) Detail of the plaques from the foundation deposit at the south-east
corner of the Second Pylon

(c) The pre-temple ground along the axis of the temple in Trench
TG1, with the brick sill bedded in the sand above

(a) Foundation deposit of Nekhtnebef as found
in the rear south corner of Temple A

(b) Complete foundation deposit of Nekhtnebef from
the rear south corner of Temple A

(c) Detail of the plaques of chalcedony, red jasper, felspar and gold
from the deposit of Nekhtnebef

(a) Profile showing the pre-temple ground and foundation
sand in Trench TG3, with the overlying deposits

(b) Sand filling in the front corner of the foundation of the First Pylon in Trench W9

(c) Kiln 2 in the late Ptolemaic level above the remains of Building N1,
with fragments of the floor of the firing-chamber

PLATE 1

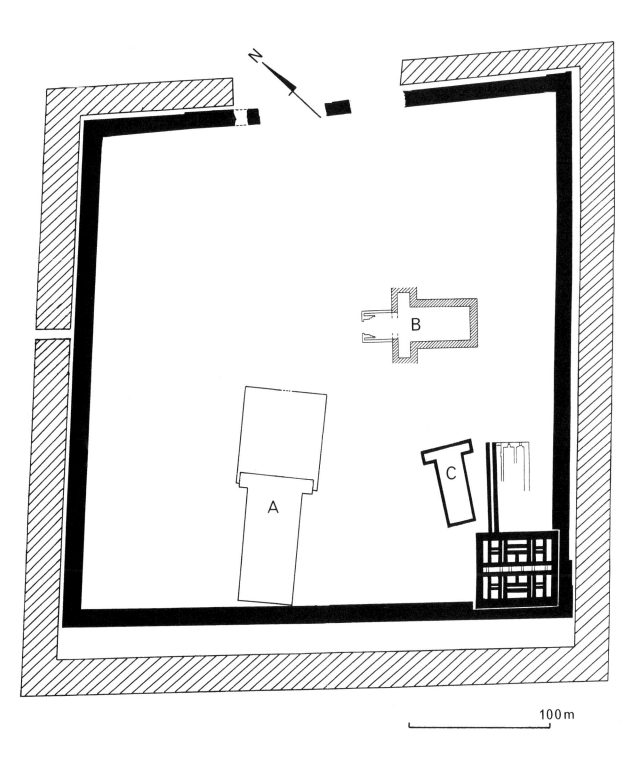

100 m

Plan of the temple complex showing the enclosure walls of Dynasties 26 and 30 and the positions of the Amun-Temple (A), the subsidiary temple of Nekhtnebef (B) and the small temple of Psamtik I (C)

PLATE 2

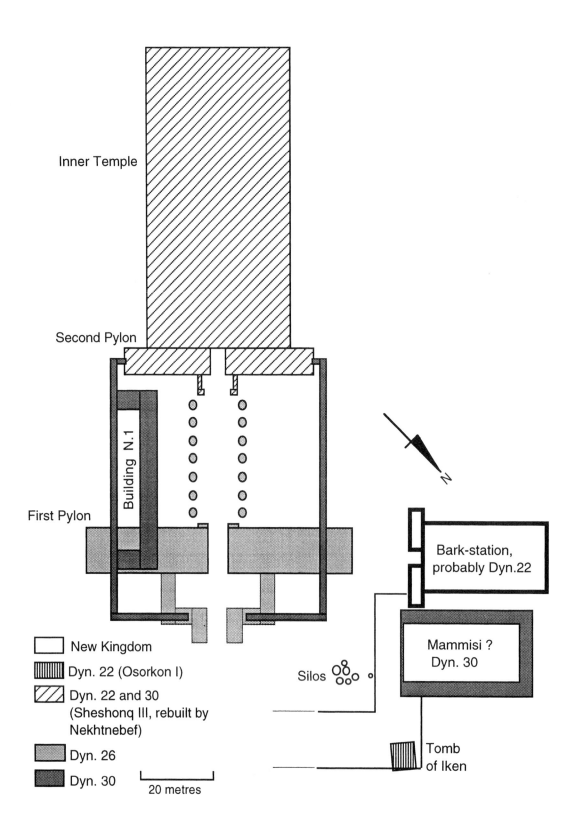

Inner Temple

Second Pylon

Building N.1

First Pylon

Bark-station,
probably Dyn.22

Mammisi ?
Dyn. 30

Silos

New Kingdom

Dyn. 22 (Osorkon I)

Dyn. 22 and 30
(Sheshonq III, rebuilt by
Nekhtnebef)

Dyn. 26

Dyn. 30

Tomb
of Iken

20 metres

Plan showing the different phases of the Amun-Temple and adjacent features

PLATE 3

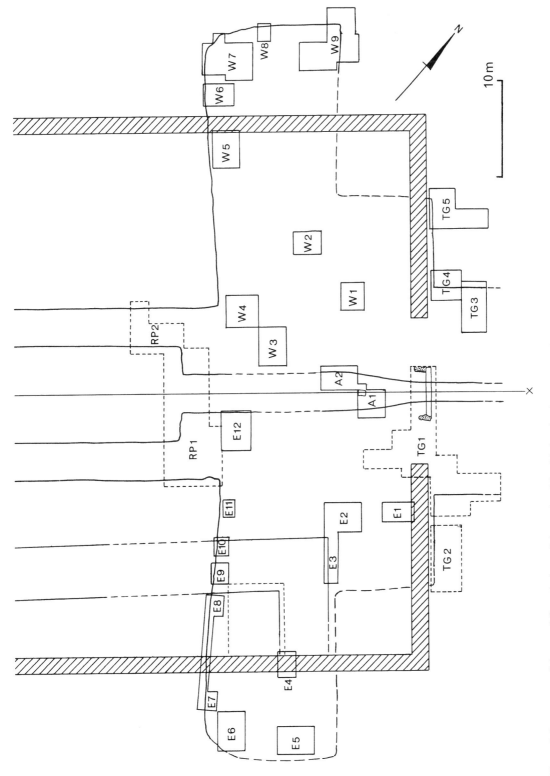

Plan of the extent of the sand foundation of dynasties 22 - 30 for the front part of the Amun-Temple with locations and numbers of excavation trenches

PLATE 4

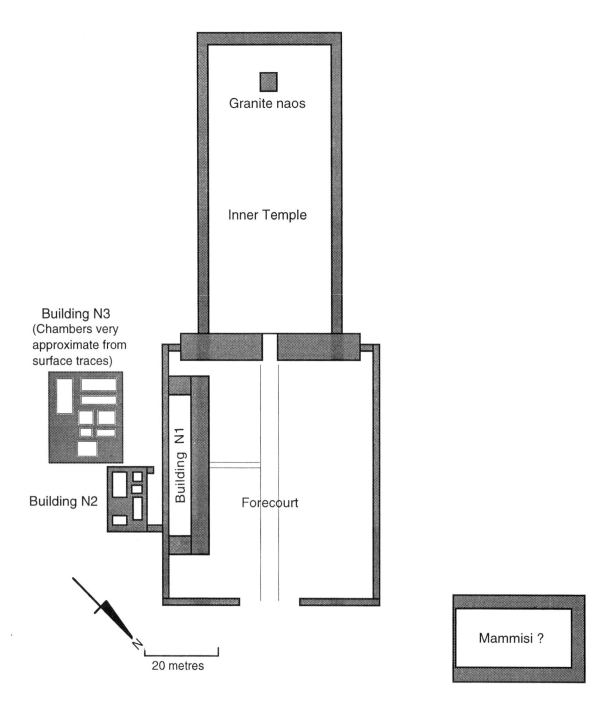

Granite naos

Inner Temple

Building N3
(Chambers very
approximate from
surface traces)

Building N1

Building N2

Forecourt

N

20 metres

Mammisi ?

Reconstructed plan of the Amun Temple and adjacent buildings in the Thirtieth dynasty and early Ptolemaic
Period

PLATE 5

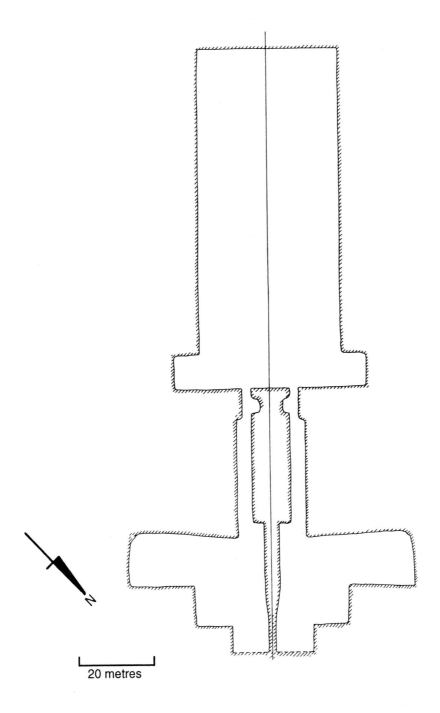

20 metres

The configuration of the sand-bed for the Amun-Temple of dynasties 22 - 26, to the same scale as the reconstruction of the temple in the following plate

PLATE 6

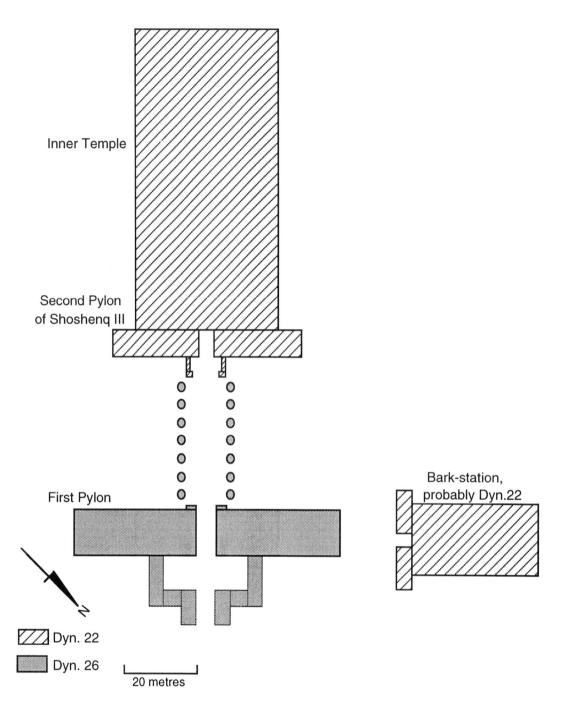

Inner Temple

Second Pylon
of Shoshenq III

First Pylon

Bark-station,
probably Dyn.22

N

Dyn. 22

Dyn. 26

20 metres

Reconstructed plan of the Amun-Temple in the Twenty-second to Twenty-sixth dynasties

PLATE 7

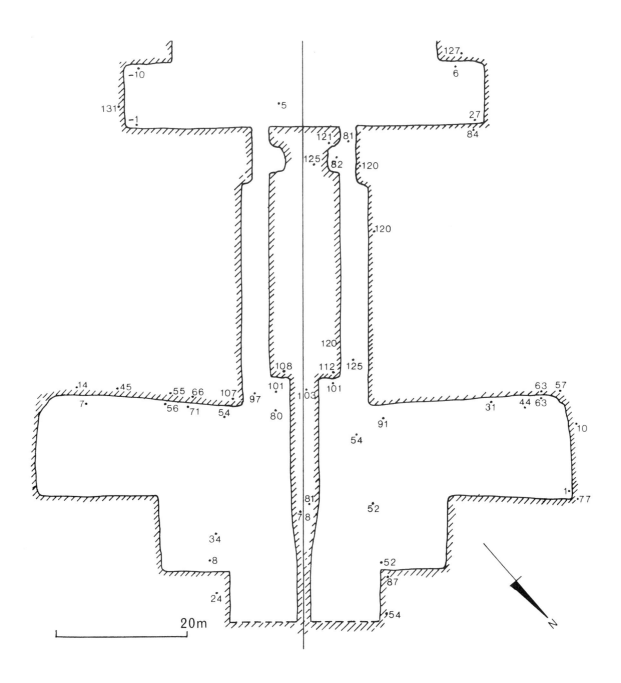

Principal relative levels on the edges of the foundation of the Amun-Temple (front part) and on the preserved heights of the sand filling

PLATE 8

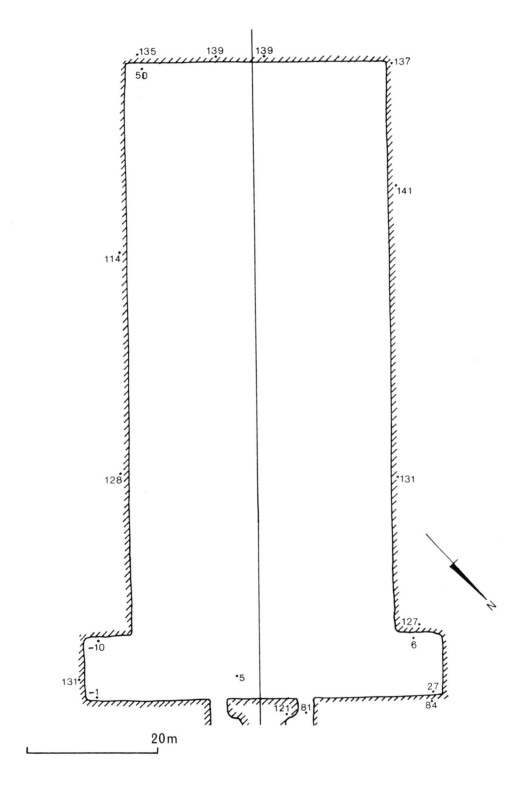

Principal relative levels on the edges of the foundation of the Amun-Temple (rear part) and on the preserved heights of the sand filling

PLATE 9

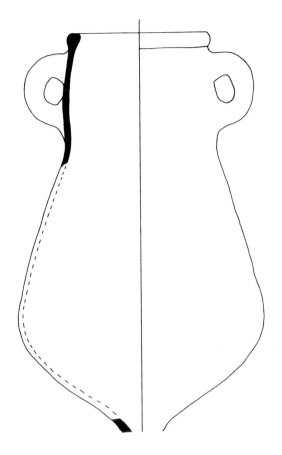

(a) Large siltware jar dumped in a pit above the north-west end of the foundation of the Second Pylon of Temple A [1:8]

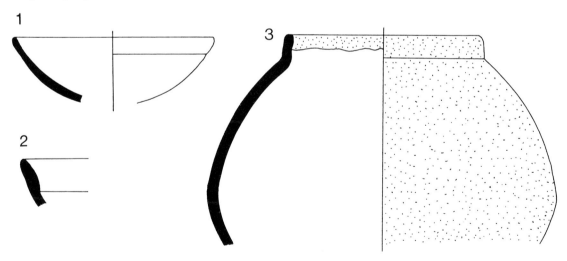

(b) Pottery from the fill outside the front of the north-west end of the foundation-pit of the Second Pylon of Temple A [1:4]

(c) Roman pottery and glass from above the north-west side of the colonnade foundation in Temple A [Nos. 1-2 at 1:4; no. 3 at 1:2]

PLATE 10

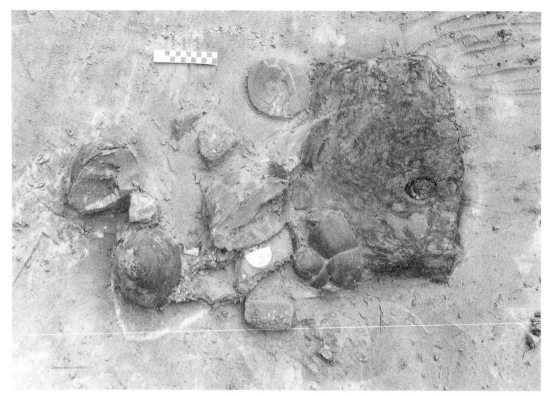

(a) Foundation deposit in the front corner of the north-west wing of the Second Pylon in Temple A

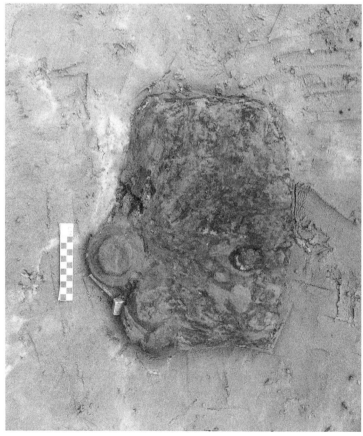

(b) Lower layer of the foundation deposit in the front corner of the north-west wing of the Second Pylon in Temple A

PLATE 11

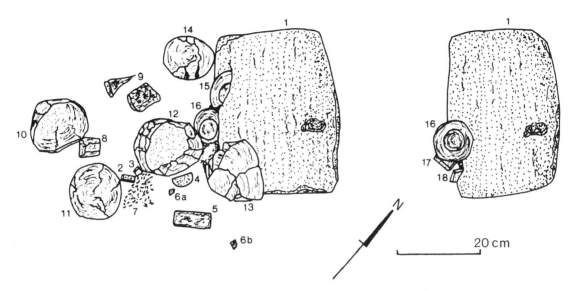

(a) Plan of the foundation deposit at the front corner of the north-west wing of the Second Pylon in Temple A

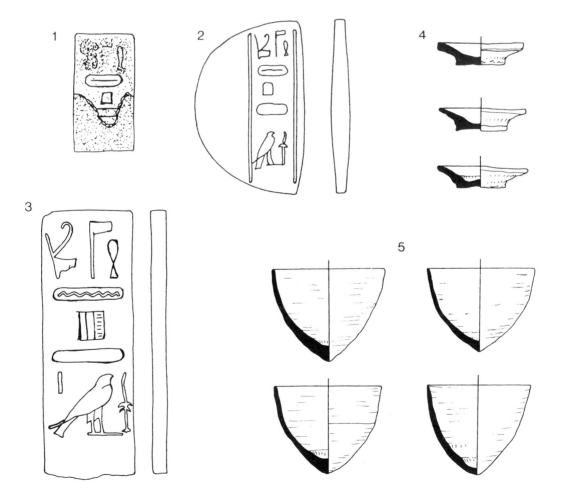

(b) Silver, calcite and bronze plaques of Hor, and pottery from the foundation deposit at the front corner of the north-west wing of the Second Pylon in Temple A [Plaques 1:1; pottery 1:4]

PLATE 12

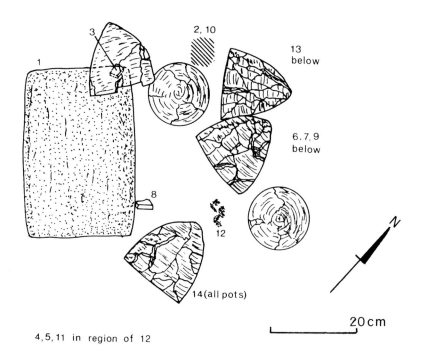

(a) Plan of the foundation deposit at the rear corner of the south-east wing of the Second Pylon in Temple A

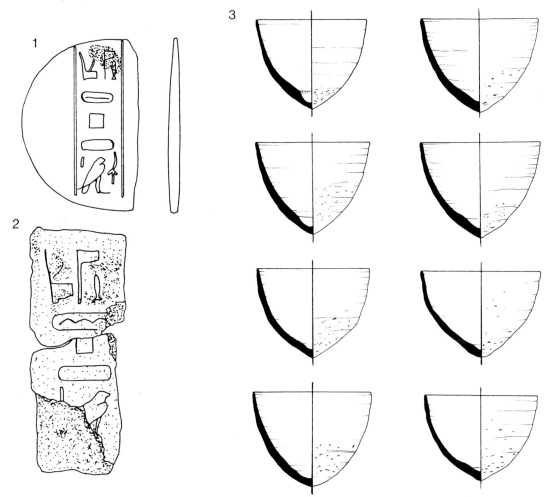

(b) Calcite and bronze plaques of Hor, and pottery from the foundation deposit at the rear corner of the south-east wing of the Second Pylon in Temple A [plaques 1:1; pottery 1:4]

PLATE 13

(a) Limestone column-drum or base re-used in the front corner of the south-east wing of the Second Pylon

(b) Excavation in front of the Second Pylon of Temple A, from the south-west. Note the curve in the edge of the foundation-pit in the foreground

PLATE 14

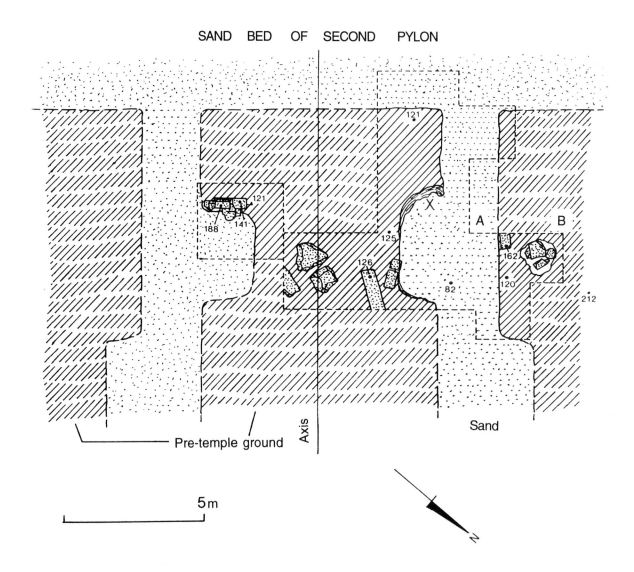

SAND BED OF SECOND PYLON

Plan of the colonnade foundation-trenches at the face of the Second Pylon

PLATE 15

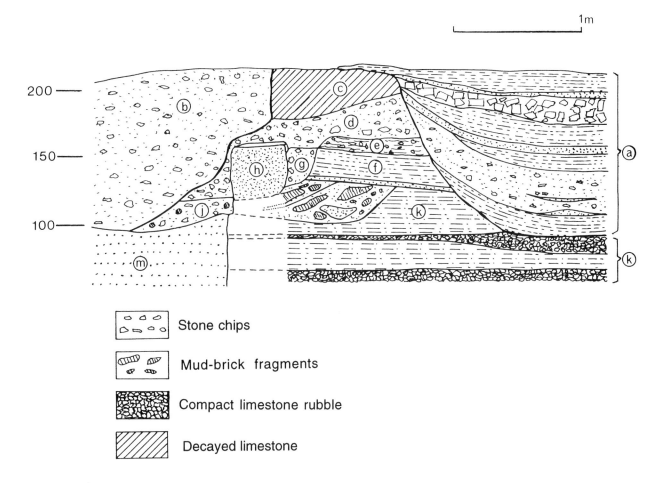

1m

Stone chips

Mud-brick fragments

Compact limestone rubble

Decayed limestone

a   Deep pit from surface, filled with successive layers of wind-laid mud, sand,
    collapsed mud brick, fill with stone chips and sherds
b   Pit above sand-filled foundation trench, refilled with loose rubble and sandy
    fill
c   Dense chips of fine limestone
d-e Stone rubble from separate destruction phases of buildings
f   Wind-laid mud
g   Trench for block (h), refilled with stone chips
h   Limestone block with red plaster on top (portion below block not dug)
j   Mud with broken bricks and stone chips
k   Pre-temple ground, consisting of alternate bands of dark mud and compact
    limestone rubble
m   Sand in the NW foundation trench for the colonnade, cut into (k)

Profile between points A and B on the plan on the preceding plate

PLATE 16

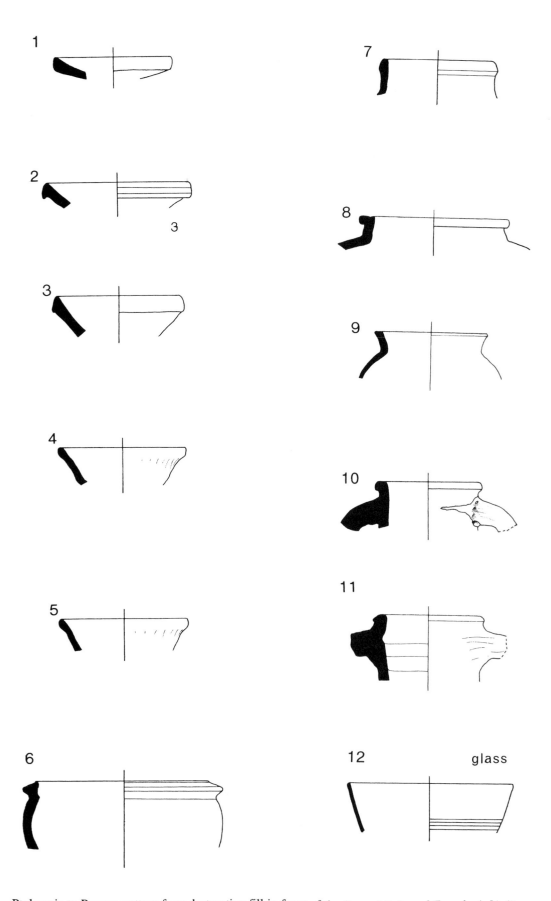

Ptolemaic to Roman pottery from destruction fill in front of the Second Pylon of Temple A [1:4]

PLATE 17

(b) Excavation in front of the Second Pylon of Temple A, showing the stone masonry to the south-east of the axis

(a) Excavation in front of the Second Pylon of Temple A, looking south-east across the axis

PLATE 18

(a) Excavation in front of the Second Pylon of Temple A, showing the stone masonry to the south-east of the axis. The curve in the edge of the foundation can be seen below

(b) The front end of the south-eastern sand-filled trench of the colonnade foundation in Area RP1, showing part of the sand bed and original ground, with a standing section of later deposits (drawn in plate 19)

PLATE 19

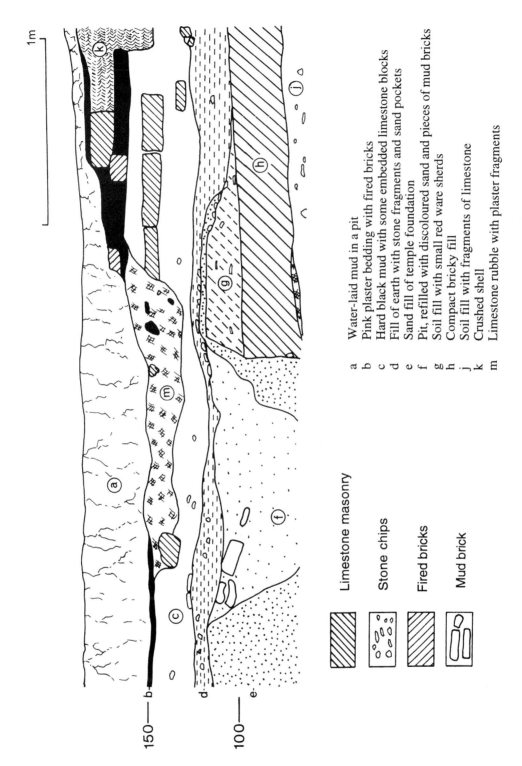

Limestone masonry

Stone chips

Fired bricks

Mud brick

a   Water-laid mud in a pit
b   Pink plaster bedding with fired bricks
c   Hard black mud with some embedded limestone blocks
d   Fill of earth with stone fragments and sand pockets
e   Sand fill of temple foundation
f   Pit, refilled with discoloured sand and pieces of mud bricks
g   Soil fill with small red ware sherds
h   Compact bricky fill
j   Soil fill with fragments of limestone
k   Crushed shell
m   Limestone rubble with plaster fragments

Profile in area RP1, through the later fill over the remains of the foundation of the First Pylon

PLATE 20

(a) Brick ring in the rear corner of the First Pylon foundation in area RP1

(b) Brick ring in the rear corner of the First Pylon foundation in area RP2

PLATE 21

(a) Remains of the ancient baulk in E12

(b) Marked axis-stone set in the front part of the foundation of Temple A

PLATE 22

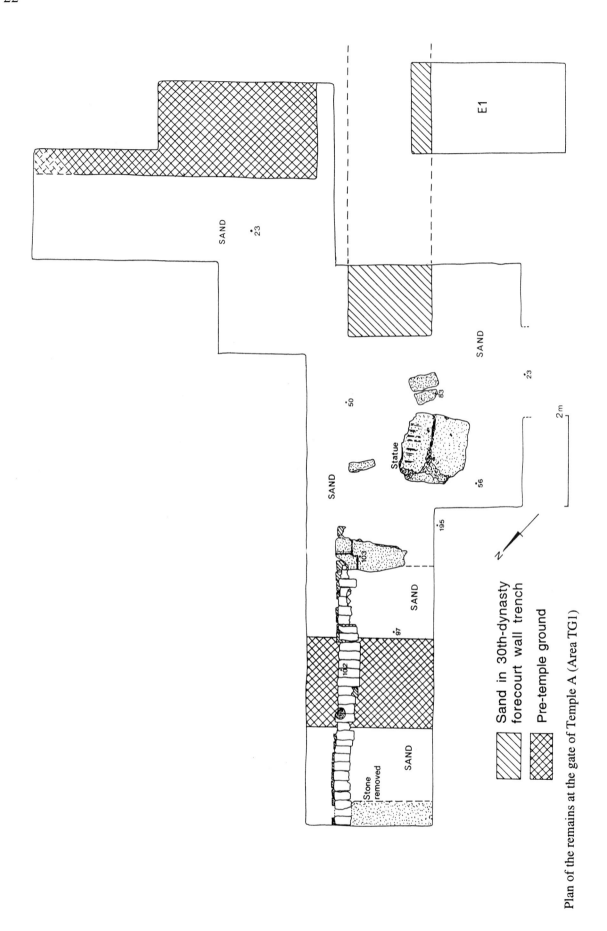

Plan of the remains at the gate of Temple A (Area TG1)

PLATE 23

(a) Brick sill at the front gate of Temple A, from the north west

(b) Brick sill at the front gate of Temple A, from the north east

PLATE 24

(a) Statue-group of Ramesses II as found in Trench TG1

(b) Limestone doorsill fragment from redeposited fill in area RP2

PLATE 25

(a) Pre-temple ground at the edge of the sand-filled foundation in the south-east part of Trench TG1

(b) Pre-temple ground at the edge of the sand-filled foundation in Trench TG3

PLATE 26

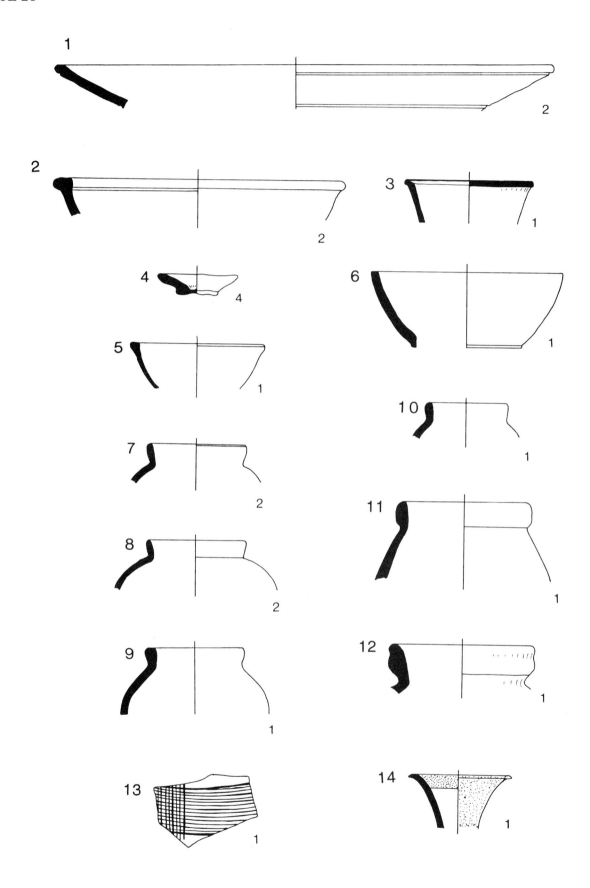

Pottery from the destruction-level above the sand-bed at the gate of Temple A, trench TG1
[Nos. 13-14 at 1:2, the rest 1:4; number of examples at lower right of figures]

PLATE 27

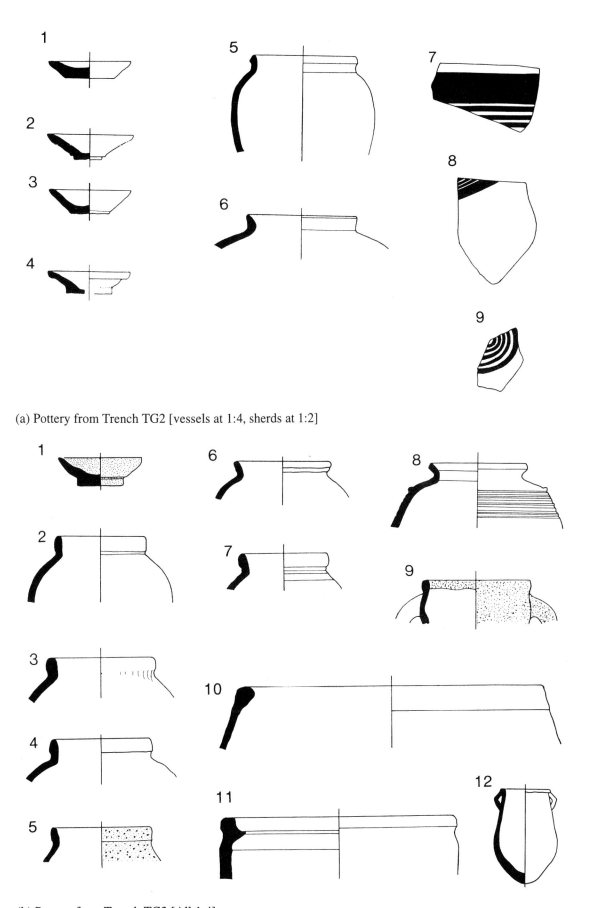

(a) Pottery from Trench TG2 [vessels at 1:4, sherds at 1:2]

(b) Pottery from Trench TG3 [All 1:4]

PLATE 28

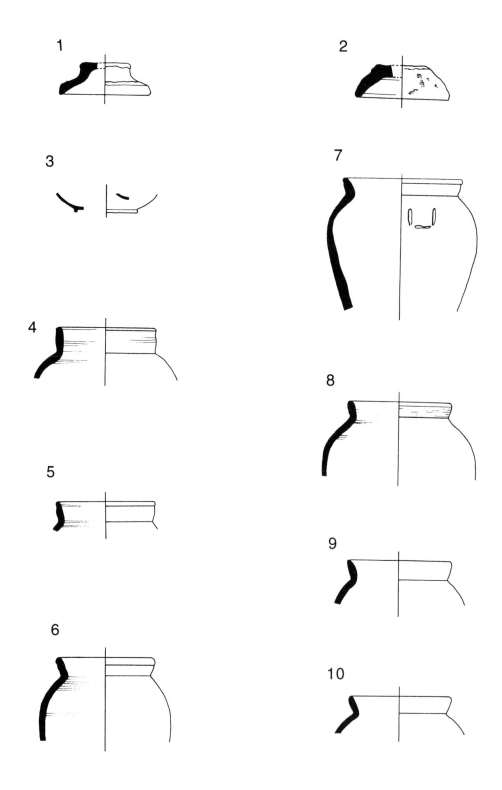

Pottery from Trench TG5 [All 1:4]

PLATE 29

(a) Basalt blocks found in the mud above the foundation sand at the south corner of Temple A

(b) Detail of the inscription on the large block shown in the foreground above

PLATE 30

(a) Ptolemaic pottery in the surface fill in Trench E1

(b) Pottery jar in the south-west section of Trench E2

PLATE 31

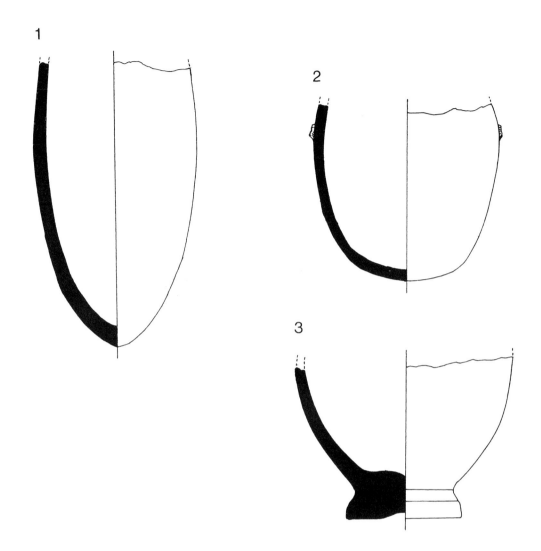

(a) Ptolemaic pottery from the surface level in Trenches E1 (nos. 1-2) and E2 (no.3) [All 1:4]

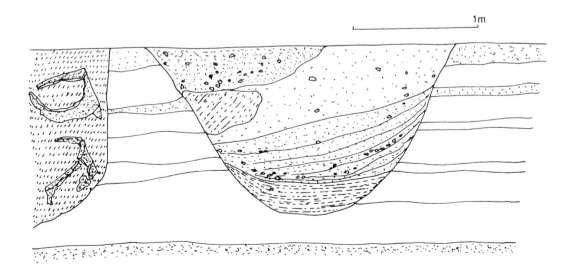

1m

(b) South-east profile of Trench E2 showing the deep Ptolemaic pits and oven fragments

PLATE 32

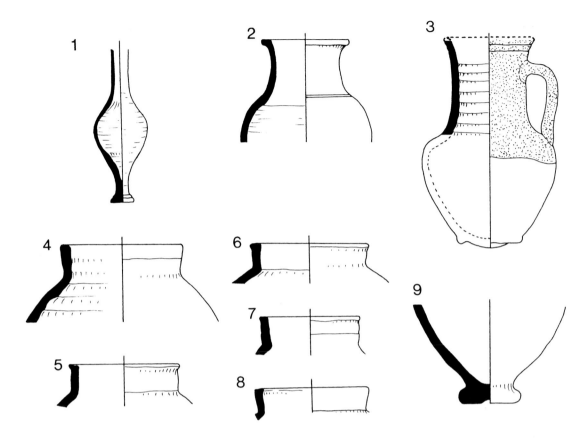

(a) Ptolemaic pottery from the surface level in the forecourt of Temple A: no. 1 from Trench E1; 2-3 from Trench E2; 4-9 from Trench E3 [All 1:4]

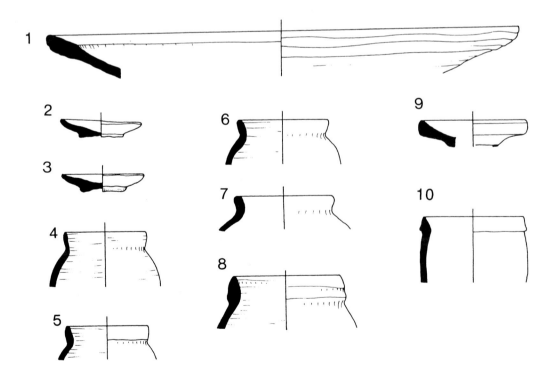

(b) Forms of Persian-period pottery from the fill above the sand-bed of the First Pylon: examples of nos. 1-8 from Trenches E1, E2 and W5; 9-10 from Trench W2 [All 1:4]

PLATE 33

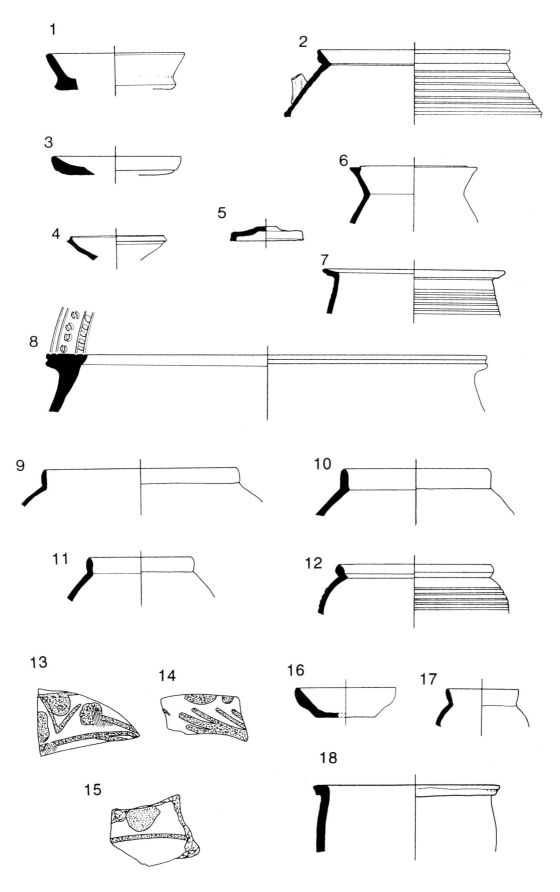

Ptolemaic pottery from the fill above the sand-bed of the First Pylon: nos. 1-2 from W3, 3-15 from RP1 and 16-18 from E12 [pots 1:4, sherds 1:2]

PLATE 34

(a) Remains of the pottery kiln in Trench E9

(b) The kiln in E9 from the south west, with the foundation sand of the First Pylon below

PLATE 35

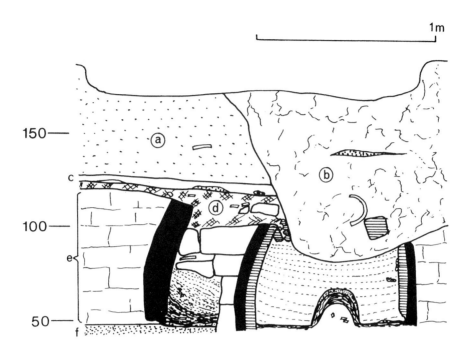

a   Compact soil fill with a few burned layers and a large red ware sherd
b   Deep mud-filled pit cut from surface into top of smaller kiln, with a sand stripe and two large sherds
c   Black burned layer with small pockets of sand at its base
d   Gritty ash fill above tops of destroyed kilns
e   Mud brick structure of two successive kilns
f   Earth fill below the earlier kiln

Profile of the renewed kiln in the north-west side of Trench E9

PLATE 36

(b)The kiln in Trench E8

(a) Debris in the kiln in Trench E8

PLATE 37

(a) Pottery jar and fragments of kiln lining in the top of a kiln between E8 and E7 (the right-hand kiln on the profile drawing in the following plate)

(b) One of the kilns in the profile between E8 and E7

PLATE 38

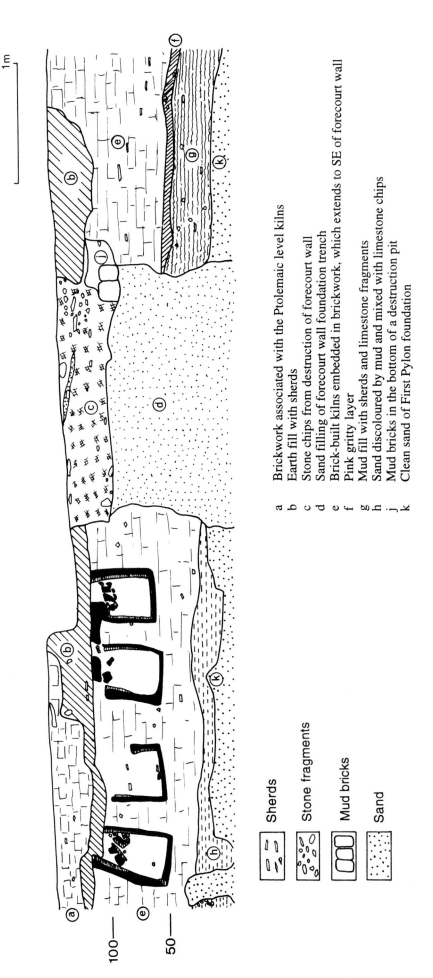

a Brickwork associated with the Ptolemaic level kilns
b Earth fill with sherds
c Stone chips from destruction of forecourt wall
d Sand filling of forecourt wall foundation trench
e Brick-built kilns embedded in brickwork, which extends to SE of forecourt wall
f Pink gritty layer
g Mud fill with sherds and limestone fragments
h Sand discoloured by mud and mixed with limestone chips
j Mud bricks in the bottom of a destruction pit
k Clean sand of First Pylon foundation

Sherds

Stone fragments

Mud bricks

Sand

Profile showing the Persian period kilns over the site of the First Pylon of Temple A

PLATE 39

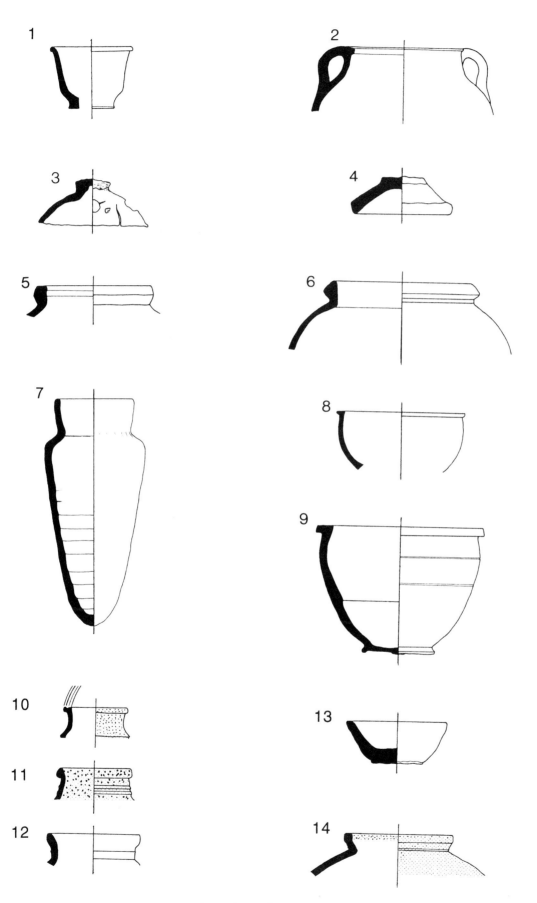

Pottery from the fill over the site of the First Pylon: nos. 1-2 from Trench E11, 3 from E10, 4-6 from E9 7-9 from E8, and 10-14 from E7 [all 1:4]

PLATE 40

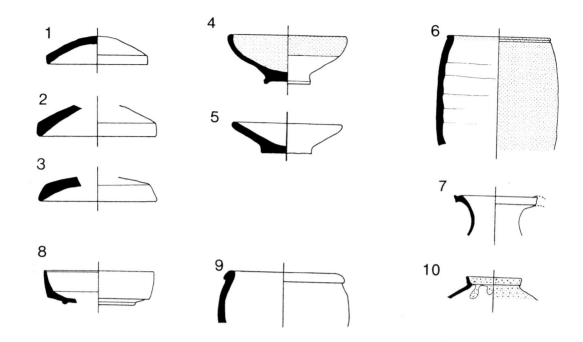

(a) Pottery from Trench E5 [All 1:4]

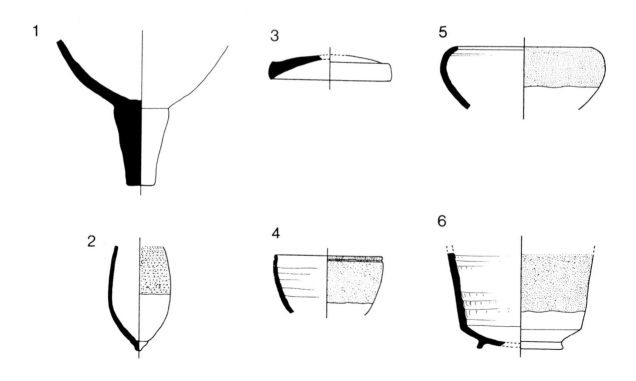

(b) Pottery from destruction fill above the rear corner of the south-east wing of the First Pylon (Trench E6): nos. 1-4 from pit in east corner; 5-6 from Ptolemaic pit in south corner [All 1:4]

PLATE 41

(a) Ptolemaic Kiln 1 and limestone pavement from the south west

(b) Limestone pavement in the ruins of the north corner of Building N1,
from the north east

PLATE 42

(a) The brick-built lime kiln in Trench W5

(b) The lime kiln in Trench W5 from above

PLATE 43

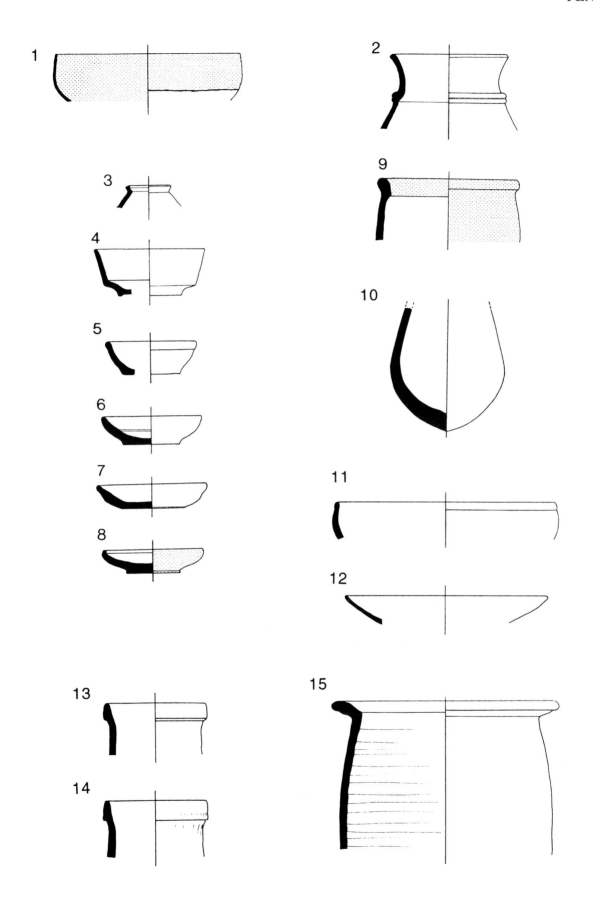

Pottery from above and around the foundation of the north-west wing of the First Pylon: nos. 1-2 from Trench W6, 3-8 from W8 and 9-15 from W9 [1:4 except no. 2 at 1:2]

PLATE 44

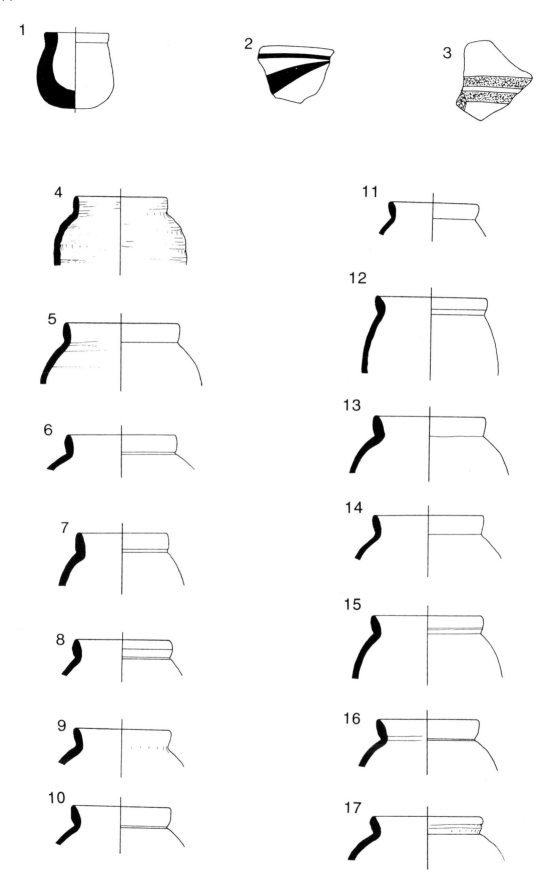

Pottery from the dump over the rear angle of the north-west wing of the First Pylon (Trench W7) [nos. 1-3 at 1:2, the rest at 1:4]

PLATE 45

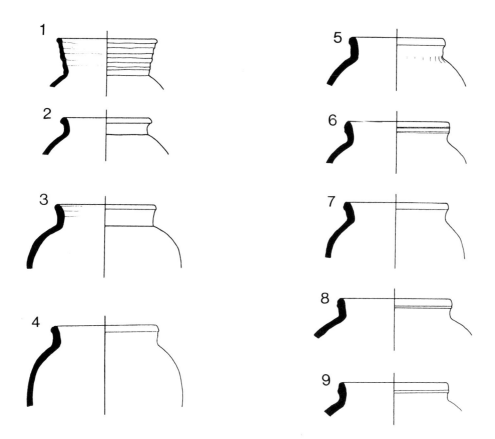

(a) Pottery from the dump over the rear angle of the north-west wing of the First Pylon (Trench W7) [1:4]

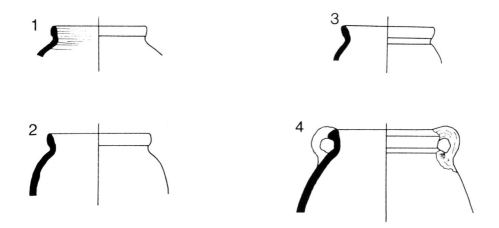

(b) Pottery from the deeper layers of the dump over the rear angle of the north-west wing of the First Pylon (Trench W7) [1:4]

PLATE 46

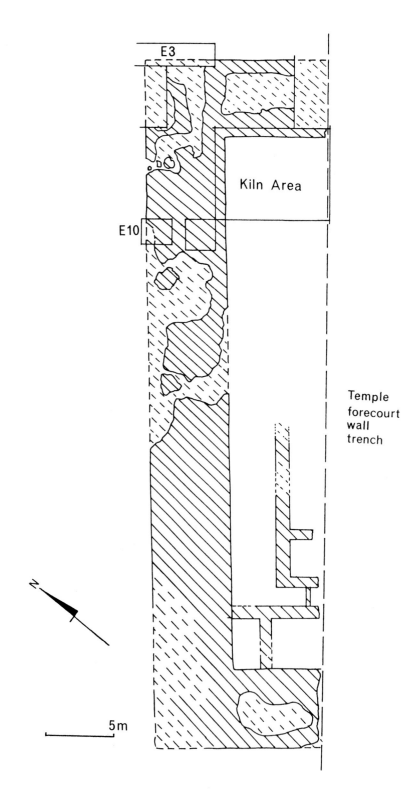

E3

Kiln Area

E10

Temple
forecourt
wall
trench

N

5m

Key plan of Building N1

PLATE 47

(a) Surface remains above the south-west end of Building N1

(b) The limestone olive-press and broken granite millstone as found at the south-west end of Building N1

PLATE 48

(a) View of the remains of Building N1 from the south west

(b) Detail of the floor of Room 3 in Building N1

PLATE 49

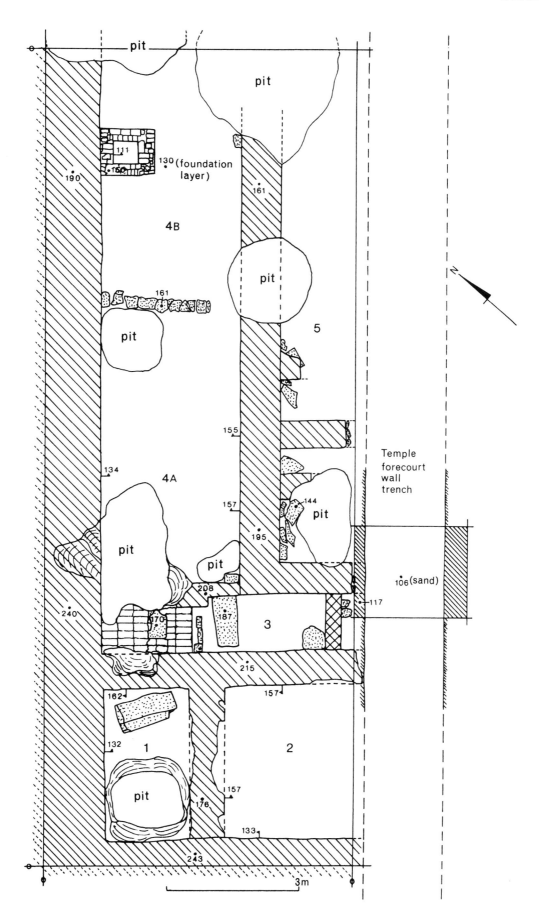

Plan of the south-west part of Building N1

PLATE 50

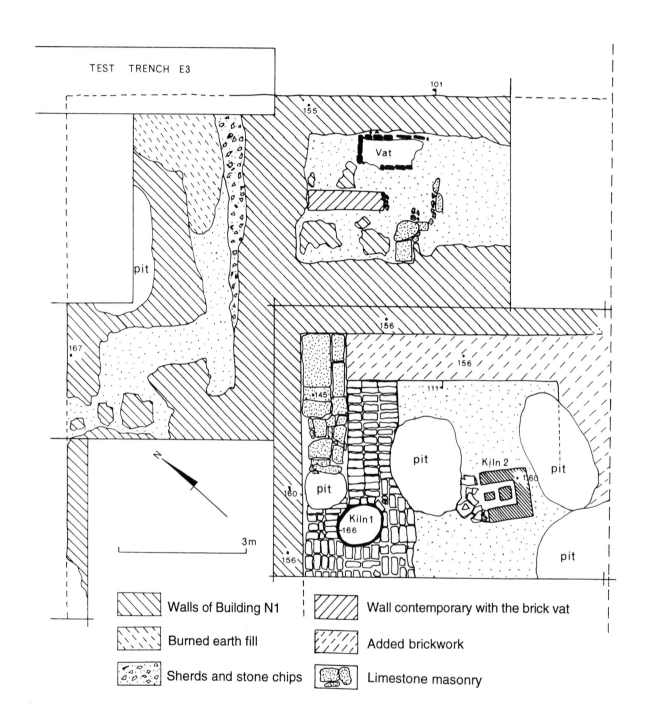

TEST TRENCH E3

Vat

pit

Kiln 2

pit

pit

pit

Kiln 1
166

pit

3m

	Walls of Building N1			Wall contemporary with the brick vat
	Burned earth fill			Added brickwork
	Sherds and stone chips			Limestone masonry

Plan of the north-east part of Building N1 and the overlying kilns

PLATE 51

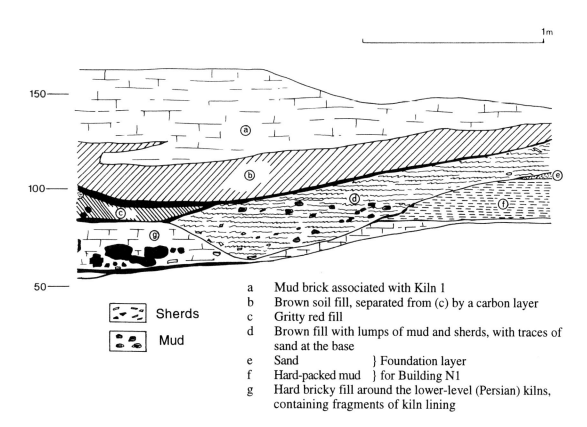

a   Mud brick associated with Kiln 1
b   Brown soil fill, separated from (c) by a carbon layer
c   Gritty red fill
d   Brown fill with lumps of mud and sherds, with traces of
    sand at the base
e   Sand   } Foundation layer
f   Hard-packed mud   } for Building N1
g   Hard bricky fill around the lower-level (Persian) kilns,
    containing fragments of kiln lining

(a) Profile below the Ptolemaic period kilns above the site of the First Pylon of Temple A

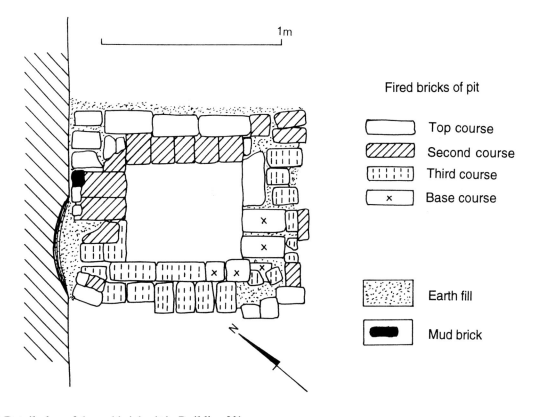

(b) Detail plan of the red brick pit in Building N1

PLATE 52

(a) View from the forecourt wall foundation to Room 3 of Building N1. The sand filling of the forecourt wall trench is visible in the foreground

(b) The square brick-lined pit through Room 4B of Building N1, showing sand from the foundation layer of the structure

PLATE 53

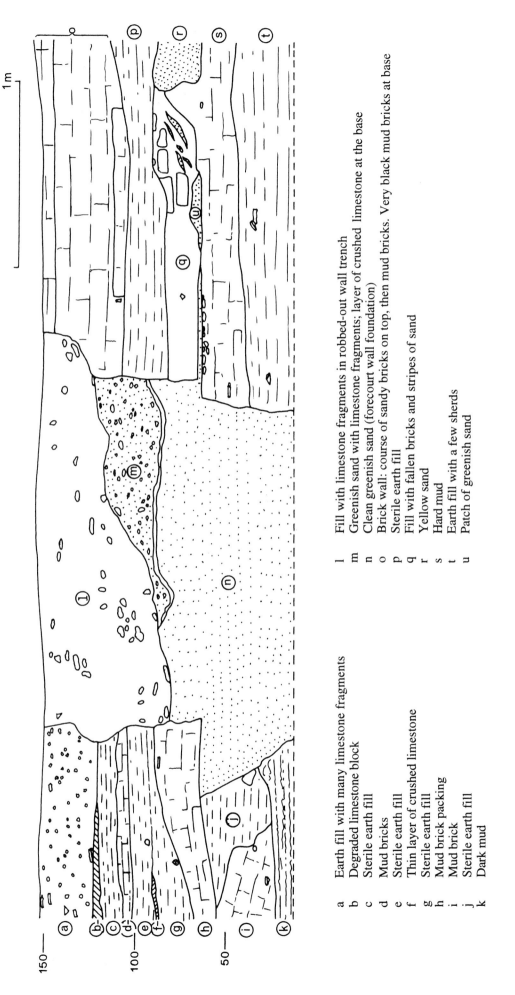

a   Earth fill with many limestone fragments
b   Degraded limestone block
c   Sterile earth fill
d   Mud bricks
e   Sterile earth fill
f   Thin layer of crushed limestone
g   Sterile earth fill
h   Mud brick packing
i   Mud brick
j   Sterile earth fill
k   Dark mud

l   Fill with limestone fragments in robbed-out wall trench
m   Greenish sand with limestone fragments; layer of crushed limestone at the base
n   Clean greenish sand (forecourt wall foundation)
o   Brick wall: course of sandy bricks on top, then mud bricks. Very black mud bricks at base
p   Sterile earth fill
q   Fill with fallen bricks and stripes of sand
r   Yellow sand
s   Hard mud
t   Earth fill with a few sherds
u   Patch of greenish sand

Profile in E4 across the foundation of the Thirtieth-dynasty forecourt wall

PLATE 54

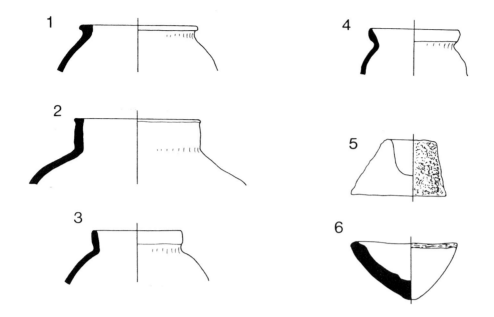

(a) Pottery from Trench E4 [Nos. 5-6 at 1:2, the rest 1:4]

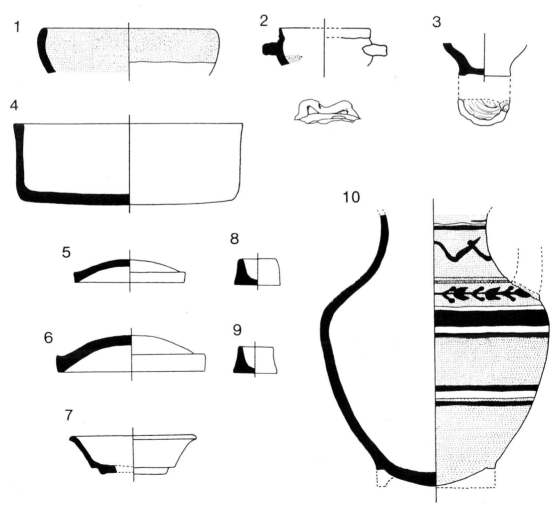

(b) Pottery from the fill over Building N1 [Nos. 1-7, 10 at 1:4; 8-9 at 1:2]

PLATE 55

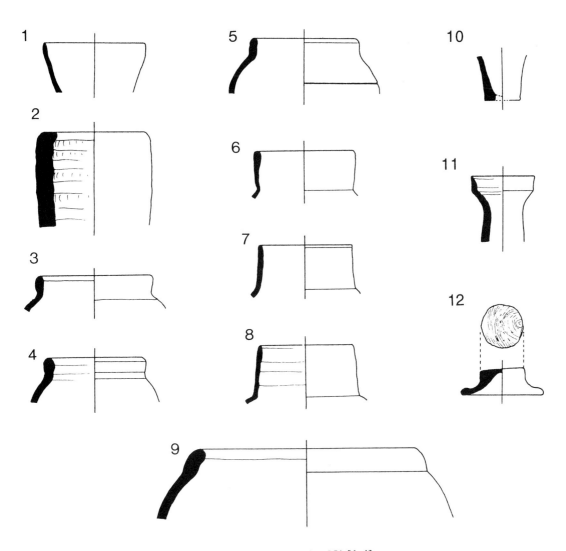

(a) Pottery from the level below chamber 4A of Building N1 [1:4]

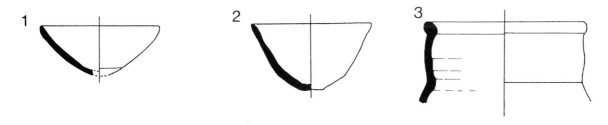

(b) Pottery from the level below chamber 4B of Building N1, near the red-brick pit [1:4]

(c) Pottery from below Building N1 in the kiln area [1:4]

PLATE 56

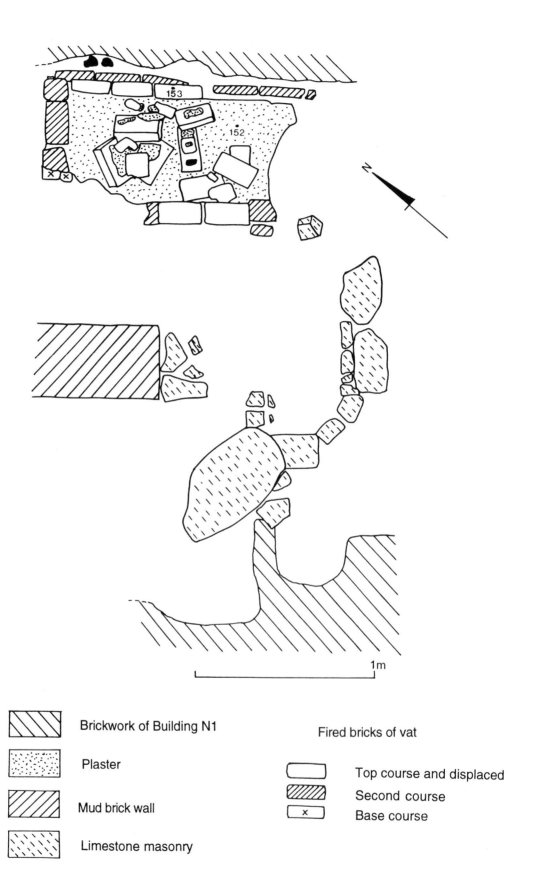

Brickwork of Building N1

Plaster

Mud brick wall

Limestone masonry

Fired bricks of vat

Top course and displaced

Second course

x Base course

Detail plan of a fired-brick structure and vat in thickness of the north-east wall of Building N1

PLATE 57

(a) Remains of the fired-brick vat in the north-east wall of Building N1

(b) The excavation of Building N1 from the east

PLATE 58

(a) The excavation of Building N2, from the west

(b) Chamber 1 of Building N2 from the south east

PLATE 59

(a) The courtyard on the north-west side of Building N2. The forecourt wall of the temple was on the left

(b) The dump of material under the west corner of Chamber 1 in Building N2

PLATE 60

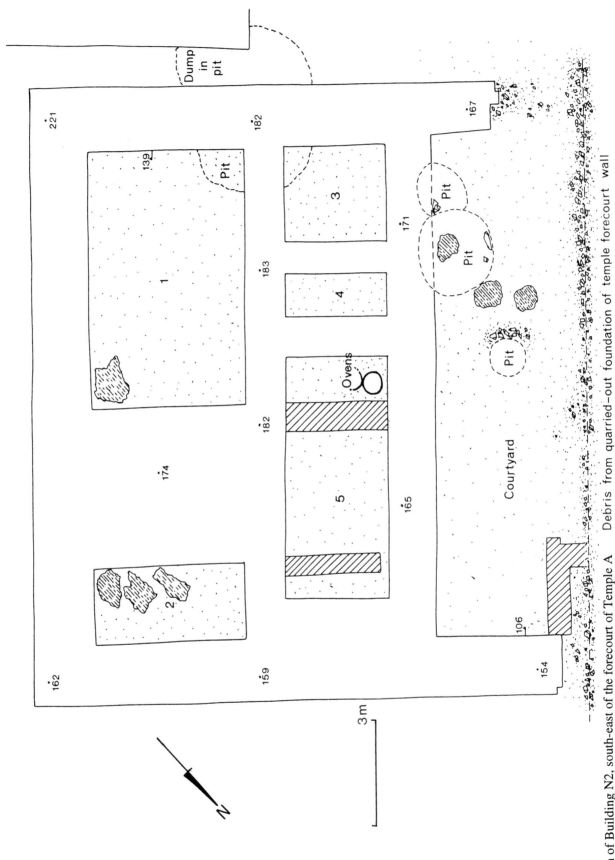

Plan of Building N2, south-east of the forecourt of Temple A   Debris from quarried-out foundation of temple forecourt wall

PLATE 61

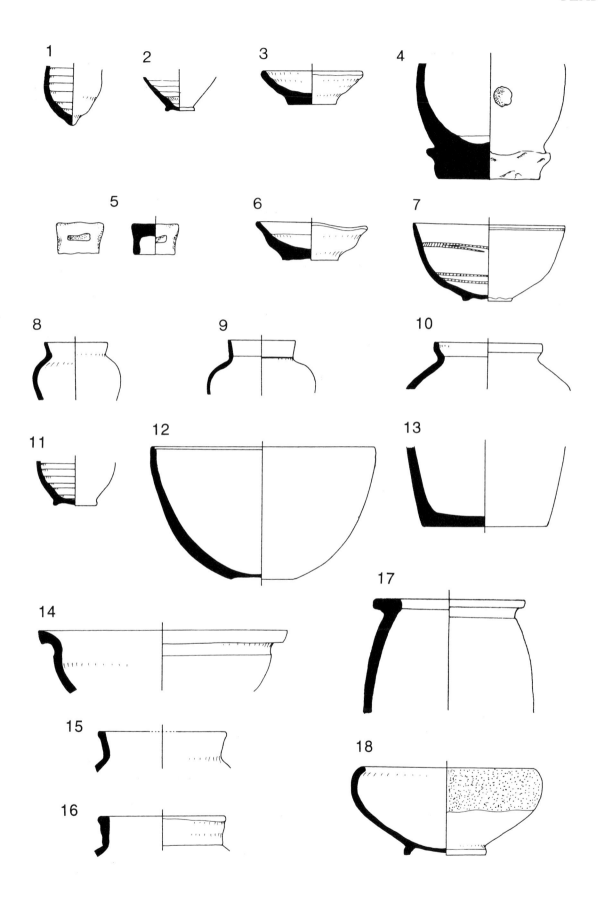

Pottery and faience from the foundation of Building N2: nos. 1-13 from Room 1 (5-13 from the SW dump), 14-16 from Room 2, 17 from Room 3 and 18 from Room 5 [Nos. 5, 12-13 and 17 at 1:2; the rest 1:4]

PLATE 62

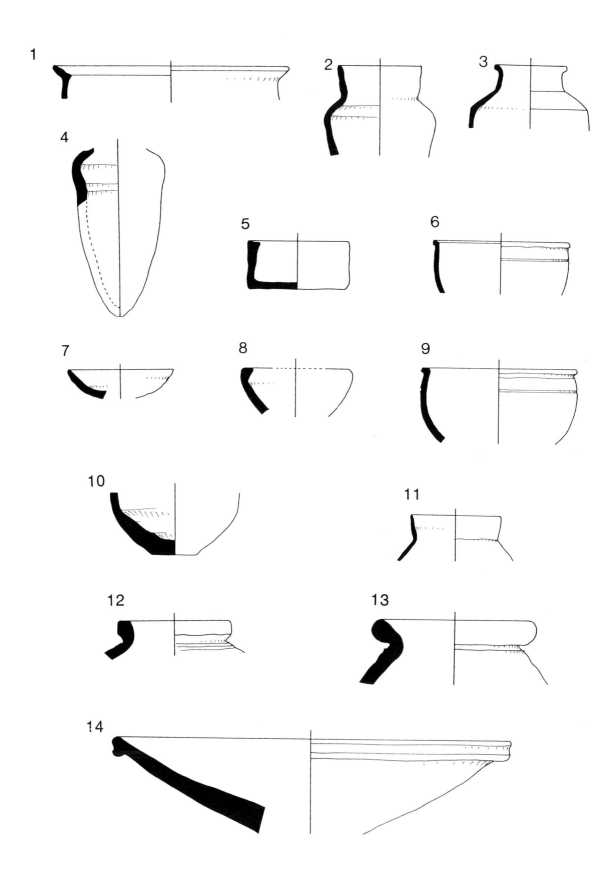

Pottery from the fill and dump between Buildings N2 and N3 [All 1:4]

PLATE 63

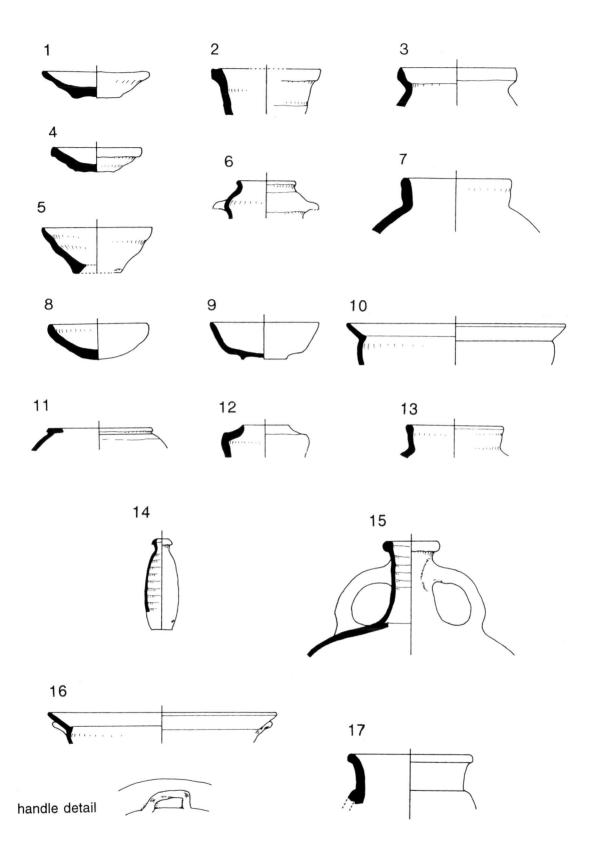

handle detail

Pottery and faience from the courtyard in Building N2: nos. 1-7 from general fill; 8-15 from pits along the wall; 16-17 near the door at the south west [All 1:4 except no. 17, which is at 1:2]

PLATE 64

(a) The partly-excavated gate in the north-west side of the Outer Enclosure, from the interior

(b) South-west jamb of the gate in the north-west side of the Outer Enclosure, from the east

(c) Brickwork of the south-west jamb of the gate in the north-west side of the Outer Enclosure, from the exterior

PLATE 65

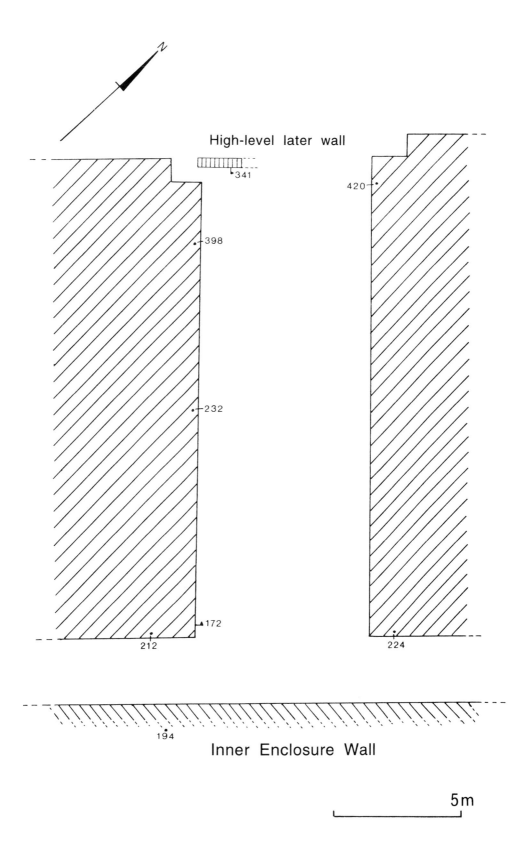

High-level later wall

341

420

398

232

172

212

224

194

Inner Enclosure Wall

5m

Plan of the north-west gate in the Outer Enclosure Wall

PLATE 66

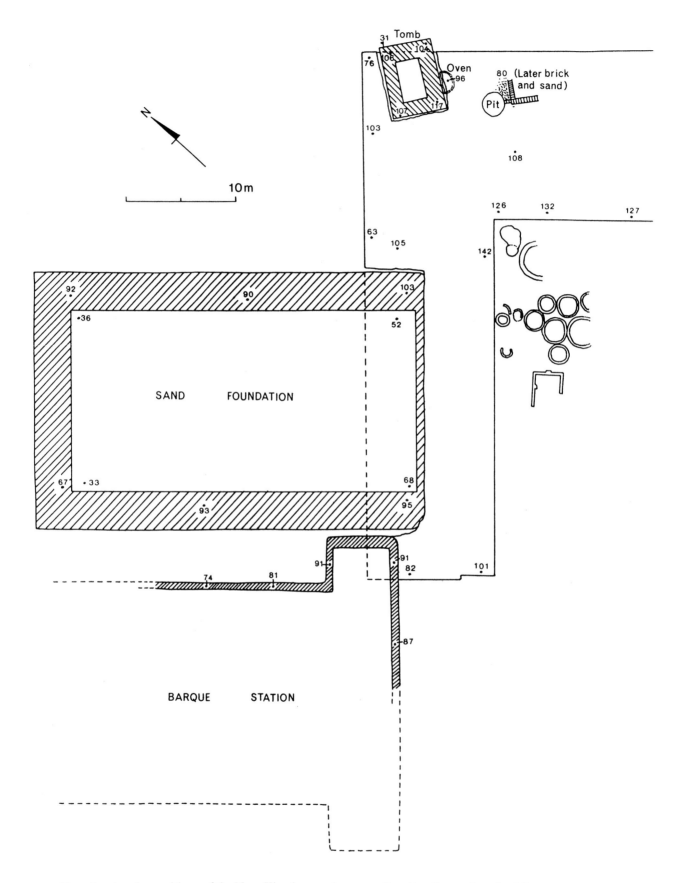

Plan showing the positions of the New-Kingdom enclosure wall, grain-silos and tomb of Iken, with the later barque-station foundations

PLATE 67

(a) Group of grain-silos inside the angle of the Ramesside enclosure wall

(b) Section through Silo 12 showing pottery in the fill

PLATE 68

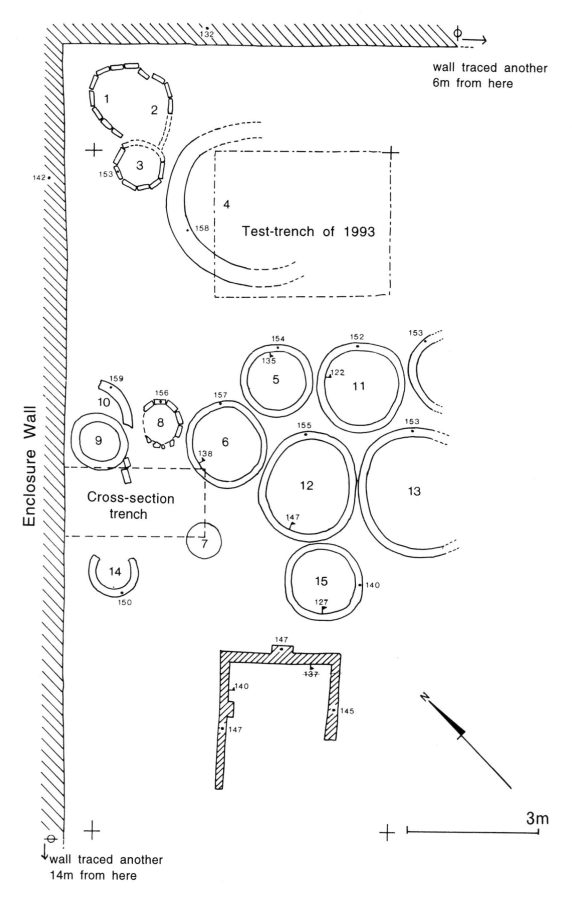

Plan of the area of grain-silos in the north corner of the New-Kingdom enclosure

PLATE 69

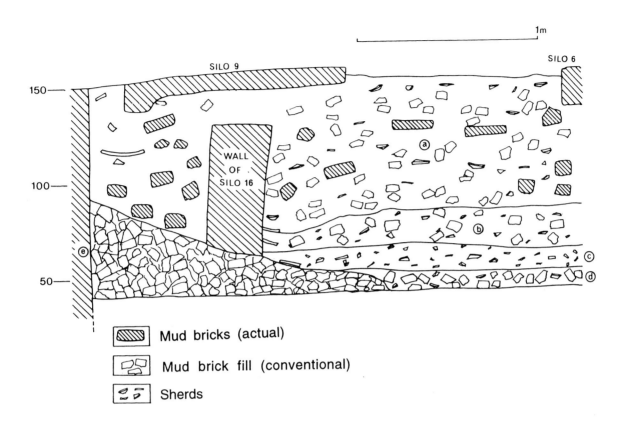

1m

SILO 9

SILO 6

150

WALL
OF
SILO 16

100

50

| Mud bricks (actual) |
| Mud brick fill (conventional) |
| Sherds |

a   Fill with sherds and broken mud bricks
b   Collapsed bricks from Silo 16
c   Fill with sherds
d   Fill with sherds and broken mud bricks
e   Collapsed bricks from enclosure wall

Section of the fill against the interior of the New-Kingdom enclosure wall in the area of the silos

PLATE 70

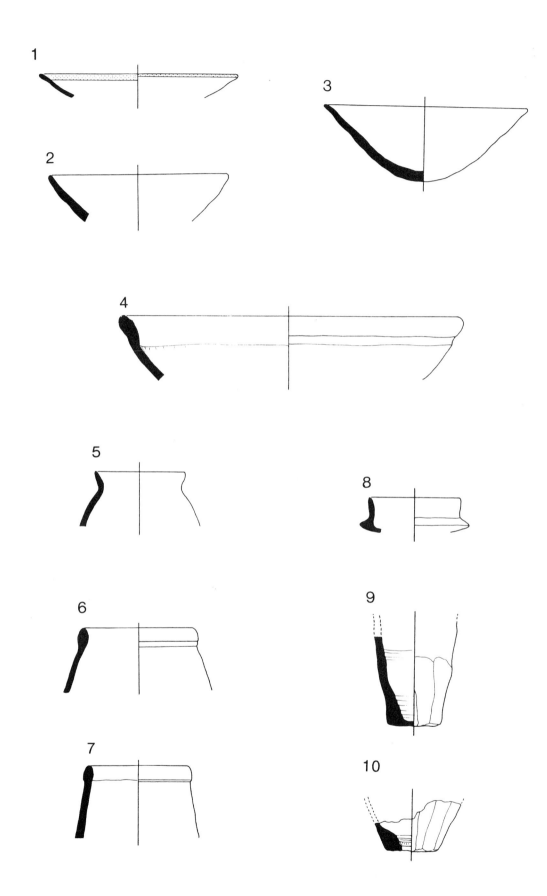

Pottery from an extension to Trench W9 in 1998 [All 1:4]

PLATE 71

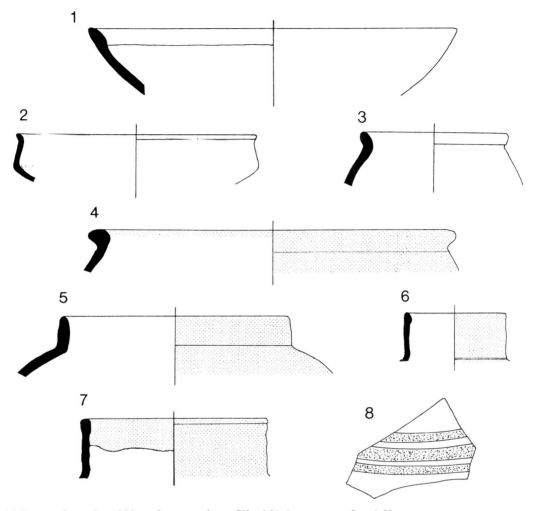

(a) Pottery from the 1993 surface test above Silo 4 [1:4 except no. 8 at 1:2]

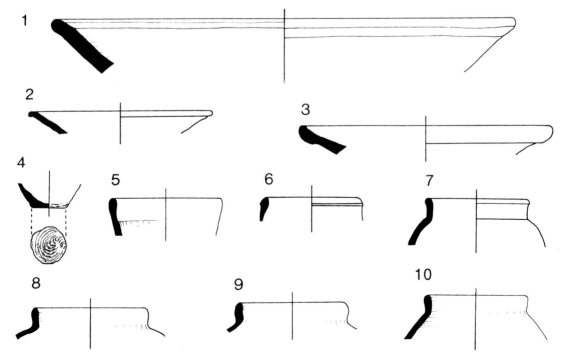

(b) Pottery from the pre-temple ground in Temple A: nos. 2-7 from in front of the Second Pylon; 1, 8-9 from Trench A2 and 10 from below the axis-stone in Trench A1 [All 1:4]

PLATE 72

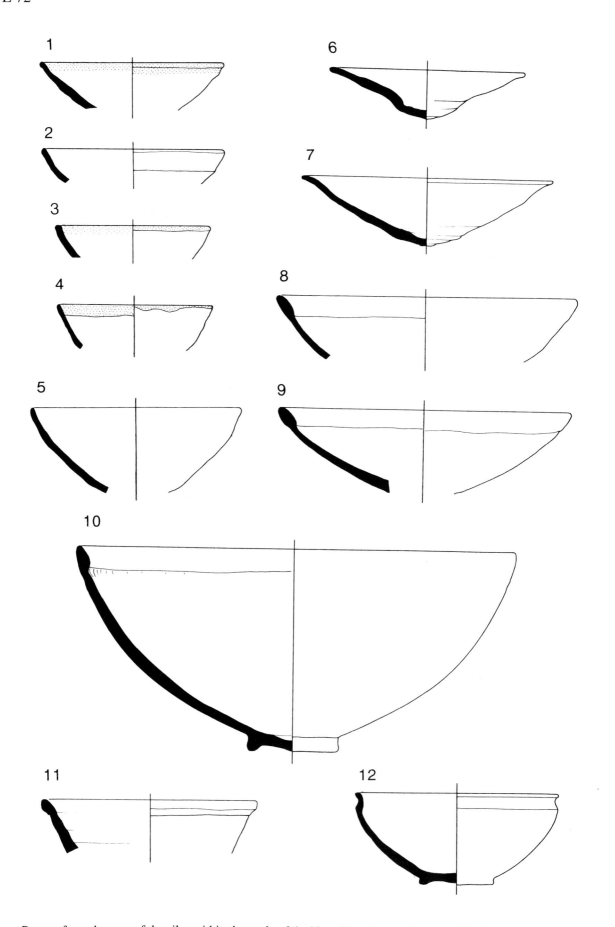

Pottery from the area of the silos within the angle of the New-Kingdom enclosure wall [All 1:4]

PLATE 73

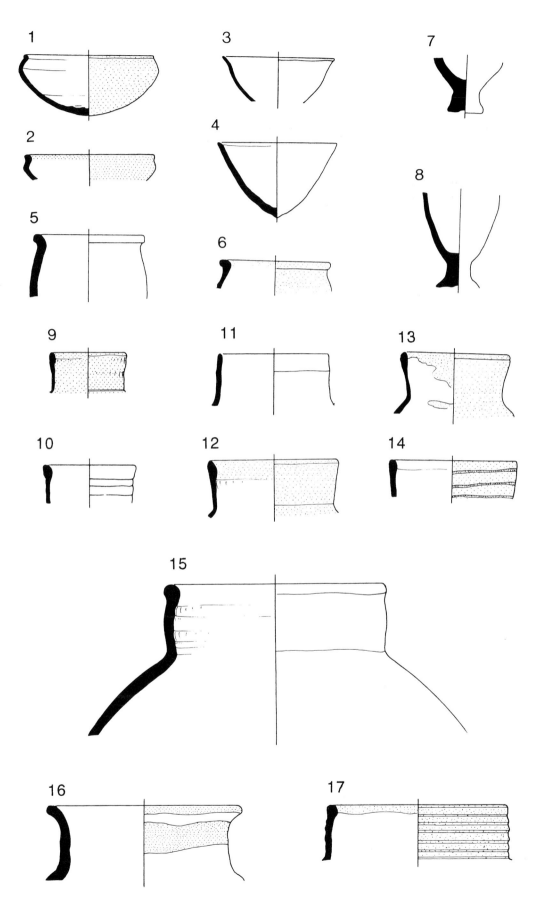

Pottery from the area of the silos within the angle of the New-Kingdom enclosure wall [All 1:4]

PLATE 74

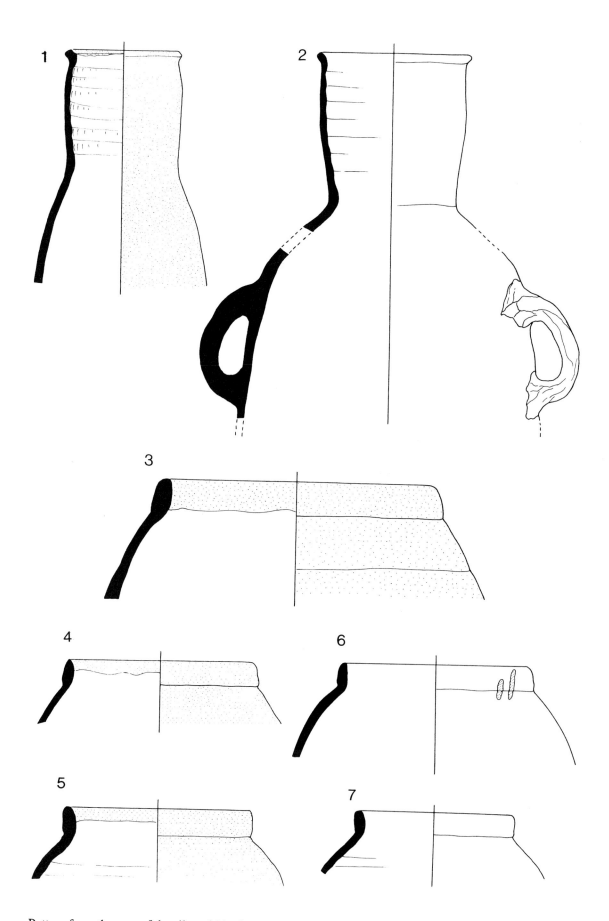

Pottery from the area of the silos within the angle of the New-Kingdom enclosure wall [All 1:4]

PLATE 75

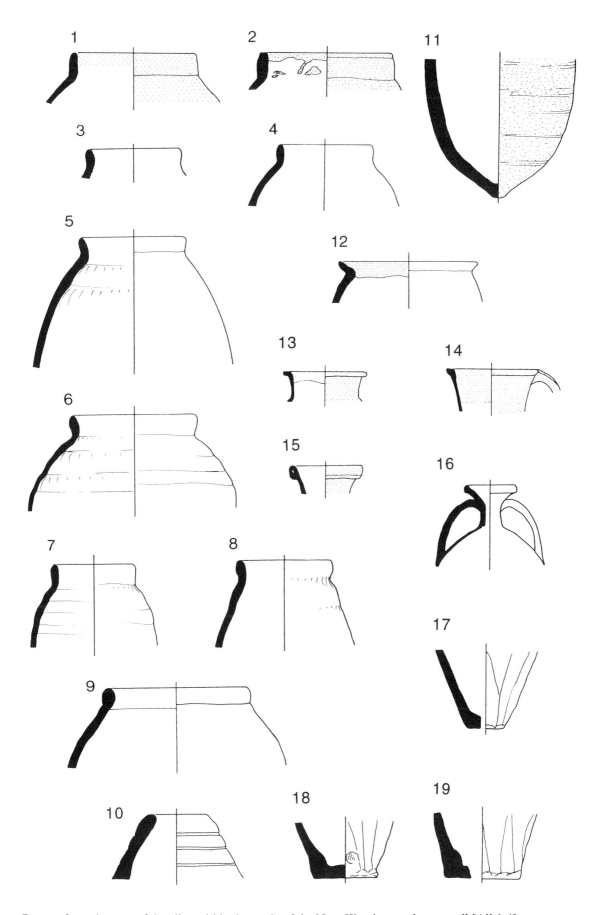

Pottery from the area of the silos within the angle of the New-Kingdom enclosure wall [All 1:4]

PLATE 76

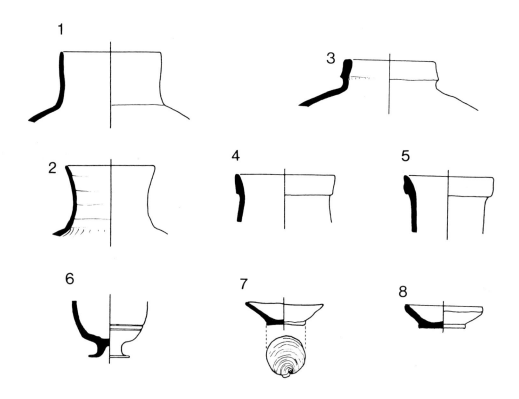

(a) Pottery from the fill above the north-east side of the New-Kingdom enclosure wall [All 1:4]

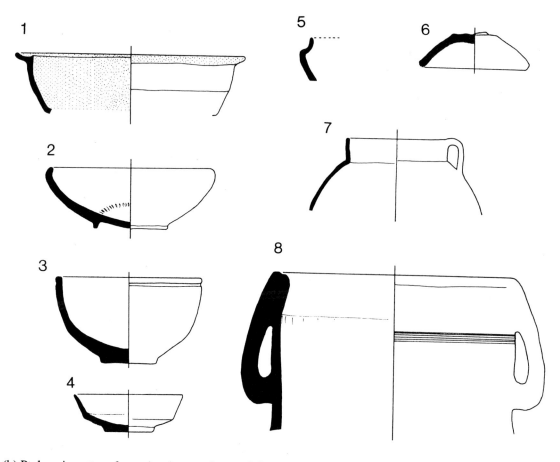

(b) Ptolemaic pottery from pits above and around the New-Kingdom enclosure wall [All 1:4]

PLATE 77

(a) Brick lining of the foundation of the Mammisi at the south-west corner

(b) The south-east corner of the foundation for the Mammisi. Some remains of the sand filling are visible

PLATE 78

(a) The tomb of Iken from the north

(b) The tomb of Iken from the south-west

PLATE 79

(a) The tomb of Iken from the east

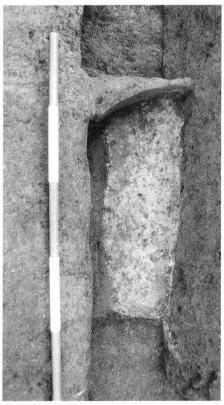

(b) Pottery oven cut by the wall of the tomb of Iken

(c) Side-view of shabtis and stone vases at the south end of the chamber

PLATE 80

(a) Group of shabtis at the south-west end of the tomb chamber, with calcite vases below

(b) The remains of the burial of Iken

PLATE 81

1

Right

Left

Catalogue: Stone objects

PLATE 82

1

 detail

Catalogue: Stone objects

PLATE 83

FRONT

Between the King and Amun   Between the King and Mut

REAR

LEFT SIDE   RIGHT SIDE

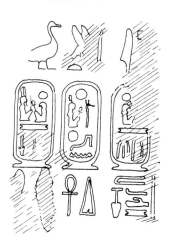

Texts from the triad of Ramesses II, Amun and Mut [1:10]

PLATE 84

2

7

3

Catalogue: Stone objects

PLATE 85

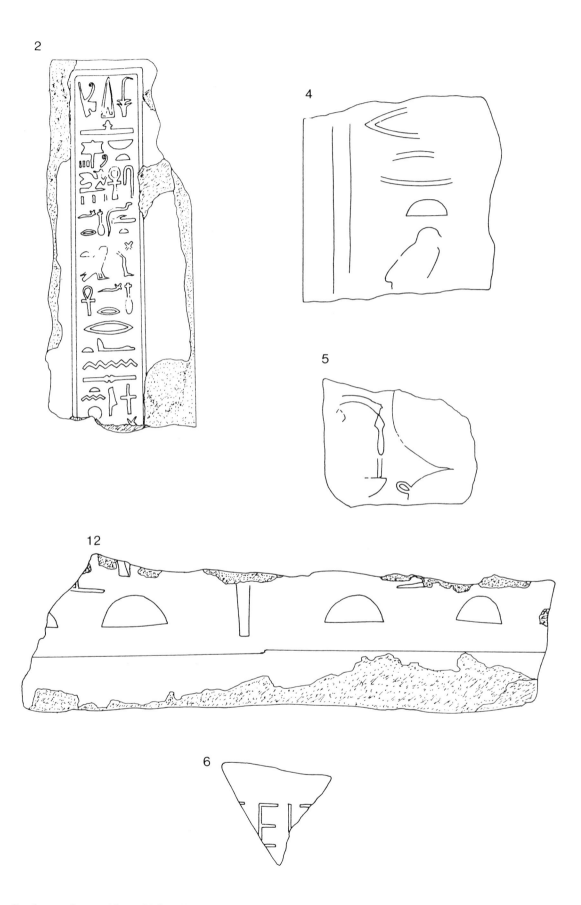

Catalogue: Stone objects [All 1:4]

PLATE 86

8

8

10

9, 10

9, 10

Catalogue: Stone objects

PLATE 87

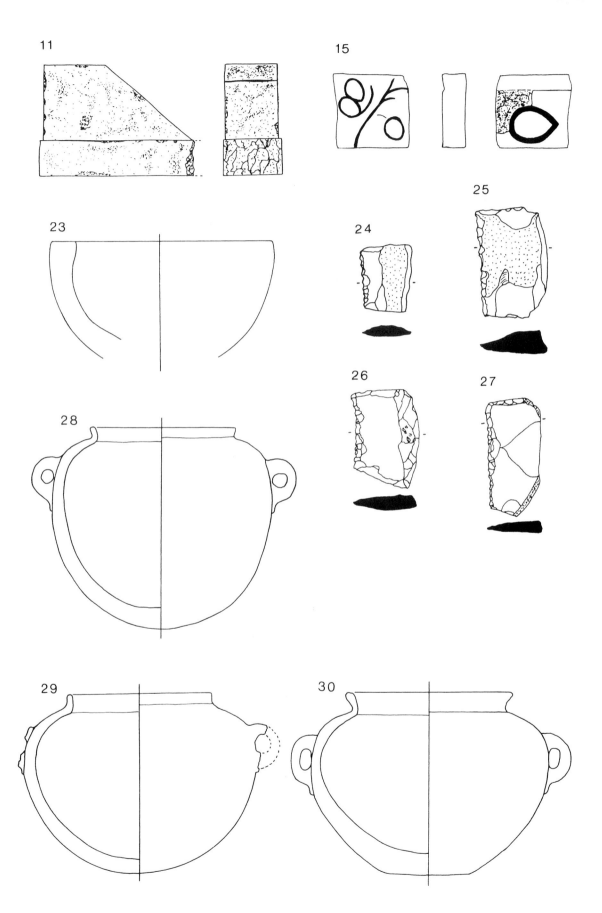

Catalogue: Stone objects [vessels at 1:4, other objects at 1:2]

PLATE 88

13

14

16

17

19

Catalogue: Stone objects

PLATE 89

22   20   21

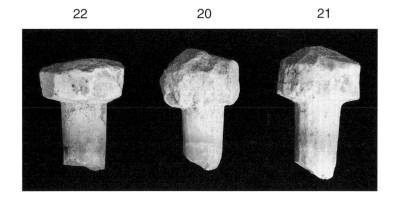

31

28   30

Catalogue: Stone objects

PLATE 90

35

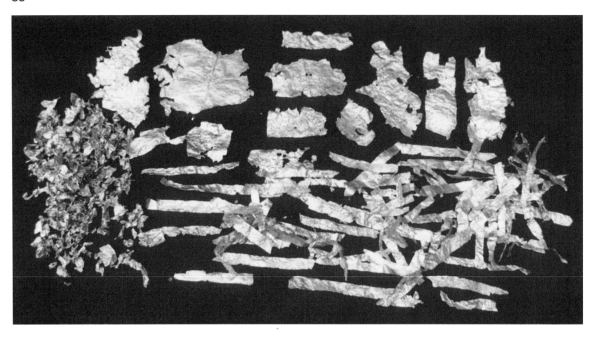

39

Catalogue: Metal and faience objects

PLATE 91

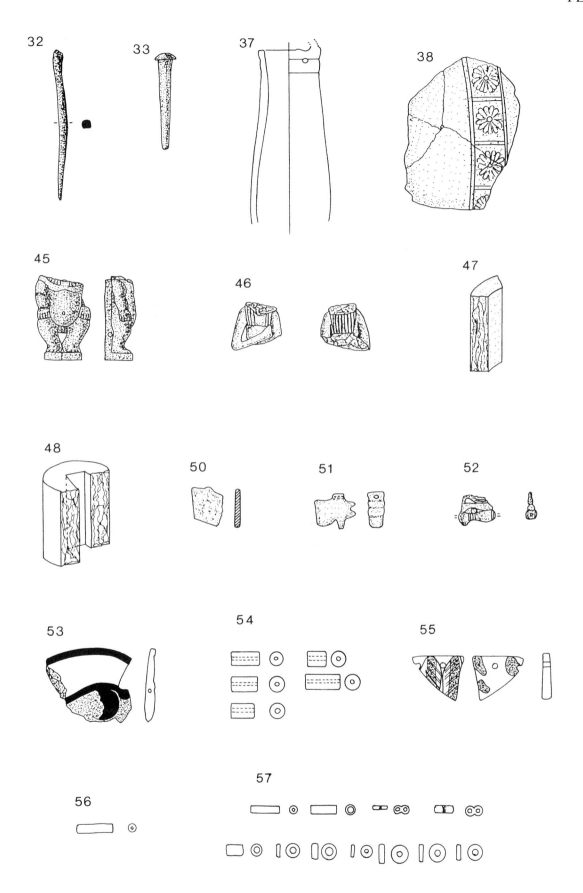

Catalogue: Metal, glass and faience objects [1:2 except 38, 51-52 at 2:3 and 57 at 1:1]

PLATE 92

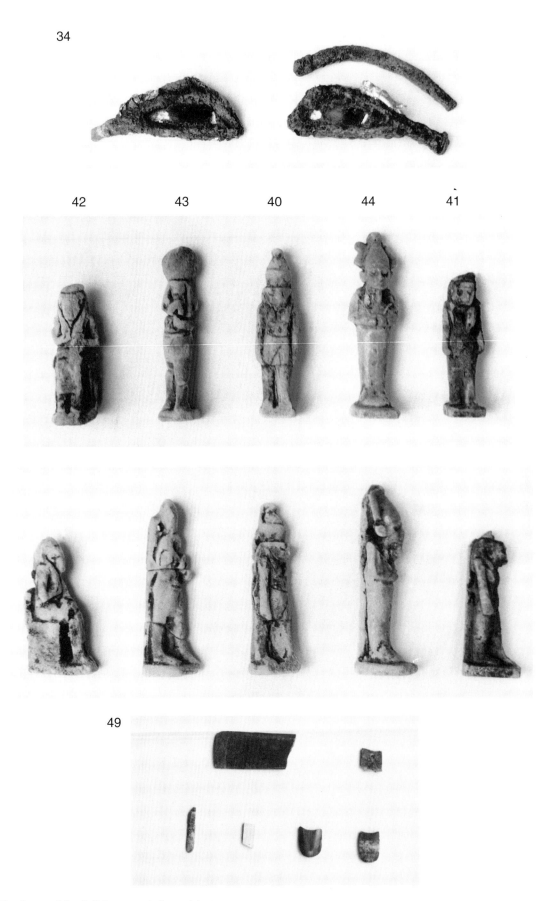

34

42   43   40   44   41

49

Catalogue: Metal, faience and glass objects

PLATE 93

58

Catalogue: Faience objects

PLATE 94

58

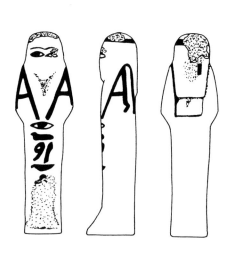

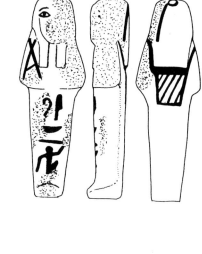

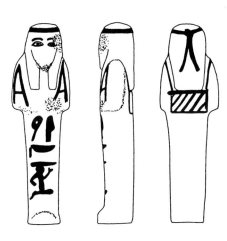

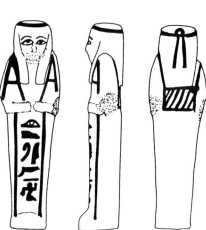

Catalogue: Examples of faience worker-shabtis of Iken [1:2]

PLATE 95

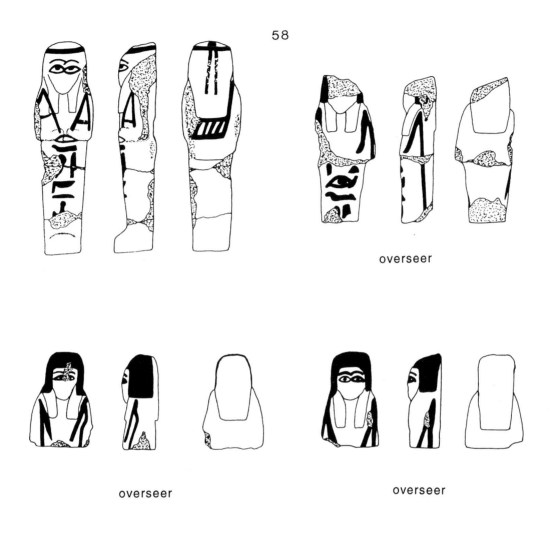

58

overseer

overseer

overseer

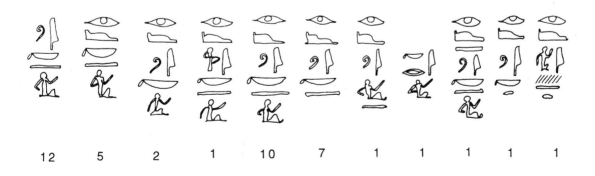

| 12 | 5 | 2 | 1 | 10 | 7 | 1 | 1 | 1 | 1 | 1 |

Catalogue: Examples of faience worker- and overseer-shabtis of Iken [1:2] and variants of shabti inscriptions with numbers of confirmed instances below

PLATE 96

Catalogue: Pottery objects

PLATE 97

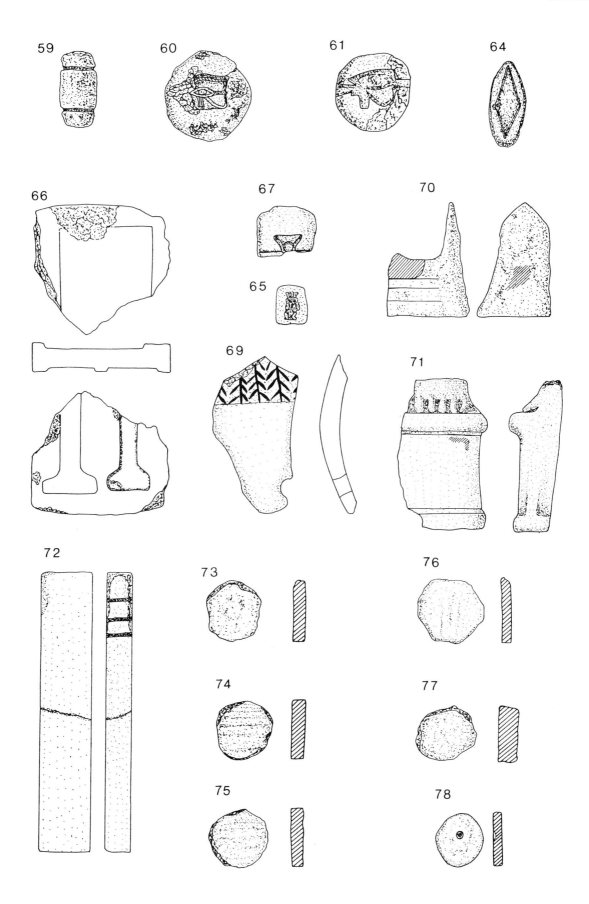

Catalogue: Pottery objects [All 1:2]

PLATE 98

81-92

96

97

98

Catalogue: Pottery objects

PLATE 99

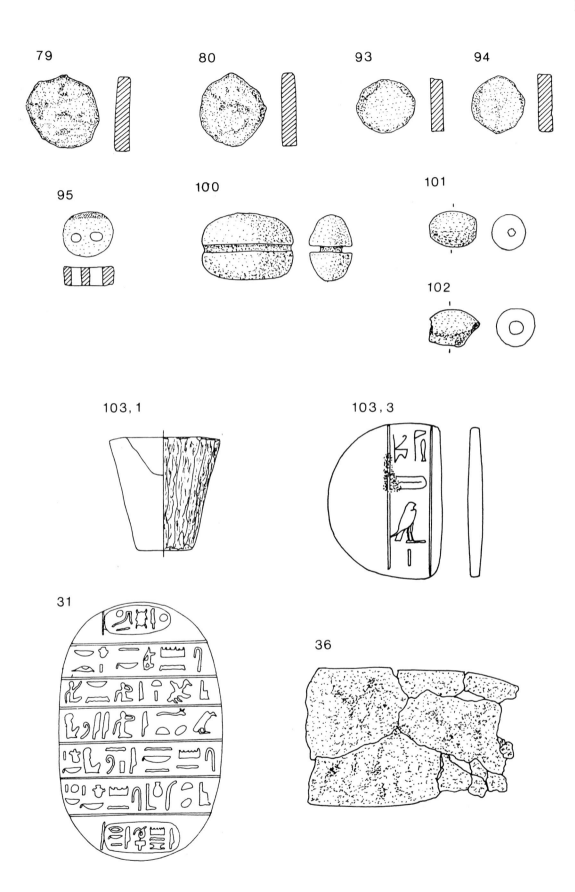

Catalogue: Pottery and miscellaneous objects [103 at 1:1, the rest at 1:2]

PLATE 100

104 (plaques and materials)

104 (pottery)

Catalogue: Foundation deposits

PLATE 101

105, 8 (cartouche)

106, 5 (cartouches)

Front

Back

105 (pottery)

Catalogue: Foundation deposits

PLATE 102

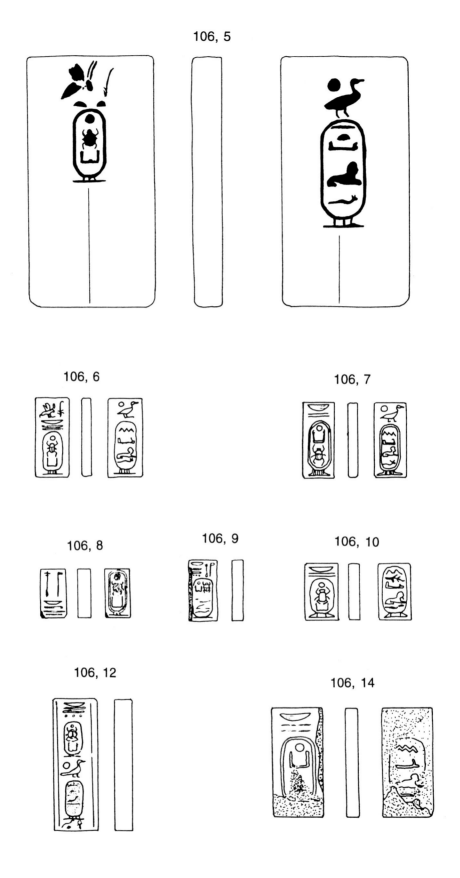

Inscribed plaques from the foundation deposit of Nekhtnebef in the south corner of Temple A [All 1:1]

PLATE 103

1

2

3

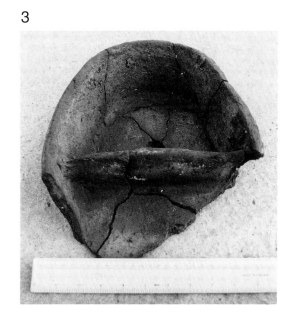

Miscellaneous pottery

PLATE 104

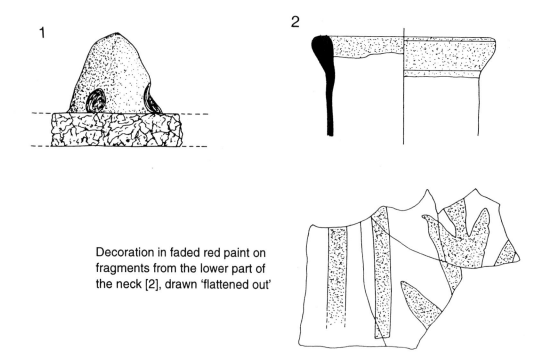

Decoration in faded red paint on fragments from the lower part of the neck [2], drawn 'flattened out'

(a) Miscellaneous ceramics [No. 1 at 1:4, 2 at 1:2]

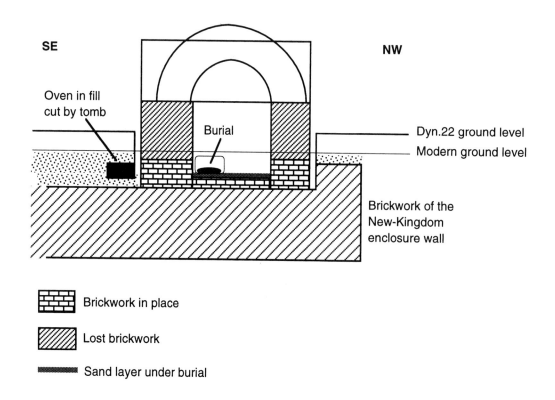

(b) Reconstructed section through the tomb of Iken, looking south-west [1:100]

PLATE 105

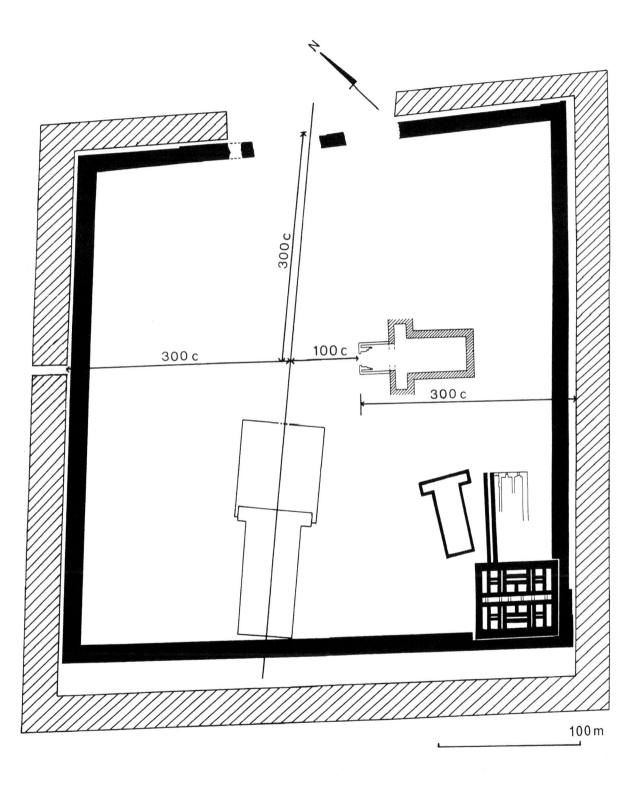

300 c

300 c

100 c

300 c

N

100 m

The design of the Thirtieth-Dynasty temple complex in cubit measurements